And Though This World
with Devils filled

american
university
studies

Series VII
Theology and Religion

Vol. 236

PETER LANG
New York • Washington, D.C./Baltimore • Bern
Frankfurt am Main • Berlin • Brussels • Vienna • Oxford

JÓN MAGNÚSSON

And Though This World
with Devils filled

A STORY OF SUFFERINGS

Translated by
MICHAEL FELL

PETER LANG
New York • Washington, D.C./Baltimore • Bern
Frankfurt am Main • Berlin • Brussels • Vienna • Oxford

Library of Congress Cataloging-in-Publication Data

Jón Magnússon, 1610–1696.
[Píslarsaga. English]
And though this world with devils filled: a story of sufferings /
Jón Magnússon; translated by Michael Fell.
p. cm. — (American university studies. Series VII,
Theology and religion; v. 236)
Includes bibliographical references and index.
1. Jón Magnússon, 1610–1696. 2. Witchcraft—Iceland.
I. Fell, Michael. II. Title. III. Series.
BF1584.I2J6613   133.4'3'094912—dc22   2004015777
ISBN 978-0-8204-7491-5
ISSN 0740-0446

Bibliographic information published by **Die Deutsche Bibliothek**.
Die Deutsche Bibliothek lists this publication in the "Deutsche
Nationalbibliografie"; detailed bibliographic data is available
on the Internet at http://dnb.ddb.de/.

Cover design by Lisa Barfield
Cover art by Sigríður Schram

The paper in this book meets the guidelines for permanence and durability
of the Committee on Production Guidelines for Book Longevity
of the Council of Library Resources.

© 2007 Peter Lang Publishing, Inc., New York
29 Broadway, 18th floor, New York, NY 10006
www.peterlang.com

All rights reserved.
Reprint or reproduction, even partially, in all forms such as microfilm,
xerography, microfiche, microcard, and offset strictly prohibited.

Printed in Germany

*This book is dedicated
to the memory of my parents*
JAMES PEMBERTON FELL *and* ELLA MAY FELL

Table of Contents

List of Illustrations	*xi*
Map	*xiii*
Foreword	*xv*
Preface	*xix*
Acknowledgments	*xxiii*
Chronology of Jón Magnússon's Life	*xxvii*
Map of Iceland	*xxix*

Introduction	1
§1. Texts Translated in This Book	2
§2. The Witchcraft Craze in Europe	3
§3. The Historical Background of Seventeenth-Century Iceland	6
§4. Schools, Administration, and Living Conditions in Seventeenth-Century Iceland	10
§5. Witchcraft in Iceland	13
§6. Sorcery and Spells in Iceland	20
§7. The Scene of Jón Magnússon's Life as a Priest	23
§8. *Síra* Jón Magnússon, Priest of Eyri	26
§9. Attitudes of Scholars Toward the *Story of Sufferings*	31
§10. The Nature of *Síra* Jón's Distresses	34
§11. *Síra* Jón's Spiritual Experiences	39
Conclusion	42

PART I

The First Part of the Story of the Sufferings of *Síra* Jón Magnússon — 59

I. **The Antecedents and Beginnings of the Attacks on *Síra* Jón At and After the End of October 1655** — 61

II.	*Síra* Jón Accuses the Kirkjuból Father and Son Before Magnús Magnússon the Sýslumaður. At an Assembly at Eyri in Skutulsfjörður, They are Required to Produce the Oaths of Twelve Persons. A Fruitless Search for Texts on Witchcraft at Kirkjuból	71
III.	The Attacks Continue into the Year 1656, but Magnús the Sýslumaður Refuses to Take any Action. *Síra* Jón Sends a Message to the Other Sýslumaður, Þorleifur Kortsson, at Bær in Hrútafjörður	83
IV.	The Father and Son at Kirkjuból Solicit Sworn Testimony. The Bodily and Spiritual Agonies of *Síra* Jón are Further Described, as well as his Admonitions to the Authorities	89
V.	Influences that Came to his Aid During his Trials	99
VI.	The Verdict on the Jón Jónssons, Father and Son, that They Should be Burned to Death	105
VII.	The Second Verdict, Regarding the Disposition of the Property of the Executed Father and Son	117

PART II

The Second Part of the Story of the Sufferings of
Síra Jón Magnússon   123

VIII.	Reflections on the Punishment of Wizards. The Assaults on *Síra* Jón Do Not Cease, in Spite of the Burning of the Jón Jónssons	125
IX.	He Attributes his Continued Sufferings to the Witchcraft of Þuríður	137
X.	Considerations Regarding Those Later Devilish Torments, of which I Believe Þuríður Jónsdóttir to have been the Primary Instigator	155

Appendix 1. Explanations of Historical Terms, Place-Names, Persons, Etc., Relevant to *The Story of Sufferings*   171

Appendix 2. Decree of King Christian IV   193

Appendix 3. The Judgment of the District Court Regarding the Two Jón Jónssons of Kirkjuból   195

Appendix 4. Four Documents Regarding the Investigation of Þuríður Jónsdóttir   201

Appendix 5. Extracts from the Minutes of the Sessions of the Althing in the Years 1656–1659, Regarding the Lawsuits Brought by *Síra* Jón Magnússon Against the Jón Jónssons, Father and Son, and Þuríður Jónsdóttir	209
Appendix 6. The Accusation Brought by Þuríður Jónsdóttir of Kirkjuból Against *Síra* Jón Magnússon	215
Illustrations	219
Bibliography	227
Index	233

List of Illustrations

Cover Design

This design, by the Icelandic artist Sigríður Schram, conveys something of the atmosphere of the book—Jón Magnússon's obsession with witchcraft, his sufferings, his compulsion to speak out, and at the same time the solace that he derived from his faith in God.

Illustrations

1. An early photograph of the spit Eyri in Skutulsfjörður taken by the photographer Sigfús Eymundsson, probably in 1868. The picture shows debris of ocean ice in Skutulsfjörður. In the center stands the Eyri church. It was newly erected when the picture was taken, and burned down in 1987. To its left are the churchyard, rectory, and rectory farm. (The preceding church had stood inside the churchyard, rather than to the south of it like the new church in the picture.) The cluster of buildings to the right of the church is the Danish trading station. The oldest still surviving building in the picture is the Danish "factor house," which was built in the latter part of the 18th century.   221
2. A wooden statue of the Virgin and Child, thought to date from about 1500, which was apparently in the possession of the Eyri church during the incumbency of *síra* Jón Magnússon and is now in the possession of the Þjóðminjasafn (National Museum). Thanks are due to the photographer Ívar Brynjólfsson.   222
3. A portrait of Bishop Brynjólfur Sveinsson.   223
4. A portrait of *síra* Páll Björnsson.   224
5. A portrait of Magnús Magnússon *sýslumaður*.   225

The photograph no. 1 taken by Sigfús Eymundsson, the statue no. 2, and the portraits nos. 3, 4, 5 are in the possession of the

Þjóðminjasafn, and I am indebted for the reproductions used here to the Þjóðminjasafn and especially to Inga Lára Baldvínsdóttir, head of its photographic division.

6. An aerial view of the modern town of Ísafjörður, looking inland from the Djúp. This picture is used by permission of the photographer Ragnar Th. Sigurðsson of "Arctic Images." 226

Map

Map of Iceland (with two inset maps, one of the West Fjords and the other of Skutulsfjörður), created by Jean-Pierre Biard, cartographer in Reykjavík, and used with his permission.

Foreword

This book from seventeenth-century Iceland, now for the first time translated into English, has no parallel in the long and rich history of Icelandic literature. Many souls in many lands were tormented in the same period and in the same manner as the author of this book. But the cries of torment here and there were not heard for very long. People prefer to forget the dark fates and events of history, especially those close to them in time. Those that are already long past awaken neither shame nor fear but often one-sided and unfair judgments.

The voice that speaks in this book was little heard and for a long time was entirely forgotten. But its words were preserved in manuscript form, and when discovered after almost two hundred years they received little attention and little understanding. More recently they have reached a wider circle of interested readers.

In his excellent introduction the translator investigates the events that caused the writer to tell this story of his tortured soul. This book is a cry of distress *de profundis*, a most remarkable firsthand documentation of the inner feelings of a man who personally experienced the cruelty and harshness of one of the mysterious plagues of history and also had the ability to make known his experience in an especially striking manner. And this account is the more remarkable for the strong, deep, and pure Christian witness that is here found in the writer. This important point, or "gold in clay" that Sigurdur Nordal first noted and pointed out, is very well handled and brought out by the translator, Dr. Michael Fell, in his Introduction. Previous discussions of this point have never shown a deeper understanding and insight into the common characteristic of all Christians, which consists in total trust in Jesus Christ and a sincere and living fellowship of the heart with Him.

The uniqueness of the book is clear from the beginning. But, having the privilege of accompanying it on its way in its English attire, I must draw attention to the unique achievement of the translator. To capture the eloquence and vocabulary of the passionate, tortured author is a difficult task. It is incredibly bold for a man who is not Icelandic and in his eighties to take upon himself the task of translating this text, and to have accomplished it extremely well. But Dr. Fell is not a novice in this area. He has previously wrestled effectively with difficult Icelandic texts. And he has exercised his powers from his youth to his elder years in scholarly research and teaching, and acquired a considerable reputation for his work—though in a totally different field.

It is my pleasant obligation to relate to the prospective readers of this book some facts about this remarkable man.

He was born in Vancouver, Canada, on 4 December 1923. His father, an Englishman, the son of a clergyman of the Anglican Church, had emigrated to Canada shortly before the turn of the twentieth century and married an American woman. Michael, their only son, has been a Canadian citizen all his life. And in Vancouver he met his future wife Daphne who, like his father, was born in England and had emigrated to Canada. They were married in 1957 and have two children—Rachel, who is a Professor of Southeast Asian Studies at Barnard College, New York, and Peter, who is an investment specialist. Daphne has been a very gracious spirit brightening his life, and their union has been strikingly beautiful.

Michael's talents were evident at an early age, and he was ahead of others in his schools both in Canada and England. He was for three years at Eton, the renowned English school. While there his interest in ancient Icelandic literature was awakened. Also he became very interested in Latin and Greek literature. One time, for example, while at Eton he received an admonition for failing to appear at the right time for dinner because he was so engrossed in reading Sophocles in Greek in his room.

Though the ancient classics tempted him and came easily to him, the areas of mathematics and physics took a yet stronger hold on him. He determined to devote himself to these scientific areas. After receiving his BA degree from the University of British Columbia in 1943 he continued his education in the field of physics at the University of California, Berkeley. He received his MA degree in this area in 1945. He then worked for one year as a Junior Research Physicist with the atomic research department of the Canadian National Research Council in Montreal. Then he returned to the University of California, Berkeley, and soon devoted his efforts totally to mathematics. He received his doctor's degree in this field in 1951. He then became an instructor in mathematics at this same university, and two years later he became an instructor at the California Institute of Technology. The next year he worked as a Research Associate at the University of Chicago. After that he was an O.N.R. Post-Doctoral Fellow at the University of Washington, Seattle. There he achieved the rank of Assistant Professor (1957), Associate Professor (1960), and Full Professor (1964). A year later he was invited to be a Professor of Mathematics at the University of Pennsylvania, Philadelphia. He accepted this position and continued his work there until he retired in 1991.

During his 40 years as a university teacher he also did considerable research in mathematics, especially in the area of functional analysis. Notable among his writings in his area of specialty is a two-volume work entitled *Representations of *-Algebras, Locally Compact Groups, and Banach *-Algebraic Bundles*, Academic Press, 1988, which he wrote in collaboration with Professor Robert Doran of Texas Christian University.

As I have already said, he is very gifted in the field of mathematics. He is also greatly talented in the area of languages, and he has never lost his passion for this field. While he was busy with research and university teaching in the area of mathematics, he found relaxation in learning Russian and Sanskrit, and reads both languages. His interest in the ancient Indian language of Sanskrit, in which there is a large and remarkable religious literature, also had its source in his interest in religion. He is by nature a man drawn to faith. He was raised in the Christian Church of his forefathers, but he left the Church and for many years he sought satisfaction for his longing for faith in the Hindu religion. By his very nature he is not satisfied with superficiality in the serious matters of life. It is not enough for him to trifle with spiritual matters as a pastime. He would rather perceive the reality that has evoked the greatest strivings of the human spirit and given it that satisfaction, that strength, that joy with which no other human experience can compare.

But he returned to the Christian faith around 1980. And, as well might be expected of such a man, he devoted himself eagerly to the study of Christian theology. At the same time his interest in Iceland was reawakened. He and his wife came to Iceland for the first time in 1980, and after that almost every year. After he retired from his teaching position they have lived here in Iceland for almost half of each year. He enrolled in the Icelandic program at the University of Iceland, and became proficient in the language in a remarkably short time. He is well read in the Icelandic literature and history of former centuries. He has also attended lectures and a program of study in theology at the University of Iceland. He and his wife have many friends and admirers here in Iceland. In their personal relationships they have much to give because of their intelligence and knowledge, and not the least because of their cordiality and their strong faith and warm understanding.

Dr. Fell has edited and written the following books during recent years:

Whom Wind and Waves Obey: Selected Sermons of Bishop Jón Vídalín. Translated into English with an introduction by Michael Fell. 1998.

And Some Fell into Good Soil: A History of Christianity in Iceland. 1999.

A Very Present Help in Trouble: The Autobiography of the Firepriest. By Jón Steingrímsson, translated into English with an introduction by Michael Fell. 2002.

And now the present book is being added to the list.

All these books are published by Peter Lang Publishing, American University Studies, Series VII, Theology and Religion. New York.

This is a great achievement for a man who has also done as much work in a completely different field as Dr. Fell has done.

Few non-Icelanders, if any, have done as much as he has done in introducing to the outside world the classical sources of Christianity in Iceland.

His initiative and contribution, it goes without saying, have been much appreciated in Iceland. He and his wife were both honored guests at the celebration of the Thousandth Anniversary of Christianity in Iceland in the year 2000. In the same year Dr. Fell was awarded an honorary doctorate by the Department of Theology of the University of Iceland.

He has already assured himself a distinguished place among the friends of my Church and nation—and even more so by this his most recent work.

Dr. Sigurbjörn Einarsson,
Former Bishop of Iceland.
At the close of 2004.
(Translated from the Icelandic by Dr. George Hanson,
of Port Townsend, Washington, U.S.A.)

Preface

The Icelandic Language, its Pronunciation and our Alphabetization

It is the policy of this book that *Icelandic words and names will be printed in their Icelandic spelling, without transliteration* (except for a few words, such as "Althing," which have already been adopted into the English language). The letters of the Icelandic alphabet that do not occur in English are the accented vowels á, é, í, ó, ú, ý, the ö (with umlaut), the vowel æ (capital Æ), and the two consonants þ (capital Þ) and ð (capital Ð).

As regards the pronunciation of Icelandic letters and diphthongs, here are a few rough indications. (For more precision, see for example Stefán Einarsson, *Icelandic Grammar, Texts, Glossary*, 1945.) In general the consonants that Icelandic and English have in common are pronounced in similar ways in the two languages. Of the several exceptions to this statement I shall mention only one: the Icelandic consonant 'j' is always pronounced like English 'y'. As for the Icelandic vowels and diphthongs:

a is pronounced like *a* in *father*.
á is pronounced like *ow* as in *cow*.
e is pronounced like *e* in *get* or *ai* in *air*.
é is pronounced like *ye* as in *yes*.
i and y are pronounced like *i* in *bid* or *pity*.
í and ý are pronounced like *ee* as in *green*.
o is pronounced like *aw* in *law*.
ó is pronounced like *ow* as in *slow*.
u is pronounced somewhat like German *ü* in *müssen*.
ú is pronounced like *oo* as in *school*.
ö is pronounced like the French *eu* in *peur*, i.e., somewhat like
   English *u* in *fur* or *burn*.
æ (really a diphthong) is pronounced like *i* in *high*.

The diphthong au is pronounced like the combination *öí*, i.e., like *eui* in French *feuille*.
The diphthongs ei and ey are both pronounced like *a* in *hate* or *ale*.

As for the Icelandic consonants which do not occur in English:

þ is pronounced like *th* in *thing*.
ð is pronounced like *th* in *this*.

Almost all Icelandic words are pronounced with the accent on the first syllable.

Since Icelandic words are not transliterated here, it is necessary to explain the somewhat motley method of alphabetizing used here in Appendix 1, the Bibliography, and the Index. This is as follows: Letters occurring in English are alphabetized as usual. As for Icelandic letters not occurring in English: The letter þ is alphabetized as if it were th, ð as if it were d, æ as if it were ae, ö as if it were o, and the accented vowels (á, é, etc.) as if they were unaccented. Moreover, in conformity with the Icelandic naming practice described below, Icelandic authors are alphabetized by their first names, while non-Icelandic authors are alphabetized by their family names.

The Icelandic Naming System

As regards names, it will help the reader to trace family connections if he or she is familiar with the Icelandic style of naming individuals—a style that has been prevalent in Iceland throughout its entire history.

In English-speaking countries a child automatically receives the family name of its parents (e.g., Smith, Jones), and in addition one or more "first" or baptismal names (e.g., John, Mary Emma), thus becoming John Smith, Mary Emma Jones, etc. In Iceland, on the other hand, most people do not have a family name. A child is given one or more baptismal names, for instance Jón or Sigurður if it is a boy, or Helga or Guðrún if a girl; and the only other name that it receives is a patronymic, consisting of the father's first name with 'son' or 'dóttir' suffixed according to sex. Thus, if an Icelander named Guðmundur Jónsson has a son Jón Ragnar and a daughter Helga, the full names of these children will be Jón Ragnar Guðmundsson and Helga Guðmundsdóttir. *The father's patronymic, Jónsson, is not inherited by his children.*

In Iceland a woman's name remains unaltered when she marries.

This difference in the manner of naming implies a difference of attitudes toward names. In English-speaking countries the family name is the most "important" of one's names. In formal conversation a person is addressed by the family name (e.g., Mr. Smith or Ms. Jones); and telephone directories, for example, list subscribers alphabetically by family name. In Iceland, on the other hand, the first or baptismal name is one's "real" name. Even in formal or official contexts one is addressed by one's first name (a custom which can seem a little strange to an Icelandic-speaking newcomer). The Icelandic telephone directory lists subscribers alphabetically by first names.

The same applies to names with titles. Take for example the title *síra* (or *séra* or sr.) of a priest (equivalent to the English "Reverend"). A priest whose name is Pétur Jónsson is spoken of or addressed in Iceland as *séra* Pétur or *séra* Pétur Jónsson, but never as *séra* Jónsson. (Foreigners, following their own custom, will usually address him as the Reverend Jónsson.)

Some Icelanders, however, have adopted family names for one reason or another, which have then been passed down through generations, usually supplanting the patronymic. The earliest example of this seems to be the distinguished seventeenth-century Icelandic scholar Arngrímur Jónsson (1568–1648), whose Latin writings on Iceland were widely read throughout Scandinavia. In deference to the naming customs of his non-Icelandic readers and colleagues he decided to adopt the family name of Vídalín (derived from Víðidalur, his parents' home district in northern Iceland). Many of his descendants in the male line adopted this family name (for example his famous grandson Bishop Jón Þorkelsson Vídalín, usually known simply as Jón Vídalín). However, one encounters no such family names in the *Story of Sufferings*.

Miscellaneous

In this book, all material quoted in English from Icelandic-language sources has been translated by Michael Fell unless the contrary is explicitly stated.

The book is of course intended for English-speaking readers, and references are given to English-language sources whenever possible. However, copious references to sources in Icelandic which are not available in English are also given for those who intend a deeper study of the subject.

Names of persons, places, institutions, administrative positions, legal terms and documents, and so forth, which occur in or are relevant to the *Story of Sufferings*, are explained in the Introduction if they are of sufficient general interest. If they are of more restricted interest but are still relevant to more than one passage, they will be found in the alphabetical listing of Appendix 1. If relevant to only one passage, they are explained in an endnote. For more precise references see the Index.

It is to be hoped that the statements made in the Introduction, Notes, and Appendices of this book are mostly accurate. However, considerable use has been made of secondary rather than primary sources, and it is only to be expected that some errors of fact and of judgment have crept in. For these the translator accepts full responsibility, and apologizes for them in advance!

Acknowledgments

The most important part of the present book is an English translation of an Icelandic text (called *Píslarsaga*) dating from the seventeenth century. As is to be expected, not only does the language and style of the original differ markedly from modern Icelandic, but the way of life to which it refers—including the whole intellectual atmosphere of the times, but also more specifically education, law, church life, trade and commerce, farming and fishing, communications, social relations between a priest and his parishioners, and so forth—all these, as well as the words and phrases describing them, have changed greatly during the intervening three and a half centuries. These changes present real difficulties for the modern translator, especially if he is not of Icelandic origin. It is therefore a pleasure for me to acknowledge the great help that I have received from several sources in bringing this work to completion.

The first is Dr. Sigurbjörn Einarsson, retired bishop of Iceland. He has graciously given of his time, in spite of many other pressing engagements, to go over the major part of my manuscript and suggest many corrections and improvements. Even more importantly, he and his late wife Magnea Þorkelsdóttir have given their friendship and unstinting help and encouragement to my wife and me over the several years during which I have been engaged in this and other translation works relating to Icelandic Christianity. He has also kindly written the Foreword to the present book.

The Foreword has been translated from Icelandic into English by Dr. George Hanson of Port Townsend, Washington, a close friend of Dr. Sigurbjörn Einarsson. My hearty thanks are due to him for his kind collaboration.

Another source of invaluable help has been Professor Margaret Cormack of the College of Charleston, South Carolina, a specialist in medieval Icelandic religious history who has worked for substantial periods of time over several years at the Árni Magnússon Institute, Reykjavík. Her contribution to this manuscript has been absolutely unique in its depth and extensiveness. In spite of numerous other commitments she has given enormously of herself, her time, and her enthusiasm to a detailed examination and improvement of my entire manuscript. She has not only greatly improved the translation itself but also used her deep knowledge of Icelandic Church history to point out deficiencies in my historical Introduction and Appendix 1, as well as editorial deficiencies. Even though I have not always agreed with her suggestions, my indebtedness to her, and to the friendship that she has displayed through her efforts to make my manuscript as reliable as possible, is very great. Her patient cooperation and innumerable suggestions have increased the quality of this book to an enormous degree.

Another scholar who has given generously of his time and knowledge to collaborate with Dr. Cormack and myself, by answering questions and making suggestions both about the historical matters discussed in my manuscript and the translation itself, is Dr. Einar G. Pétursson of the Árni Magnússon Institute, Reykjavík. He is a specialist in the culture of seventeenth- and eighteenth-century Iceland and therefore eminently suited to the task.

Dr. Robert Cook, retired professor of English at the University of Iceland, has also been extremely helpful. He has gone over the entire manuscript and made numerous editorial suggestions.

I have also received important help from Einar Már Jónsson, instructor in Scandinavian languages and civilization at the Université de Paris IV, who has recently (in 2004) published a French translation of the *Píslarsaga*. When he and I learned of the existence of each other's work, we exchanged manuscripts, and he has kindly permitted me to make use of his manuscript for the improvement of my English version. He has also carefully gone over my Introduction and Appendix 1, suggesting many improvements. Many of the Notes contained in his French translation have also been illuminating to me.

I want to express my gratitude also to Már Jónsson, docent in the Department of History of the University of Iceland, for clarifying my translation of the material of Chapter VII.

I also want to record my gratitude to Professor Einar Sigurbjörnsson of the Theological Faculty of the University of Iceland, one of the outstanding scholars in the field of the religious history of Iceland. He has gone over the long Introduction, and has always been helpful in giving detailed answers to questions regarding the history of Christianity in Iceland. In addition, conversations with him over the past several years have helped to give me a better understanding of the religious climate of Iceland in past centuries.

Special thanks are also due to Inga Lára Baldvinsdóttir, head of the photographic division of the National Museum of Iceland (Þjóðminjasafn Íslands), who has supplied me with the historic photographs included in this volume.

I owe the aerial photograph of the modern town of Ísafjörður to the photographer Ragnar Th. Sigurðsson, of "Arctic Images."

Acknowledgments

The design on the cover of this book is the work of the Icelandic artist Sigríður Schram, and I want to express my special thanks to her for her imaginative work.

The map of Iceland and the West Fjords contained in this book is the work of the Reykjavík cartographer Jean-Pierre Biard.

My daughter, Professor Rachel Fell McDermott of Barnard College, New York, has given me valuable editorial advice, for which I am most thankful.

Many thanks are also due to the Icelandic Ministry of Education and the Ministry of Justice and Church Affairs, both of which have granted me subsidies toward the expenses of publishing this book.

I would be remiss if I did not express my appreciation of the splendid facilities provided by the National and University Library of Iceland and also of the Árni Magnússon Institute in Reykjavík, and of the friendliness and helpfulness of the staffs of both institutions, which have contributed much toward making my translation work a pleasurable experience.

Last but by no means least, I owe an enormous debt of gratitude to my wife Daphne, who for forty-nine years has provided an atmosphere of peace, understanding, and good humor in which projects such as the present book could be carried out with joy and concentration.

Chronology of Jón Magnússon's Life

Jón Magnússon born at Auðkúla, N. Iceland	around 1610
Decree of King Christian IV regarding punishment of sorcerers	1617
Jón Magnússon's first experience of abandonment by God	1627
Jón Magnússon graduates from Skálholt school	1630
Death of Bishop Oddur Einarsson of Skálholt	1630
Síra Jón (i.e., Jón Magnússon) becomes assistant priest at Vatnsfjörður	1633
Síra Jón becomes priest of the parish of Ögur, West Fjords	1635
Síra Jón reprimanded by Bishop Gísli Oddsson for negligence	around 1635
Death of Bishop Gísli Oddsson of Skálholt	1638
Brynjólfur Sveinsson becomes bishop of Skálholt	1639
Síra Jón installed as priest of Eyri	1644
"Demonic attacks" on *síra* Jón begin	October 21st, 1655
Court at Eyri orders the two Jón Jónssons to collect oaths testifying to their innocence of sorcery	December 14th, 1655
The two Jón Jónssons arrested by the *sýslumaður*	March, 1656
The two Jón Jónssons condemned to be burned	April 9th, 1656
The two Jón Jónssons burned to death	April 10th, 1656
Verdict on the disposition of the property of the two Jón Jónssons	April 11th, 1656

Second round of *síra* Jón's torments begins, when *síra* Jón and Erlendur Ormsson go to Kirkjuból and reprove Þuríður	August 29th, 1656
Síra Jón receives a blessing from Randíður Ólafsdóttir. Þuríður flees from Kirkjuból and takes refuge at Holt in Önundarfjörður	September, 1656
Síra Jón writes to the dean, *síra* Jón Jónsson, a letter of accusation against Þuríður	January 9th, 1657
A court of five priests calls *síra* Jón's accusations against Þuríður "baseless," and permits her to receive the sacrament	May 27th, 1657
Síra Jón twice attends the Althing to press his case against Þuríður	1657, 1658
Þuríður is acquitted of the charge of sorcery by a local court at Mosvellir	autumn 1658
Síra Jón writes what is now called the *Píslarsaga*	winter 1658–1659
The acquittal of Þuríður approved at the Althing session	1659
Þuríður brings suit against *síra* Jón, accusing him of persecuting her	spring 1660
A synod meets at Holt to discuss Þuríður's suit, but no conclusion is reached	May 29th, 1660
Síra Jón's son Snorri is ordained as assistant to his father	1665
Snorri loses his priestly status after fathering an illegitimate child	1669
Episcopal visitation to Eyri shows the parish affairs there to be in good order	1675
Síra Jón resigns as parish priest at Eyri	summer 1689
Síra Jón moves into Kirkjuból to live there with his son Snorri	spring 1690
Síra Jón hands over the parish to his successor	May 27th, 1690
Síra Jón is bedridden	by the middle of 1692
Síra Jón dies	1696
First census in Iceland records one Þuríður Jónsdóttir, living on a croft in Dýrafjörður, mother of the farmer's wife, 65 years old	1703

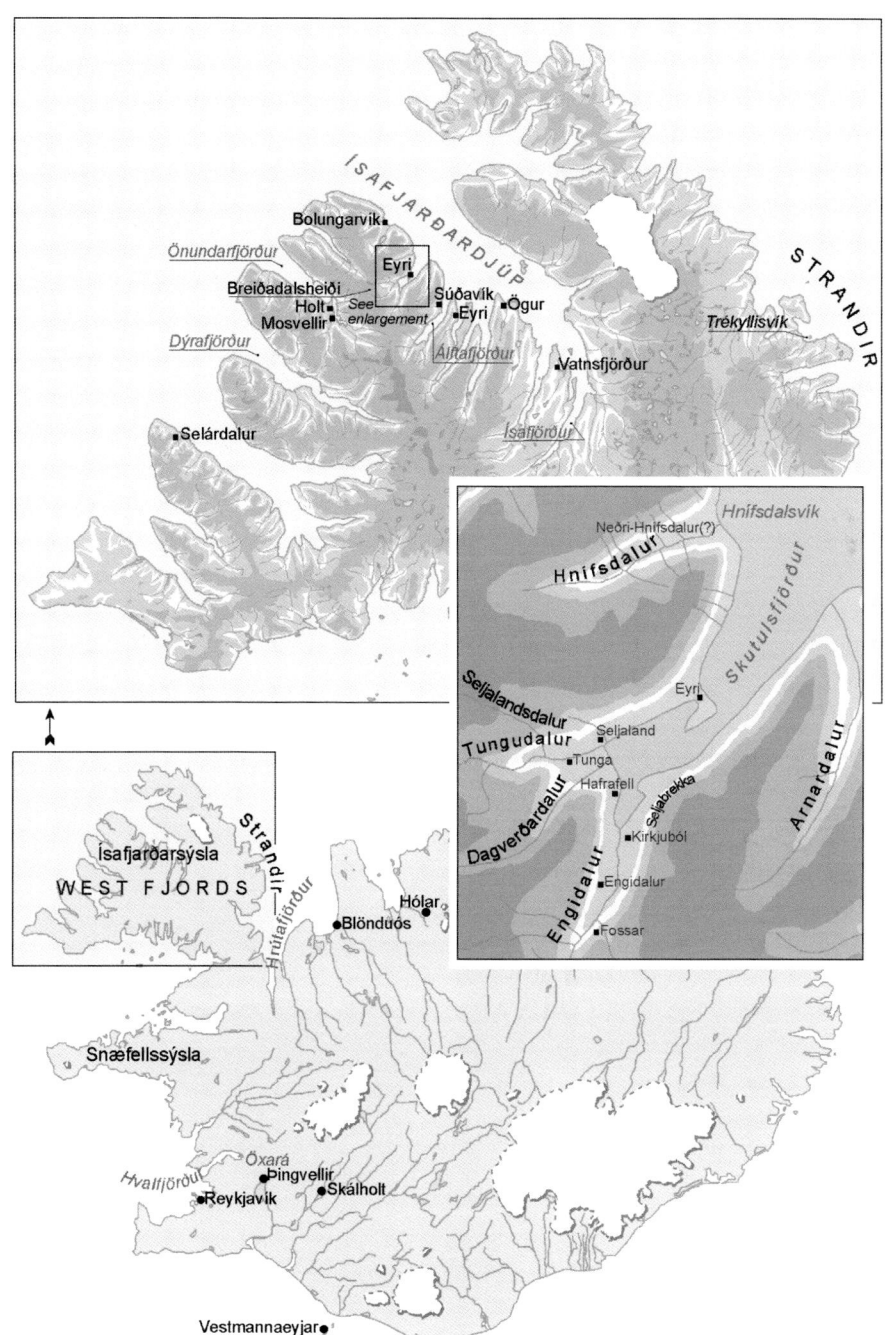

Map of Iceland, with two inset maps, one of the West Fjords and the other of Skutulsfjörður.

Introduction

The Jón Magnússon with whom this book is concerned was the younger of two brothers with identical names who lived and became well known in Iceland in the seventeenth century. The elder of the two Jón Magnússons became a learned (Lutheran) priest and distinguished poet; but he never enters our story. The younger Jón Magnússon, nicknamed *þumlungur* (Icelandic for "thumb," perhaps because he was of short stature), was born about 1610 and lived until 1696. In 1643 he became priest of the parish of Eyri on Skutulsfjörður in the West Fjords, where the town of Ísafjörður now stands. (At that time there was no town there, only a farming and fishing community of probably between 200 and 250 people.) There, late in the year 1655, he and his family and household became subject to strange physical and mental sufferings which, being a firm believer in the reality and efficacy of black magic, he attributed to black magic practiced on him by a father and son, both named Jón Jónsson, who lived on a nearby farm, had a reputation for practicing magic, and seem to have hated him. He importuned the local magistrates to have the Jón Jónssons punished on the basis of the anti-witchcraft laws currently in force in the Danish realm. At first they were unwilling to take up his case. But *síra* (that is, the Reverend) Jón Magnússon found a champion in a senior law official of northwest Iceland, one Þorleifur Kortsson, an avid witch-hunter who had already consigned other alleged sorcerers to the flames. With his help the Jón Jónssons father and son were both convicted of sorcery and burned to death in April 1656. But *síra* Jón's sufferings did not cease with the death of the two supposed culprits. So he concluded that some other individual must be practicing demonic arts against him, and he fixed upon Þuríður, the daughter and sister of the two Jón Jónssons, as the evident evildoer. He accused her of witchcraft before the magistrates. But she seems to have been a well-behaved and attractive young woman, and had powerful friends who helped her to assemble enough sworn testimony to her innocence to get her finally acquitted in the local court in the fall of 1658. Þuríður now turned the tables on *síra* Jón, and brought suit against him, accusing him of maligning and persecuting her. Unfortunately we have no records of the final outcome of Þuríður's case.

Síra Jón's response to all this was to take up his pen, and (probably in the winter of 1658–1659) he wrote an autobiographical document to which later writers have given the title *Píslarsaga*[1] (translated here as *A Story of Sufferings*), in which he describes the sufferings of himself, his wife, his household, and indeed his whole district, and also presents in detail the evidence by which he pins the blame for them on the alleged sorceries practiced by the Jón Jónssons and Þuríður. In the process he also severely castigates the negligence and indifference of most of the Icelandic magistrates of his day to what he regards as the terrible and sinister evil of sorcery. By good fortune a copy of this document has survived to the present day. The present book contains the first translation of it into English.[2] Though not always pleasant to read, it is thought by Icelanders to have considerable literary merits. It should also be of great intrinsic interest to historians of the European witchcraft craze of the sixteenth and seventeenth centuries, being one of the few extant autobiographical accounts from that era of the feelings and struggles of a priest who not only felt called upon by God to ferret out and extirpate the diabolical evil of sorcery, but was himself caught up in it and suffered untold torments which he firmly believed to be its effects.[3]

§1. Texts Translated in This Book

Jón Magnússon's original manuscript of the *Píslarsaga*, probably written in the winter of 1658–1659, has been lost for centuries. Fortunately a copy of it was made around the middle of the eighteenth century by *síra* Jón Sigurðsson, the priest who from 1730 onward ministered in *síra* Jón Magnússon's parish of Eyri.[4] This copy came into the possession of a manuscript-collector named Jakob Langebek in Copenhagen, who died in 1775; it is now preserved in the Royal Library of Copenhagen (catalogued as number NKS 1842 4to). Long forgotten, it was first brought to the attention of modern scholars by the Icelandic geographer Þorvaldur Thoroddsen in the last decade of the nineteenth century. Since then it has appeared in three printed Icelandic editions[5]— in 1914 (edited by Sigfús Blöndal), in 1967 (edited by Sigurður Nordal), and in 2001 (edited by Matthías Viðar Sæmundsson). These three editions differ greatly in the material that they include. By far the most complete is the 2001 edition. This contains: 1) The *Píslarsaga* proper, including four supplementary apologetic tracts by Jón Magnússon[6] defending his legal proceedings against sorcerers; 2) surviving legal documents connected with these lawsuits; 3) relevant extracts from the minutes of the proceedings of the Althing from the years 1656 to 1659; 4) surviving letters to and from Jón Magnússon; and 5) other surviving letters, reports of episcopal visitations, and so forth, bearing on Jón Magnússon's parish and in general on sorcery in the West Fjords.

Introduction

As for the present book, it begins (following this Introduction and the Chronology of Jón Magnússon's life) with the *Píslarsaga* proper, except that I have omitted all but the first of the four supplementary apologetic tracts mentioned above. (In this I follow the example of Sigurður Nordal, who in his 1967 edition omits the last three on the grounds that they add little to the argument of the first one). Moreover, in order to facilitate references I have divided the *Píslarsaga* into ten chapters, Chapter X being the first supplementary tract (*Viðlit historíunnar* ....). (No such division is made either in the surviving manuscript or in any of the three printed Icelandic editions of the *Píslarsaga*.) Of the ten chapters, Chapter VI is the official verdict reached by the local court which condemned the two Jón Jónsons to be burned to death for the crime of sorcery, and Chapter VII is the official disposition of the property of the two deceased "criminals"; both of these chapters are court documents, and neither is the work of *síra* Jón Magnússon himself.[7]

Following Chapters I to X are six Appendices. Appendix 1 is an alphabetical list of explanations of geographical names, names of individuals, institutions of Church and state, important legal documents, facets of religious and cultural life, units of measurement, and so forth, that are relevant to the *Story of Sufferings* (i.e., the *Píslarsaga*) but are not adequately explained in this Introduction. The five Appendices 2 to 6 are translations of other short documents contained in the 2001 edition of the *Píslarsaga*: Appendix 2 contains an important decree by the Danish king, first published (in Danish) in 1617, regarding the punishment of sorcerers in his domains. Appendix 3 gives a preliminary judgment pronounced by the district court regarding the two Jón Jónssons. Appendix 4 contains four documents bearing on the prosecution of Þuríður for witchcraft. Appendix 5 is a collection of extracts from the minutes of the sessions of the Althing from 1656 to 1659, bearing on the lawsuits initiated by *síra* Jón. Finally, Appendix 6 contains the charges brought against *síra* Jón Magnússon by Þuríður Jónsdóttir, after her acquittal, for having groundlessly slandered and persecuted her as a sorceress.

§2. The Witchcraft Craze in Europe

For an understanding of the events described in the *Story of Sufferings* one must say a few words about the witchcraft craze in Europe.

Magic or sorcery may be defined as the alleged art of harnessing supernatural forces or spirits, by the performance of specific acts, so as to bring about desired ends in this world—such as the acquisition of property or money, success in love or in battle, the healing of disease, the causing of good or bad weather, the raising of the ghost of a dead person, or the harming or destruction of an enemy. A man who practices this art is called a sorcerer or wizard or warlock; a woman who does so is a sorceress or witch. It is usual to distinguish between "white" magic and "black" magic. The former is practiced to secure beneficial ends, such as the healing of disease or good weather for fishing; the latter aims at causing harm to one's enemies.

In the early Middle Ages the Church in western Europe largely took the attitude that sorcery was wicked nonsense, that the heathen spirits imagined in its rites were delusions and had no objective existence.[8] But by the fifteenth century the Church's predominant attitude had begun to change: the spirits invoked in the practice of sorcery were now held to have an objective existence and to be demons, ministers of Satan. The adoption of this attitude spread rapidly after 1486, when two Dominican monks, Jacob Sprenger and Heinrich Kramer, with authorization from a papal bull by Pope Innocent VIII, published an encyclopaedic "study" of witchcraft, demons, and the proper means of combating them. It was entitled *Malleus Maleficarum* (the Hammer of Witches), and was a major factor in promoting the witchcraft craze which afflicted western Europe for two centuries and did not subside until about 1700.[9] The fantasies propounded in this book became the accepted doctrine regarding magic and demons during this long period, the basis of the persecution and burning of tens if not hundreds of thousands of supposed witches and wizards, of whom the vast majority were women. The book is an extraordinary and frightening example of the perversities into which a whole society can be plunged by reasoning based on a literal interpretation of scripture. The central figure in the whole structure is the devil, Satan, who with his fiends is supposed to be engaged in a campaign to destroy the right relationship of man with God in Christ. As Satan first beguiled Eve, who then lured Adam to his fall (see *Genesis*, Chapter 3), so (the authors proclaimed) women are even now the morally weaker sex, more susceptible than men to evil emotions. They are the primary agents through whom the devil makes his assault on the human race, though certainly men are not excluded from this role. Principal among the fantasies that developed regarding sorcery was the "witches' sabbath." Witches (and wizards too) were supposedly transported magically to large gatherings presided over by Satan himself, at which blasphemous parodies of the Christian Eucharist took place, accompanied by orgies in which the witches and wizards had sexual intercourse with fiends, or even with Satan himself. Witches were required to perform various abominable acts demonstrating their loyalty to the devil, such as killing and devouring newborn (unbaptized) infants. The truth of these fantasies was said to be confirmed by the confessions of numerous imprisoned witches and wizards. Most of these confessions were extracted by torture, though some seem to have been the product not of torture but of diseased imagination. Building on the flimsy fabric of such confessions, the theologians and Inquisitors of the Church racked their brains to construct a "rational" theory of demonology—to explain in "naturalistic" terms, for example, how the devil and his fiends, who are immaterial, could assume bodies in which to have sexual relations with humans, and whether they could conceive (demonic) offspring by so doing!

Because of the immense danger in which the human race stood from these attacks of Satan, it was considered the duty of Christians to use every possible means to exterminate witches and wizards. Those convicted of witchcraft were executed by being burned alive (though in England the prescribed penalty was more humane—death by hanging). To escape the agonies of torture, accused women (and men also) would often not only confess to being witches themselves but would implicate those of their friends and neighbors whom they imagined (or thought it expedient to imagine) that they had also seen at witches' sabbaths; and so the lists of those destined for burning multiplied.

The Protestant Reformers, though they rejected the authority of Rome, did not reject the excesses of the witch-hunters. Luther himself maintained that death by burning was a just punishment for sorcerers.[10] The Protestant evangelists largely accepted and took over the demonology of the *Malleus Maleficarum*, and burnings of sorcerers continued in areas which they had converted. In particular this was the case in Denmark, whose king in 1537 had decreed the abolition of the authority of Rome and the establishment of the Lutheran faith in his dominions, including Iceland.

It is not possible to give an accurate estimate of the number of convicted witches who were burned or hanged in the centuries (fourteenth to seventeenth) of the European witchcraft craze. Educated guesses range from about 50,000 up to 300,000. The most intensive witch-hunts, in England and Scotland at least, took place between 1590 and 1650.[11]

But the demonology of the witch-hunters was not without its critics. Platonism and Neoplatonism were being revived in Renaissance Europe at the very time of the burgeoning of the witchcraft craze, and many of the representatives of this school were courageously outspoken in their criticism of demonological fantasies. Among these were the Platonist philosopher Cornelius Agrippa (1486–1535), the mathematician Girolamo Cardano (1501–1576), and the medical doctors Johann Weyer (1515–1588) and Reginald Scot (1530–1599).[12]

One should not imagine, however, that these critics were scientific rationalists in the modern sense. They did not deny the existence of devils and witches, but maintained that the vast majority of those condemned and burned for witchcraft were not witches at all but victims of mental disease. The witches' sabbaths and the attendant orgies which these people confessed to participating in were unreal, they said, the products of diseased imagination. True witches indeed existed, and *they* should be burned—not for attending (non-existent) witches' sabbaths, but for their ungodly lives, manifested in all sorts of blasphemies and in acts of sorcery which, whether effective or not, showed a wicked desire to harm others and manipulate spirits for their human ends.

In the eyes of these critics the demonology of the *Malleus Maleficarum*, and of its subsequent exponents such as Nicolas Rémy and Jean Bodin, was a string of absurdities violating common sense. In the first place, could witches and wizards really be magically transported over long distances to attend witches' sabbaths? Could humans really have sexual intercourse with fiends, or do any of the acts of sorcery attributed to those in the devil's service, which involve upsetting the course of nature? Even the *Malleus Maleficarum* admits that only God can perform miracles; human beings can only do so if God Himself permits them. But would God give permission to demons and sorcerers to upset the course of nature? Surely, said Weyer, Scot, and their fellow liberals, it is simpler to suppose that all that the devil and his agents the genuine sorcerers can do is to deceive, vitiate, and misdirect the mind and senses of poor human beings, so that the latter *seem* to see and experience miracles which are in fact unreal.[13]

By placing their emphasis on mental illness rather than on diabolical possession, and by responding to it medically and with compassion, liberal doctors like Weyer and Scot took the first steps toward undermining the intellectual basis of the witchcraft craze, though they were not able to stem the tide of hysteria and fanaticism in their own day.[14]

§3. *The Historical Background of Seventeenth-Century Iceland*

Let us turn now to Iceland, and present a few facts about its history which will help in the understanding of Jón Magnússon's document.

For a lucid one-volume account in English of the history of Iceland from its first settlement to modern times, the reader is referred to Gunnar Karlsson's book, *Iceland's 1100 Years: History of a Marginal Society*.

To begin with, Iceland, as far as we know, is the only country in Europe which had no aboriginal inhabitants before the arrival of the first recorded permanent settlers. These arrived, mostly from Norway and the British Isles, during the period known as the Settlement Age, from A.D. 870 to 930—one of the manifestations of the explosion of Scandinavian energies during the so-called Viking Age. For nearly four centuries (from the Settlement Age to about 1260) this scattered community of settlers in Iceland formed an independent nation, not subject to the rule of any king, native or foreign. Around 930, at the conclusion of the Settlement Age, the Althing (general assembly) was founded to promulgate laws, to maintain law and order, and to strengthen a sense of community among the settlers. This assembly convened for about two weeks each summer on the plain of Þingvellir, by the banks of the river Öxará in southwest Iceland, and was therefore often referred to as the *Öxarárþing* (Öxará Assembly). It continued to meet annually at Þingvellir every summer for many centuries—in fact until 1798. The principal organ of the Althing was the *lögrétta* (law council), which at first carried out both the legislative and judicial functions required to hold the new community together. It did not however have executive powers; the enforcement of its laws was left to leading chieftains who, it was expected, would voluntarily undertake to punish lawbreakers. By 960 the system had been extended through the creation of a number of subsidiary local *þing*s (assemblies[15]) whose purpose was purely judicial—to try local lawbreakers and to refer to the Althing only the most difficult cases. In 1117 the first step was taken toward the codification of the country's law. The completed lawbook, preserved in thirteenth-century manuscripts, was called *Grágás* (Grey Goose).

Perhaps the most important decision ever taken by the Althing was the adoption of Christianity as the official religion of Iceland in the year 1000.[16] About a century later Iceland was divided into two bishoprics, supervised by two bishops with their respective seats at Skálholt in south Iceland and Hólar in north Iceland. Each of these bishops operated a school at his diocesan seat, primarily for the training of priests. These two schools lasted until about 1800 (when they were abolished and replaced by a single school located near the present capital city of Reykjavík). During the seventeenth century the diocesan schools at Skálholt and Hólar were the only schools in Iceland.

In 1096 or 1097 a Tithe Law was instituted in Iceland by Gissur Ísleifsson, one of the early pre-Reformation Icelandic bishops, with the support of the country's chieftains. The purpose of it was to ensure the viability and independence of the Church. It obligated every man and woman above the age of sixteen, whose property was worth at least three ewes, to pay a yearly tax (10% of his or her income, or 1% of his or her total worth). The proceeds of this tax were divided evenly between the bishops, the priests, the Church, and the poor. The Tithe Law remained largely in force even after the Reformation, except that thereafter the bishop's portion of the proceeds of the tax went mostly into the coffers of the Danish king.

The independence of Iceland from foreign domination lasted for almost four centuries. Its final demise came about through the concentration of power in the hands of a few ambitious chieftains and the escalation of bloody feuds among them exacerbated by two factors: First, as was mentioned above, the Althing had no centralized executive power with which to curb outbreaks of violence. Secondly, the kings of Norway had long cast greedy eyes on Iceland, and did not hesitate to use the civil strife among Icelandic chieftains as a tool for achieving control over the country. Finally, exhausted by the internecine feuds of their leading men, the Icelandic people agreed, around 1260, that Iceland should accept the status of a dependency of Norway and should pay taxes to the Norwegian crown, and that in return the latter should guarantee law and order to the country.

The period from the Settlement Age up to the loss of independence around 1260 is generally referred to as the Commonwealth Period (Icel. *Þjóðveldisöld*) of Icelandic history.

Around 1280 a new codification of Icelandic law was drawn up by the Norwegian king and largely accepted by the Althing, called the *Jónsbók* (Jón's Book). This was an important event, since the *Jónsbók* was to form the core of Icelandic law for the next four hundred years. As might be expected, much of the material of the old *Grágás* was taken up into the new lawbook.

In 1397 the so-called Kalmar Union took place, uniting the three countries of Denmark, Norway, and Sweden under the hegemony of Denmark. Norway, and therefore Iceland also, now became a dependency of Denmark. The status of Denmark as ruler of Iceland was to last for more than five centuries, until Iceland finally threw off the last traces of its subservience to Denmark in 1944.

Until the Reformation the Church in Iceland was under the authority of the pope and the Roman Catholic Church, and was administered ultimately from Rome. However, the Reformation changed all that. In 1534 King Christian III, an ardent Lutheran, came to the throne of Denmark, and in 1536 severed all religious ties with Rome. In 1537 he issued a Church Ordinance, decreeing the establishment of the Lutheran Church order in all his dominions, including Iceland.[17] The Ordinance was of course bitterly opposed by the two Roman Catholic bishops in Iceland. But the king's military might could not long be resisted, and the last flame of resistance was stamped out in 1550 with the execution of Jón Arason, the last Roman Catholic bishop of Hólar. With this event Lutheranism became the established form of Christianity in Iceland. The general pattern of the liturgy of the church services remained unchanged; but the Danish king now replaced the pope as head of the Church in his domains, taking responsibility for all Church affairs, including the appointment of bishops and priests.

In the wake of the Reformation all the nine monasteries and convents that had existed in Iceland up till then were abolished, and their revenues (consisting mostly of the rents from the properties which they owned) reverted to the royal treasury. The privilege of managing the properties that had formerly belonged to each monastic institution—of placing tenants on its farm properties, collecting rents, sending taxes to the king, and so forth—was auctioned off by the Crown to the highest bidder, who then became the monastic proprietor (Icel. *klausturhaldari*) for that monastic estate.

Even though imposed at first by decree from above, Lutheranism soon began to take root among the people. This can be attributed largely to a succession of wise and capable Lutheran bishops who occupied the sees of Skálholt and Hólar during the first Lutheran century. Foremost among these was Guðbrandur Þorláksson (1542–1627), bishop of Hólar for the record period of fifty-seven years (from 1570 to his death). This prodigiously energetic man made use of the one and only printing press in Iceland (originally brought to Hólar by Bishop Jón Arason) to publish a torrent of about a hundred books of Christian devotion, including the first complete Icelandic translation of the Bible (published in 1584) and the Graduale (first published in 1594), which in its successive editions became the standard liturgical handbook for the Icelandic Lutheran Church for the next two hundred years. Another very important innovation, for which he was directly or indirectly responsible, was a royal decree of 1579 which subsidized promising Icelandic students to study at the University of Copenhagen.

Almost contemporary with Bishop Guðbrandur was Oddur Einarsson (1559–1630), bishop of Skálholt from 1589 to his death. Bishop Oddur cooperated enthusiastically with his northern fellow bishop in disseminating the latter's printed works. He had received an excellent education abroad, even studying mathematics and astronomy under the famous Danish astronomer Tycho Brahe. Living as they did at the dawn of the Age of Science, both he and Bishop Guðbrandur showed a keen interest in scientific pursuits. Bishop Guðbrandur made a remarkably accurate measurement of the latitude of Hólar; and Bishop Oddur wrote an essay, *Íslandslýsing* (Description of Iceland), in which he propounded an explanation of volcanic eruptions which, while far from acceptable nowadays, at least made no appeal to supernatural agencies. At the same time it must be remembered that in the seventeenth century scientific pursuits were still heavily colored by occult speculations. Tycho Brahe and other men of science at that time were influenced by Neoplatonism. This ancient school of Graeco-Roman philosophy had been revived in Europe during the Renaissance, especially by Cornelius Agrippa (1486–1535), whose book *De Occulta Philosophia* propounded a "scientific mysticism," according to which the world was not merely material but was permeated with spirit and occult forces that could be known and manipulated by means of astrology and other "higher knowledge." So it is not surprising that Bishop Oddur found his scientific training quite compatible with belief in the reality of the supernatural and the efficacy of sorcery.

These few words about the intellectual background of Bishop Oddur Einarsson are of some relevance since, as we shall see later, he became the foster father of Jón Magnússon, the subject of this book, and the supervisor of the school in which the latter received his education.

Another shining light in the history of seventeenth-century Iceland was Brynjólfur Sveinsson (1605–1675), bishop of Skálholt from 1639 to 1674— the period during which the events described in this book took place. He had been co-rector of a prominent school in Denmark before his episcopal appointment, and was a strict disciplinarian and capable administrator. But at the same time he was a man of great culture and broadmindedness. Among his first acts as bishop was a decree that a synod (Icel. *prestastefna*) of priests of his diocese should be held annually in conjunction with the session of the Althing, at which internal affairs of the Church should be discussed and decided, so far as possible, without interference from the secular authorities. His broadmindedness was illustrated on three occasions when boys in his own diocesan school were found to have been experimenting with magic. He seems to have felt that their fault was youthful curiosity rather than deliberate malice, and he protected them from the severest penalties. Similarly, he used his authority to protect and encourage that remarkable self-taught Icelandic farmer, writer, philosopher, and man of the people Jón Guðmundsson the Learned (1574–1658), who studied and tested everything that he saw, including white magic, and thereby incurred the wrath of some leading men who would like to have seen him burned. Moreover, when Bishop Brynjólfur's friend and relative *síra* Páll Björnsson wrote to him asking him to press for legislation facilitating the conviction of sorcerers by relaxing the requirements for proof of their guilt, he declined to comply with *síra* Páll's request, pleading lack of leisure to consider the matter.

Bishop Brynjólfur's name is never mentioned in the *Story of Sufferings* (doubtless for reasons of political expediency), but his influence is strongly felt, especially in connection with the appearances of Jón Magnússon at the Althing in 1657 and 1658.[18]

§4. *Schools, Administration, and Living Conditions in Seventeenth-Century Iceland*

A few words should be said about the two diocesan schools in the seventeenth century. These were intended primarily for the training of priests, and the core of the school curriculum was the study of Latin. Graduation from either the Skálholt or the Hólar school was the only educational prerequisite for ordination to the priesthood. Only boys were admitted to the schools at that time. Girls were effectively debarred from any formal schooling until late in the nineteenth century. In spite of the poverty of the schools and the harshness of the living conditions there, a boy who applied himself diligently could acquire a good classical education; he would read extensively from the classical Latin authors, and would even be taught to write Latin poetry. Diligence in study was encouraged by a liberal application of corporal punishment. During the seventeenth century the total number of students enrolled in both diocesan schools at any one time was on the average at least forty-eight, of whom about ten would have graduated each year. Of these it seems that on the average about two journeyed each year to Copenhagen and entered the university (though only a small minority of these completed the course of studies there).[19]

As for the administration of government, the Danish king was of course the highest authority in the land, but until 1662 his decrees required the assent of the Althing before they became law in Iceland. In that year the so-called Decree of Absolutism made the king an absolute monarch, whose edicts became law in his domains even without the confirmation of any legislative body. From that time onward the legislative function of the Althing declined almost to nothing, and the latter became essentially a court of law—the highest in the land.

The highest government official for Icelandic affairs was the governor (Icel. *hirðstjóri* or *höfuðsmaður*). The governors throughout the seventeenth century were all foreign, and seldom came to Iceland. They exercised their authority through their bailiffs (i.e. representatives, Icel. *umboðsmaður*, plural *umboðsmenn*, or *fógeti*, plural *fógetar*) in Iceland, who were Icelanders living at Bessastaðir (the headquarters of the Danish presence in Iceland), near the present capital of Reykjavík. The governor of Iceland during the period of the events of this book was an unusually enlightened man named Henrik Bjelke. He seems to have taken a genuine interest in promoting the welfare of Iceland, and was exceptional among governors in that he visited the country quite frequently.

Also serving under the governor were two law-men (Icel. *lögmaður*, plural *lögmenn*), one for the northern and western districts and the other for the southern and eastern districts. The main function of these was to preside over the court sessions of the Althing (Icel. *lögrétta*). Since his duties involved considerable expenses, a *lögmaður* would often be granted proprietorship of certain royal properties as well as a fixed salary and the proceeds of fines. The status of a *lögmaður* carried with it a very considerable prestige.[20]

A man who had a seat in the *lögrétta* and participated in the reaching of verdicts (at least in the seventeenth century) was called a *lögréttumaður* (plural *lögréttumenn*). According to the *Jónsbók* the number of these should be eighty-four (though not all of these would be seated in the *lögrétta* at any one session). A quota of *lögréttumenn* was chosen from each district by the local *sýslumaður* or his deputy (see below). A *lögréttumaður* had to be a reasonably affluent farmer, since he was under obligation to attend the sessions of the *lögrétta*. He was compensated for the travelling expenses that he incurred in so doing, and his status as a *lögréttumaður* carried with it a degree of honor that raised him above the generality of farmers.[21]

One recognized Icelandic legal procedure in the seventeenth century for establishing the innocence of an accused person is worth special mention, since it plays an important role in our story. This was the procedure of compurgation, in which the accused was required to muster a specified number of persons (compurgators) who would swear an oath that they believed him or her to be innocent of the crime in question. In trials for serious offenses such as witchcraft the required number was twelve, and the compurgation was then called an *oath of twelve* (Icel. *tylftareiður*).[22]

For administrative purposes Iceland was divided into districts (Icel. *sýslur*, plural of *sýsla*), which in the seventeenth century were twenty-one in number. The chief administrative officer in each *sýsla* was the sheriff (Icel. *sýslumaður*, plural *sýslumenn*). He was the overseer of the local district court (Icel. *héraðsdómur*), in which criminal cases would first be tried. Serious crimes, especially those involving capital punishment, could be referred to the *lögrétta* at the Althing, which served as a court of appeal. One of the more onerous duties of a *sýslumaður* in the seventeenth century was the custody of accused persons, since Iceland had no prisons at that time. If a *sýslumaður* lived outside his *sýsla*, he might well get his *sýslumaður*'s duties there performed by a deputy (Icel. *lögsagnari*).[23]

The most important *sýsla* in the story of this book is the Ísafjarðarsýsla, which includes all the land bordering the Ísafjarðardjúp in the West Fjords (see the map). At the time of the events described in the *Story of Sufferings*, this large *sýsla* had two *sýslumenn*—one, Magnús Magnússon, for the western part of it, and the other, Þorleifur Kortsson, for the northern part. Since Þorleifur lived in a different *sýsla*, he had a *lögsagnari*, a wealthy man called Gísli Jónsson, who managed the affairs of the northern part for him.

As for trade between Iceland and the outside world, in the seventeenth century (in fact, from 1602 to 1787) it was carried on exclusively by a Danish trading company which purchased the right to this monopoly from the Danish king.[24] About twenty-six trading stations (Icel. *kaupstaðir*), managed by Danish merchants, were scattered around the coast of Iceland, where the local people could go to buy imported goods (foodstuffs, wood, fishing tackle, etc.) and to sell their own produce (mostly woolen garments and fish). Not only were harsh punishments imposed on Icelanders who tried to do business with foreigners outside of the authorized trading company; but to each trading station was assigned a definite geographical area around it, and people were even prohibited (regardless of inconvenience) from doing business with any trading station other than the one in whose area they lived. Also, the Danish merchants who operated the trading stations were forbidden by their government to live in Iceland during the winter months. They were obliged to return to Denmark for the winter, leaving their stores locked and inoperative.

A few words on the construction of Icelandic farm dwellings are in order here.[25] In the seventeenth century (and much later) Icelandic farm dwellings—and churches—were low structures built largely of stone and turf. Wood, being mostly imported from abroad, was expensive and therefore used sparingly on the poorer farms; it provided supports and beams for the roof, and

Introduction

also inside panelling of the walls and flooring for those who could afford it.[26] Each farm dwelling had of course several rooms—the *baðstofa* (communal room, where people slept and did indoor work), *skáli*[27] (guest bedroom), kitchen, pantry, smithy, cowshed, and so on. Each of these was separately roofed; from the outside they had the appearance of small separate but adjacent houses. The rooms were connected on the inside by a long corridor leading in from the main entrance. A conspicuous indoor fitting of Icelandic farmhouses (often mentioned in the *Story of Sufferings*) was the *pallur*, or platform, a wooden surface raised above the general floor level, especially lengthwise along the wall of the *baðstofa*, furnished with one or more steps and intended for people to sit or rest on.[28] The walls, of stone and turf, could be several feet thick. The outer layer of the roof was of turf. Construction of a good turf roof was very skilled work. If the pitch of the roof was too little, the rain would not run off and the roof would leak; if it was too great, storms might wash the turf away. Because of the harsh climate and the scarcity of bushes and trees, peat and cowdung were the commonest heating fuel for the poor, and heat had to be jealously conserved. Windows were tiny, being made (in all but the wealthiest farms) not of glass but of animal membranes, and intended not for ventilation but only to admit a little sunlight. Some, though inadequate, provision was made for the escape of kitchen smoke through a hole in the roof. One can easily imagine how damp and malodorous the atmosphere in such farm dwellings must have been. But, knowing nothing else, the average Icelander of past centuries did not complain.

§5. *Witchcraft in Iceland*

What headway did the European witchcraft craze make in Iceland?

Two separate questions are involved here: The first is the question of the extent to which magic, both white and black, was practiced in Iceland throughout its history; and the second concerns the extent to which such practice was considered wicked and punished in different epochs. In §2 of this Introduction the European witchcraft craze was briefly considered from the standpoint of the second of these questions. In this section, about Iceland, mention will be made of the first as well.

Cases of magic and sorcery are recorded in the *Íslendingasögur* (Sagas of the Icelanders) and the *Sturlunga Saga*, which were written in the thirteenth and fourteenth centuries; and the lawbooks *Grágás* and *Jónsbók* (see §3) lay down harsh penalties for the practice of black magic. But white magic was still a subject of controversy at the begining of the seventeenth century, indeed, up to about 1650. Was it legitimate to invoke good spirits to achieve good ends by white magic?[29] The best-known defender of the legitimacy of white magic at that period was Jón Guðmundsson (1574–1658), nicknamed the Learned,[30] who has already been mentioned in §3. One of his most famous exploits was the laying of a troublesome ghost in 1611. In his opinion there was a gradation of supernatural beings, from the purely evil (demons) to the purely good (angels), with elves and *huldufólk* in between.[31] He clearly had sympathizers in high places. Bishop Guðbrandur Þorláksson of Hólar seems to have adopted a lenient attitude toward white magic and to have been helpful to Jón the Learned, employing him in literary work and getting his son accepted into the Hólar school. Later on Bishop Brynjólfur Sveinsson of Skálholt also helped and encouraged Jón the Learned (see §3).

But attitudes toward white magic were already changing in Iceland around 1590. A critical point came in the year 1592, when Bishop Oddur Einarsson of Skálholt made the following pronouncement at a synod of priests:

> As for those who practice magic, sorcery, conjurations, the carving of runes, the writing of charms against colic, and other such diabolism, pretending thereby to cure people's ills and sicknesses, if they refuse to mend their ways after three Christian admonitions, they must be punished by their priest according to the Ordinance and excluded from the sacrament. The same applies to those who desire to have this [magic performed for them] by others. For we believe that such acts are attended with terrible blasphemy.[32]

In 1617 King Christian IV of Denmark issued a decree to the effect that all sorcery, whether white or black, was evil and illegal and must be harshly suppressed throughout his domains.[33] In 1630 this decree was read out at the Althing in Icelandic translation, and thereafter became law in Iceland. White magic was declared to be a stratagem of the devil to lead people astray into worse things. It was even debated whether or not it was legitimate for scholars to study magic, black or otherwise, as a scientific pursuit.[34]

In 1627 a priest by the name of Guðmundur Einarsson wrote a treatise called *Hugrás* attacking Jón Guðmundsson the Learned, whom *síra* Guðmundur regarded as an emissary of Satan sent to mislead people by habituating them to the "milder" forms of sorcery. In it he castigates Icelandic *sýslumenn* for neglect of the king's decree of 1617. According to *Hugrás* there is no gradation of supernatural beings: all spirits other than angels are satanic.

In 1637 Jón the Learned was sentenced at the Althing to permanent exile from Iceland for practicing white magic and misusing God's name. But the king lightened the sentence, permitting him to take up residence in eastern Iceland—perhaps because sorcery was less of an issue there than in his native district of western Iceland.

At any rate, by the middle of the seventeenth century it seems to have been generally agreed by the ruling classes in Iceland that *all* practice of magic, white and black alike, was criminal and deserved the harshest punishment.

Belief in the reality and efficacy of magic both black and white, and fear of those who had a reputation as adepts in black magic, was rampant among all classes, not only among simple uneducated people but among priests and magistrates as well.[35] Nevertheless, in Iceland the campaign against witchcraft was slow in getting started, and was consistently milder than on the European continent. Not until 1625 was the first person (a man) burned to death for sorcery in post-Reformation Iceland; and subsequently no sorcerer was burned until 1654. The total number burned in Iceland for sorcery during the seventeenth century was about twenty-one—a small number in comparison with most European countries, even in proportion to population. Of these, seventeen were explicitly convicted of practicing black magic; two were burned for the practice of white magic; and of the remaining two we are not told the nature of the sorcery for which they paid the supreme penalty.

Of the twenty-one persons burned for sorcery in seventeenth-century Iceland only one was a woman.

Of course not all witchcraft trials ended in burnings; some defendants received lesser punishments (e.g., flogging or exile), and others were acquitted. The total number of witchcraft trials in Iceland after the Reformation was about 120. About three quarters of these took place in the half-century between 1646 and 1695. About half of the witchcraft trials originated in the West Fjords (although, according to the 1703 census, the West Fjords were home to only about fifteen percent of the total population of Iceland). As regards sex, only ten of the defendants in the witchcraft trials were women.[36]

Why was the witchcraft craze in Iceland much less intense than elsewhere in Europe? It is true that, by the middle of the seventeenth century, leading churchmen and magistrates of Iceland generally held that converse with spirits for any worldly purpose, and therefore all witchcraft both white and black (and even the mere possession of manuals of witchcraft), was devil-worship and therefore a rejection of God, and as such should be suppressed and severely punished. But various factors tended to mitigate the extent to which this suppression was carried out in Iceland. Two facts are significant here: First, the evidence adduced to convict sorcerers in Iceland was in general more factual and observable than on the continent—for example, evidence of the possession of manuals of magic, and of their use with intent to cause harm (or even healing) to others. Secondly, it seems that in Iceland judicial torture was hardly ever applied to obtain evidence of guilt. These facts in themselves prevented enthusiastic Icelandic prosecutors from multiplying the number of witchcraft suspects in the ways that were open to their counterparts on the continent.

Most of the Icelandic civil magistrates and Church leaders, while giving lip service to the condemnation of all forms of sorcery, were reluctant to take the initiative in pressing charges of witchcraft in the courts, as the king's decree of 1617 required them to do. Indeed, on this point, where the 1617 decree clearly conflicted with the traditional procedures laid down in the old Icelandic lawbooks, many Icelandic magistrates simply bypassed the former. (We shall see in the *Story of Sufferings* how intensely *síra* Jón Magnússon campaigned against this reluctance.) As we have seen (in §3), an outstanding example of this lack of fanaticism was Brynjólfur Sveinsson, bishop of Skálholt from 1639 to 1674, who, though a stern disciplinarian who believed that sorcery was very evil, resisted pressure to facilitate the prosecution of sorcerers according to the standards of Danish law (see §3). In fact, most of the burnings for witchcraft in Iceland were the work of a small number of zealous magistrates who had been educated in Germany, where the witchcraft craze was at its peak. Chief of these was a man named Þorleifur Kortsson, whom we will meet later on.

One naturally asks: to what extent was the relative mildness of the witch-hunt in Iceland due to the infiltration of the ideas of Cornelius Agrippa, Johann Weyer, and their fellow liberals? Some Icelanders certainly held similar ideas at that time. For example, we find Gísli Oddsson, son of Bishop Oddur Einarsson and himself bishop of Skálholt from 1632 to 1638, surmising that the elves or "hidden people," so frequently encountered in Icelandic folklore, are in fact nothing but delusions, optical illusions, manufactured by demons.[37] Moreover, along with cases in which insanity and demonic possession are identified (see Note 35), seventeenth-century Iceland also yields instances in which a clear distinction is made between natural and demonic causes of insanity.[38]

A few Icelanders of the seventeenth century were aware of, and receptive to, the work of liberals like Weyer. Such was the priest and scholar *síra* Páll Björnsson (1621–1706), whose book *Kennimark kölska* (*Character Bestiae* = The Mark of the Beast) is the most outstanding work on sorcery produced in Iceland in the seventeenth century.[39] This is an immensely learned work, quite moderate in tone, and full of curious anecdotes about tricks that the devil has played on mankind during its long history. In this book he quotes several times from the writings of Weyer, Cardano, and Agrippa, but only once from the *Malleus Maleficarum*. This indicates that the ideas of Weyer and his ilk were at least known in Iceland at the time.[40]

Síra Páll, like his contemporary *síra* Jón Magnússon, was a firm believer in the reality and efficacy of black magic (and in fact was instrumental in getting several persons burned to death for sorcery). So it is not surprising that he is not always an unqualified admirer of Weyer. He writes:

> The word "sorcery" may at some time have meant certain harmless skills and know-how. But at present sorcery is in such bad odor among all good men that the only meaning it conveys is the diabolical expertise which makes use of staves

Introduction

dipped in blood, sinister runes and carvings, spells, dead men's bones and fat, conjurations, and countless ceremonies involving the perversion of God's word and sacraments, to establish a contract between the devil and the sorcerer for the breaking down of God's kingdom and the building up of the kingdom of darkness. Thereby many have suffered irreparable damage to their health and happiness, according as our God has permitted it, to the everlasting damnation of those who will not cease from studying and practicing [this art] by hand and voice. So the word ["sorcery"] appears to be used in too mild a fashion by those who refer to acts of sorcery as tricks (*praestigia*) or illusions, as Weyer has done by the title of the book that he has written about sorcery [see Note 12]. In these days works are known by their fruits; and many an innocent person has been murdered and tortured by the devils that these sorcerers have dispatched against him for the purpose. For it has sometimes been found, and indeed stated by them, that they are able to dispatch whomever they wish, to bring about every kind of mishap. So to call [these acts] tricks and illusions is to do the least possible justice to [the reality of] sorcery and the sorcerer's art.[41]

Nevertheless, in other contexts *síra* Páll approves the more liberal ideas of Weyer. He accepts, for example, the view that only God can do real miracles. Sorcery can never do miracles or change the course of nature; it can at most *appear* to do so. Thus, appealing to the authority of St. Augustine, he writes:

An Egyptian man was once in frantic pursuit of a girl and changed her into a mare; but she was restored to her normal state by the holy Macarius.[42] The best justification of this story is given by Augustine in his book *De Spirit [sic!] et Anima*,[43] [where he says]: Human cogitation and conjecture would assert that by some feminine art or diabolical potency humans can be changed into animals, in so far as their necessary functions are concerned, and that after doing whatever [they are meant to do] they are restored to their proper nature. They do not take on the mental state of the animals [into which they are transformed], but keep their own understanding. Here we must recognize that these devils cannot create a new nature; the most they can do is to make something *appear* to exist which does not exist.[44]

As a biblical example of such "sorcery through illusion" *síra* Páll quotes the ability of Pharaoh's sorcerers to imitate Moses' miracle by turning their staffs too into serpents.[45]

Even more importantly, *síra* Páll, following Weyer, makes a clear distinction between mental illness and sorcery. So we find him saying:

One must be very careful not to blame sorcery whenever something appears to take place contrary to our experience, which through ignorance we are unable to explain—for example, when people are plagued with depression [Icel. *melancholia*], which is due to a black, turbid fluid in the body that often leads the mind and brain astray. .... Here the devil, our enemy, lies in wait to interject himself and to attack the [sick] person at his weakest point. But in all this there is no sorcery involved.[46]

But in spite of his sympathy with views of witchcraft that were considered liberal at the time, *síra* Páll was never in any doubt that evil spirits were on the rampage, and that their power to torment poor human beings and lead them astray was very real, even if the "miracles" that they seemed to do were illusive. Thus, he was convinced of the existence and malignancy of elves and "hidden people."[47] His conviction that sorcerers, the human dupes of the devil, deserved the severest possible punishment has already been mentioned.

It seems to me that the relatively easygoing attitude of most Icelandic priests and magistrates toward witchcraft, so vigorously attacked in the *Story of Sufferings*, was the cause rather than the effect of their receptivity to the kind of ideas promoted by Weyer and his fellow liberals. The attitudes of the latter seem to have been in harmony with what most educated Icelanders already believed. Indeed, as I have already observed, Weyer did not condemn all witch-burnings; he simply pressed for greater caution and restraint in distinguishing between real witches (who *should* be burned) and those whose only sin was some form of insanity.

From a pastoral point of view also, at least two of the leading ecclesiastical figures of seventeenth-century Iceland, namely Bishop Guðbrandur Þorláksson and Bishop Brynjólfur Sveinsson, were not slow to point out the spiritual evils of an obsession with demonology. The demonology of the *Malleus Maleficarum* instilled the idea that the devil fights against God by using his henchmen, the sorcerers, to inflict material disasters on poor human beings, and must be fought in turn by human beings with material violence (burnings). But in fact only God is mightier than the devil, and the primary weapons of both are spiritual, not material. Satan's real victories lie not in inflicting material disasters, but in making human beings despair of their salvation. The only way to foil this strategy of Satan is to turn one's mind from the power of sin and the devil to the infinitely greater salvific power of God in Christ. In fact, even tangible human misery does not originate in black magic, but in the benevolent purposes of God.

Thus, in the preface to a book published by him in 1597 Bishop Guðbrandur writes:

> Among God's children are some God-fearing persons who are terrified of God's wrath, eternal damnation, and the merited punishment of their sins, but in spite of all cling trustingly to God's gracious promises. Some of these have strong and sturdy faith in the promises of God's grace. Others are weak, and pass through storms and strong passions aroused by the devil, being tormented in their consciences because of the multitude and gravity of their sins. [Accordingly, this book is directed against] this poisonous infatuation of the soul which we call hopelessness or despair, [and finds medicine for it] in the Lord's garden [i.e., in the holy scriptures].[48]

One also sees enlightened ideas in Bishop Brynjólfur's comment contained in a letter that he wrote to a parish priest in 1656:

> The reason why the devil has such power in our country is that people have such fear of him. The more the heart and mind are busy with the fear of the devil, the more the fear of God and true faith lose ground. Why does the Lord suffer and permit the enemy to work such derangement in the Christian Church? It is because people's hearts are lukewarm and do not sincerely hold fast to almighty God, but are disloyal to Him, fearing the devil as well as God, whereas fear, like love and faith, are owed to God alone. That is one cause among others, I think, that gives scope for the mischief done by the devil's henchmen in our country. But the devil is an arrogant spirit, and cannot bear to be treated with contempt. So his courage droops in the presence of a genuine fear of God, prayer, and practice of Christian living.[49]

Here we see a clear perception of Weyer's insight—that the effects of sorcery are due primarily to the upset condition of the victim's mind.

Here a warning is in order: one must not exaggerate the prevalence of witchcraft in seventeenth-century Iceland, as if there were little else to occupy the minds of Icelanders in that period. The obsession with witchcraft shown in the behavior of our subject *síra* Jón Magnússon was not typical of seventeenth-century Icelanders. The sorcery cases tried in the courts originated mostly in the northern and western parts of the country; in the south and east sorcery cases were relatively rare.[50]

Indeed there *was* another development of consuming interest to many contemporary Icelanders, namely, the literary revival of the seventeenth century. The high point of this revival was the *Passion Hymns* of the poet-priest *síra* Hallgrímur Pétursson (1614–1674), a collection of fifty hymns of meditation on the passion of Christ, first printed in 1666, which have had more influence on Icelandic Christianity since his time than any other book except the Bible. In the *Passion Hymns* there is only one explicit mention of witchcraft (Hymn 14, verse 11), and that is quite peripheral. Most of the prose and poetry produced in seventeenth-century Iceland was centered on the Christian life, and was didactic, mystical, or devotional in character. But there was also a great deal of literary work of a secular nature. Indeed, multitudes of unprinted manuscripts from the seventeenth century, both religious and secular, in both prose and poetry, survive in the National Library of Iceland and in other places, testifying to the eagerness of the Icelandic people of that era to participate in literary pursuits.

Other aspects of cultural revival also captured the imaginations of many seventeenth-century Icelanders. One was the renewal of interest in their old Saga Age literature, stimulated by the enthusiasm of scholars abroad. Three outstanding representatives of this pursuit were Bishop Brynjólfur Sveinsson,

Bishop Þorlákur Skúlason (bishop of Hólar from 1628 to 1656), and the poet *síra* Hallgrímur Pétursson.

Also, the sixteenth and seventeenth centuries were the era of the birth of modern science.[51] The Royal Society of London for the promotion of science was founded in 1660. In Iceland too the movement had made itself felt by the seventeenth century. By 1650 physics and mathematics were being taught to some extent in the diocesan schools of Skálholt and Hólar. As was mentioned above, Bishop Oddur Einarsson of Skálholt studied under Tycho Brahe in Copenhagen, and Bishop Guðbrandur Þorláksson of Hólar determined the latitude of Hólar with surprising accuracy. Most remarkable was the case of *síra* Páll Björnsson, also mentioned above, that wide-ranging scholar whose interests encompassed science and technology and who corresponded with the Royal Society of London, and who nevertheless was a burner of sorcerers par excellence.[52]

Thus the seventeenth century was a period of startling contradictions, in Iceland as elsewhere in Europe.[53]

As the seventeenth century approached its end, the sense of the urgency of eradicating witchcraft was dying down, in Iceland as in the rest of Europe (see Note 14). The last person in Iceland to be burned for sorcery was a man called Sveinn Árnason, consigned to the flames in 1683. Two years later one Halldór Finnbogason was burned to death, not strictly speaking for sorcery but for persistent and boastful blasphemy and for making a pact with the devil in a dream. In 1690 an Icelander called Klemens Bjarnason was sentenced at the Althing to be burned for sorcery, but his sentence was commuted by the Danish king to permanent exile. The last recorded Icelandic trial for sorcery took place in 1720, when three men were sentenced at the Althing to pay fines for dabbling in magic.[54]

So ends the story of civil punishment for magic in Iceland. But, needless to say, the belief in and practice of magic did not entirely die out, but has persisted on the periphery of society throughout the eighteenth and nineteenth centuries and perhaps even up to the present day.

§6. *Sorcery and Spells in Iceland*

What was involved in seventeenth-century Icelandic magic?

In answering this question this translator is aware that he stands on shaky ground. First, he himself is not a specialist in the area of magic and spells. Secondly, among scholars who have devoted time and effort to the subject there is disagreement on important aspects of it, for example: 1) the relationship between the *galdrastafir* (magical staves) and the pre-Christian runic alphabet, and 2) the mental qualities and attainments required of a prospective sorcerer.

We shall begin by asking: what were the procedures by which a seventeenth-century Icelandic sorcerer would cast his (or her) spells? The primary sources available for answering this question are the surviving manuals of magical lore from that period. These are very few in number—a fact that should not surprise us, considering the zeal with which the authorities of Church and state destroyed such manuals in their campaign to eradicate sorcery.

Two sources of Icelandic magical lore will be mentioned here. During the period (1639–1674) when the scholarly Brynjólfur Sveinsson was bishop of Skálholt, it was discovered that some of the schoolboys at the Skálholt school were in possession of an old dilapidated manual of magic,[55] which we shall refer to as the *Skálholt manual*. The bishop had it destroyed, but not before he had arranged to have a (still extant) index of its contents made.[56] His index lists the purposes for which the eighty magical procedures (spells and talismans) described in the manual were supposed to be effective, but (for reasons easy to surmise) refrains from describing the procedures themselves.

But the most important and revealing of the sources of our knowledge of the Icelandic magical lore of the times is the manuscript known as *Íslensk galdrabók* (Icelandic Book of Magic). It was probably compiled during the first half of the seventeenth century,[57] and finally found its way into the Antikvarisk-Topografiska Arkivet in Stockholm, Sweden, where it still resides. It has been published in printed editions three times in the twentieth century, in 1921 (by Natan Lindqvist), 1989 (by Stephen Flowers), and in 1992 (by Matthías Viðar Sæmundsson).[58] It prescribes forty-seven spells and talismans—both their procedures and the purposes for which they are intended. It is a unique monument to the culture of magic in the seventeenth century, the most complete Icelandic relic that we possess of the kind of book whose very possession could at that time doom men and women to be burned or at least flogged or exiled.[59]

Let us look first at the purposes for which the magic is prescribed, and then at the procedures themselves. As regards the purposes, there is a close parallel between the Skálholt manual and the *Íslensk galdrabók*. In both we find the following categories of spells:

1) Spells for protection against danger, and for gaining the upper hand in conflicts.
2) Spells for protection against thieves.
3) Spells for healing diseases.
4) Spells for acquiring prosperity.
5) Spells for acquiring profitable knowledge of circumstances and propitious times.
6) Spells for causing injury to the property and persons of others.
7) Spells for inducing unnatural deep sleep in others.
8) Love-spells for attracting a woman.

One does notice a difference, however: there are proportionately more love-spells and "black" magic in the Skálholt manual than in the *Íslensk galdrabók*, and conversely more "white" magic in the latter than in the former.[60]

What about the procedures, or spells, or magical rites themselves? One or more of three elements seem to enter into every magical rite from the *Íslensk galdrabók*: 1) graphic signs, 2) spoken or written words, 3) natural substances.[61]

1) The graphic signs used are either written on paper or carved on wood, and can be either letters of the runic alphabet or combinations of these in fixed stylized patterns. The latter are called *galdrastafir* (magical staves), and each had its name by which it was known, and its own potency. Among the most important of these was the Ægishjálmur (literally, helmet of awe or terror), whose basic form was a fourfold or eightfold cross with branches at its terminals.[62]

2) The spoken or written words (spells or conjurations) are used either independently or to activate the graphic signs.[63] Sometimes they consist of Christian prayers (often in garbled Latin); but often they contain appeals to one or more heathen (pre-Christian) gods. In this connection one must remember that, both in the Judaeo-Christian and in the heathen tradition, names are very powerful links to the person named: to know the correct name of a god or human person is to gain power over him.

3) Certain natural substances—e.g., blood, some kinds of wood (in which the runes and *galdrastafir* were to be carved), and certain herbs—were thought to be powerful elements of a magical rite.

It is important to remember that the tradition of magic and sorcery had descended from pre-Christian times. So it is not surprising that the names of the pre-Christian deities very often appear in the conjurations associated with sorcery. The same applies to the runic alphabet, which prior to the coming of Christianity was the only alphabet known and used in Iceland, and so became associated with heathendom. Indeed, some have conjectured that the *galdrastafir* themselves were formed from runic letters that denoted the names of heathen gods, or from the numerology associated with them.[64]

Stephen Flowers has argued that the role of a trained seventeenth-century Icelandic sorcerer was not merely to follow mechanically a memorized routine ritual procedure. Indeed, the above three elements of a magical ritual were "thought to be conduits or doorways through which various powers or entities are directed to do the will of the magician. The actual physical sign seems to have little power on its own; it is only in combination with the will of a trained magician that any results can be expected. That is why, in the folktales concerning the famous sorcerers of Iceland's past, such emphasis is placed on their scholarly characters and on the fact that the signs had to be learned by a process that involved more time and effort than just memorizing their external forms."[65] The signs and symbols were more than just material shapes with a form and a symbolic meaning. In addition there was the "power of the symbol," which lay hidden in the symbol and had to be harnessed and quickened, bringing about a mysterious contact between the symbol and what was symbolized. The most essential element in this mysterious quickening, empowering process was the mind (*hugur*) of the sorcerer himself. No ingredient of a magical rite could be effective in itself, unless the *hugur* of the sorcerer cooperated to empower it.[66]

According to the dominant demonology of the seventeenth-century western Church, the spirits that were thus harnessed by the *hugur* of the sorcerer working on the ingredients of his magical rite were necessarily diabolical. That is why theologians were commonly in agreement that *there cannot be magic unless the sorcerer makes deliberate contact with the devil*. The seventeenth-century Icelandic priest and scholar Arngrímur Jónsson wrote: "Everyone must realize that runes have no magical power in and of themselves, but only in so far as the sorcerer [who uses them] has fellowship with the devil. At that point the staves are no longer just runes; they have become magical and demonic staves, and only those who are proficient in this art can put them to use."[67]

According to this interpretation of sorcery, there is no essential difference between white and black magic.

It is worth observing that in general a clear distinction was made between sorcery on the one hand and extrasensory perception, such as second sight or clairvoyance, on the other. The latter is an inborn ability to perceive spirits and was considered morally harmless, while the former is a wilfully cultivated skill in manipulating spirits and, as we have seen, was generally regarded in the seventeenth century as highly sinful.

§7. The Scene of Jón Magnússon's Life as a Priest

Before turning to the life of Jón Magnússon, it will be well to describe the locale in which he spent his life as a priest.

After his ordination to the priesthood he lived for the rest of his life in the so-called West Fjords (Icel. Vestfirðir). This is a large rugged mountainous peninsula, deeply indented by numerous fjords, that projects out from the northwest corner of Iceland into the Arctic Ocean toward the east coast of Greenland some 180 miles away. It is somewhat like a fan in shape, about 100 miles across at its widest point, and is joined to the rest of Iceland by a relatively narrow isthmus, about thirteen miles wide. The largest of the fjords that indent it, and the one that penetrates most deeply into the heart of the West Fjords, is the so-called Ísafjarðardjúp, or Djúp for short—which incidentally provides very productive fishing grounds for the local inhabitants. At its mouth, where it enters the Arctic Ocean, the Djúp is about eleven miles wide; and its total length (from its mouth to the bottom of its longest branch) is about forty-six miles. The Djúp itself is indented with numerous subsidiary fjords. One of these, about five miles long, near the mouth of the Djúp on its south side, is called Skutulsfjörður; and it is this small fjord, and the valleys bordering it, that form the scene of most of the grisly events described in this book.

Let us look a little more closely at Skutulsfjörður. On both sides it is hemmed in by rocky mountains (a little more than 2000 feet high) whose steep slopes reach down almost to the water. At the bottom of the fjord rise somewhat lower hills; and these divide the land there into three grassy valleys, the largest and easternmost being Engidalur, then Dagverðardalur, then Tungudalur on the west. One of these, Dagverðardalur, if followed to its upper end, leads to the steep and formidable pass Breiðadalsheiði which travellers until recently were obliged to negotiate in order to journey south from Skutulsfjörður to the neighboring fjord, Önundarfjörður. (In 1996 the necessity of crossing this pass was obviated by the opening of a tunnel through the mountain.) But the most outstanding geographical feature of Skutulsfjörður is a large gravel spit (Icel. *eyri*),[68] which projects out into the fjord from roughly the middle of its west bank, extends more than halfway to the opposite bank, and then curves sharply south, forming a protected natural harbor (called Pollur, or pool) on its inland side. The twentieth century has seen a bustling town, Ísafjörður by name, grow and develop on this spit. It can rightly be called the capital of the West Fjords, and its population, together with that of surrounding smaller communities, now numbers about 4000. Its main economic support is the fishing industry, but at present it also boasts cultural enterprises such as a good music school.

But in the seventeenth century there was no town in Skutulsfjörður,[69] only the scattered evidences of a poor rural community. On the western end of the spit stood the local parish church, called Eyrarkirkja ("the church of the spit"), with its graveyard, and also the rectory and farm belonging to the church, which were called simply Eyri.[70] Toward the southern tip of the spit was the local trading station, called Neðstikaupstaður, operated by Danish merchants.[71]

The Eyrarkirkja, like all the churches in the West Fjords, belonged to the (southern) diocese of Skálholt. The first extant mention of the Eyrarkirkja occurs in the enumeration of churches (Icel. *kirknatal*) by Bishop Páll Jónsson of Skálholt, dated 1200. Later it is mentioned in the inventory of Bishop Vilchin of Skálholt,[72] dated 1397, according to which it was relatively prosperous. But in 1597 the church suffered serious damage from a wanton attack by English pirates, and evidently the damage had not been fully repaired even by the mid-seventeenth century when Jón Magnússon became the incumbent. An inventory from the year 1644—the year when *síra* Jón Magnússon took over as priest of Eyrarkirkja—describes the church in general terms: The interior of the church was panelled, at least in part. The nave and the choir both had board floors, and were presumably separated by a partition (serving, as in most churches, to enhance the sense of the holiness of the altar and sanctuary). Benches were arranged along the choir side of the partition and on the south side of the nave (where the men sat), and the church owned a tolerable set of priestly vestments, an altarpiece, a silver chalice with a paten, a baptismal basin, and other necessities. But other parts of the report present a picture of dilapidation: The church's two small windows were of glass, of which one was cracked. There was a tattered and unusable chasuble, an old worn-out altar cloth, a cracked bell, an old Bible with a decayed binding, and so on. However, it seems that in the later years of his incumbency Jón Magnússon did accomplish substantial renovation of the church and its possessions. During his incumbency the Eyrarkirkja owned a handsome painted image of the Virgin Mary and Child, apparently carved about 1500, which is now in the keeping of the National Museum of Iceland.[73]

In the seventeenth century the parish of Eyri—that is, the community for whose spiritual welfare the priest at Eyri was responsible—consisted of twelve farms, several of which are mentioned in Jón Magnússon's text. These were: Neðri-Hnífsdalur, Fremri-Hnífsdalur, Bakki, Eyri, Seljaland, Tunga, Hafrafell, Engidalur, Fossar, Kirkjuból, Fremri-Arnardalur, and Neðri-Arnardalur. Of these, the first three and the last two lie in valleys (Hnífsdalur and Arnardalur) that open into the Djúp just west of and just east of Skutulsfjörður respectively. Eyri itself, as we have seen, lies on the spit; and the remaining six farms are located in the valleys at the bottom of Skutulsfjörður. In addition there were three or four crofts (Icel. *hjáleiga*, smaller farms split off from the main ones). These farms were not all one-family units. Most of them housed two, three, or even more households (Icel. *býli*)—each of the latter including not only extended family members but also servants and laborers (and perhaps paupers quartered on them by the local authorities).[74]

To get an idea of the population and number of households in the Eyri parish in Jón Magnússon's time, we are obliged to appeal to the census[75] and Farm Register of 1703, compiled seven years after *síra* Jón's death and some forty-five years after the events described in this book. According to these, the total population of the Eyri parish in that year was 228; and the total number of households there was 39. (Thus the average number of members of each household must have been about six. These figures were presumably not too different in the 1650s.) From the Farm Register we also learn that the estimated values of the different farms were widely different: Kirkjuból was considered the most valuable and Bakki the least (being of about one fourth of the value of Kirkjuból).[76]

The farm in the parish of Eyri most important in our story, apart from the priest's farm at Eyri, is Kirkjuból. Around 1650 it was home to three households: one was that of the two Jón Jónssons (who were to be burned to death in 1656 for sorcery); another was that of Snæbjörn Pálsson (who was also later to be suspected of sorcery); and the third was that of Sturli Bjarnason (whom *síra* Jón describes as a pious man, and who witnessed against the Jón Jónssons). One feature of Kirkjuból that set it apart from other surrounding farms was that from Catholic times it had had its own church attached to it—the Kirkjubólskirkja. This was not a full-fledged parish church but was subordinate to, and served from, the parish church at Eyri. It was called a half-church or chapel (Icel. *hálfkirkja, bænhús*), and the local people would receive the sacrament there. The church at Kirkjuból plays a significant role in Jón Magnússon's story, as the reader will see from the opening page of the *Story of Sufferings*.

§8. Síra *Jón Magnússon, Priest of Eyri*

Jón Magnússon was born around 1610 in northern Iceland, not far from the present town of Blönduós. His father was a parish priest, and one of his brothers, also named Jón Magnússon,[77] became a well-known priest, scholar, and poet (who, however, never figures in our story). When our subject lost his mother at an early age he was taken as a foster child into the home of Oddur Einarsson, the capable and scholarly bishop of Skálholt from 1589 to 1630, and in due course entered the Skálholt school, where he completed his education in 1630. Since Jón Magnússon tells us that he always remembered his foster parents with deep respect and affection,[78] it is quite likely that his own attitudes toward religion and the supernatural were influenced by those of Bishop Oddur.[79]

In those days graduation from either the Skálholt or the Hólar school was the only educational prerequisite for ordination to the priesthood. In 1633 Jón Magnússon was ordained to be assistant priest to *síra* Gísli Einarsson (brother of Bishop Oddur) in Vatnsfjörður in the West Fjords; and it is as *síra* Jón (i.e., the Reverend Jón) that we shall refer to him henceforth. From 1635 to 1643 he served as priest at the parish of Ögur, also in the West Fjords. Here he met his wife-to-be, Þorkatla Bjarnadóttir, the widow of a priest named Snorri Hákonarson. She already had two children, a son Bjarni Snorrason and a daughter Rannveig Snorradóttir, by her first husband. While serving as priest at Ögur *síra* Jón wrote a letter to Bishop Gísli Oddsson, who had succeeded his father Oddur Einarsson as bishop of Skálholt, complaining that his work load was too much for him, and received in reply a reprimand for laziness![80]

In 1643 *síra* Jón was called to be parish priest at Eyrarkirkja (after the preceding priest, *síra* Ólafur Jónsson, had been dismissed for adultery). By 1655 he and Þorkatla had a young son named Snorri. He remained at Eyri for the rest of his working life, and here the unhappy events took place which have made him famous (or infamous!).

At the farm Kirkjuból in the parish of Eyri, there lived a father and son, both called Jón Jónsson. It seems certain that both the Jón Jónssons had strong grudges against *síra* Jón. For one thing, the younger Jón Jónsson had previously courted *síra* Jón's stepdaughter Rannveig, but his request to marry her had been refused by the priest, for reasons unknown.[81] Another contributing cause may have been the stern rebuke delivered publicly at a church service by *síra* Jón to the younger Jón Jónsson for having in a fit of anger punched one of the servant women at Kirkjuból and knocked her over.[82] Moreover, both the Jón Jónssons were practitioners of sorcery, and both of them later confessed to having practiced their magical arts against their priest.[83] In October 1655, while they were apparently so engaged, *síra* Jón (and indeed his family and household to a lesser extent as well) began to suffer extraordinary and distressing symptoms of illness, accompanied by a strong sense of being persecuted by demons. The detailed course of events is graphically described in the *Story of Sufferings*, so there is no need to outline it here. But, to show how excruciating the sufferings were that *síra* Jón experienced during the period 1655–1656, I will insert here the following quotation from the *Story of Sufferings*:

> These torments were neither human nor within the bounds of human understanding. They were not like natural diseases, which I have often experienced in my lifetime, both as a youth and as an older man, and some of which have pushed me to the brink of death. Compared to these devilish tortures human sicknesses are nothing but chaff and trifles. ...... Sometimes it was as if I were being squeezed and squashed under an enormously heavy weight, as when a worm is squashed or cheese is compressed, so that every ounce of strength was drained out of me; and along with the crushing weight I felt as if my body were being jabbed with small red-hot glowing needles....... Sometimes I felt as if I were being transfixed through the side that I was lying on with a spike that seemed to pierce through the body between my ribs, so that I expected it would be the death of me. Sometimes I lay in a blazing fire, struggling for breath. I felt sure that the flames from the fire were leaping through my entire body, especially my chest, and flashes of fire seemed to erupt from my fingers, so that I felt convinced that I was going to burn to ashes. ...... At times the flesh on my bones felt as if it were crawling with a mass of worms, seething and twisting in a most ghastly and abhorrent manner. And yet all this was but a trifle compared with the interior tortures that assailed me, ... far surpassing all torments that can be expressed in words.[84]

To *síra* Jón it was beyond all doubt that the causes of all his sufferings and those of his household were the spells put upon him by the two Jón Jónssons. He therefore pressed charges against them before Magnús Magnússon and

Gísli Jónsson, the local *sýslumaður* and *lögsagnari* (deputy *sýslumaður*). The primary accusation against them was that they practiced sorcery, a crime against God and His word and against the laws of the country and the king. He further accused them of causing demonic attacks on him, his household, and others of the district, which threatened to reduce the life of the whole community to a shambles. He himself had been reduced to such a state of suffering, sickness, and debilitation that he could no longer perform the duties of his priestly office. Whether from inertia, or inexperience,[85] or from a suspicion that *síra* Jón was mentally unbalanced, Magnús Magnússon was at first unwilling to take up the case. But, whatever his sufferings, *síra* Jón's drive and persistence had not abated. At his insistence the two magistrates convened a local court at Eyri in December 1655 to investigate the matter, at which Jón Magnússon presented what he considered to be conclusive proof that the two Jón Jónssons had practiced wicked sorcery against him and his household. The evidence presented by *síra* Jón was basically twofold: 1) clairvoyant people had seen the devil masquerading under the form of the two Jón Jónssons, and 2) *síra* Jón's sickness increased each time that the Jón Jónssons approached his church or rectory. The court's decision[86] was that the only way for the Jón Jónssons to establish their innocence would be the time-honored legal procedure known as the *tylftareiður*: they must muster twelve men (compurgators) willing to swear an oath affirming their innocence, and were to be given a certain amount of time in which to assemble the compurgators.[87] *Síra* Jón was furious at this outcome, since instead of causing the immediate arrest of the father and son it would grant them an extra period of liberty during which to practice their sorcery against himself and his household. However, he soon enlisted the support and cooperation of a new and more enterprising ally, the *sýslumaður* of the northern part of the Ísafjarðarsýsla, Þorleifur Kortsson by name, who only a year before had shown his mettle by getting three alleged sorcerers burned to death in Trékyllisvík, another remote area of the West Fjords. The outcome of the joint efforts of *síra* Jón and the three magistrates was that the Jón Jónssons, father and son, being unable to assemble the required number of compurgators, were arrested and put in irons, and on 10 April 1656 were both burned to death (on the site of the present Ísafjörður airport). Chapter VI of the *Story of Sufferings* contains the official verdict passed on the two sorcerers on 9 April 1656, summarizing the evidence for their guilt as collected by the court.

It is worth noting that the evidence against the Jón Jónssons, based largely on their own confessions and summarized in the official verdict, makes no mention of any conscious *pact* between them and the devil.[88]

Even after the death of the Jón Jónssons, the intense physical and spiritual sufferings of *síra* Jón continued intermittently for a while, to his great disappointment. During this period he wrote a letter to *síra* Páll Björnsson of

Selárdalur asking for his advice and prayers. *Síra* Páll not only responded with a letter of consolation, but took the trouble of travelling the long distance from Selárdalur to Eyri to visit *síra* Jón (though we have no record of any effects produced by the visit). But this spell of sufferings finally ended, and *síra* Jón enjoyed a remission that lasted through the summer months of 1656, during which he was able to resume some farm work and priestly duties.

But the remission was not permanent. In August of 1656 a new round of torments began in earnest. Surely these too were due to sorcery. While the Jón Jónssons were alive, *síra* Jón had found that his sufferings intensified when either the father or son passed by close to his farm. After August 1656 he noticed that his torments were intensified on the approach of Þuríður Jónsdóttir, a young woman who was daughter and sister to the two Jón Jónssons. It must, he thought, be she whose sorcery (presumably learned from her father and brother, and practiced in revenge for their deaths) was responsible for these new tortures. A crucial hardening of his attitude toward Þuríður came when on 29 August 1656 he made a call on her at Kirkjuból, accompanied by a glib talker and vagrant named Erlendur Ormsson,[89] who had gained the priest's confidence by setting himself up as a pious Christian and devout enemy of all witchcraft. Both Erlendur and *síra* Jón berated Þuríður harshly for her sorceries, and demanded that she should repent. Þuríður's response to these diatribes was almost complete silence, interpreted by *síra* Jón as sinful hardheartedness. This and other supposedly demonic manifestations strengthened *síra* Jón's conviction that it was indeed she whose witchcraft was to blame for his renewed sufferings. And the renewed tortures that followed this meeting, which he describes as follows, turned his conviction into a sense of certainty:

> I rode homeward from Kirkjuból as evening drew on........ When I reached home and sat on the bed in the *skáli*, I felt as if my face were being attacked by the biting of gnats. Thereafter I began again to suffer agonizing torments. They were especially violent for three nights, most of all on the third. Not until that time did I realize how savage were the racking tortures that the devils could cook up. In my sleep I felt as if I were being drawn out limb from limb and then, in between, slammed and snapped together again into fetters. Never do I remember having experienced this kind of torture—never in all the former attacks of witchcraft, as far as my memory reaches—except on this one occasion.[90]

About a week after this "pastoral" call, *síra* Jón paid another visit to Þuríður, in the course of which (according to Þuríður's later accusation against him[91]) he spat in her face. Foreseeing the persecution in store for her, Þuríður now fled from Kirkjuból and took refuge with an influential family that was friendly to her. This was the family of *síra* Jón Jónsson, priest of a parish in a neighboring valley and the district dean, whose wife, Halldóra Jónsdóttir, was a forceful individual with high family connections in her own right.[92] In due course *síra* Jón brought charges of sorcery against Þuríður, intending to have her burned to death if he could, as he had already done to her father and brother. But by now the authorities had lost confidence in *síra* Jón's accusations, and Þuríður's protectors were influential enough to stymie the proceedings. Later, in May 1657, five priests met at Holt to consider the case against Þuríður (in particular, her request for permission to receive the sacrament at Holt), and concluded "that her behavior was Christian, and that the case against her was mere conjecture and insinuation."[93] At this point *síra* Jón saw no other recourse than to present his case before the highest court of the land, the Althing, which met at Þingvellir in June of each year. Sick as he was, in June 1657 he made the long journey from Eyri to Þingvellir. Though the magistrates there paid lip service to the 1617 edict of King Christian IV, his complaints did not lead to any serious steps against Þuríður, as he found to his disappointment on his return home. Later in the year 1657 he renewed his demands for an investigation of his charges against Þuríður, and journeyed to the 1658 session of the Althing, where the case was again discussed in the presence of both him and Þuríður. But *síra* Jón's charges were now clearly viewed with even more skepticism than in 1657. In particular, Erlendur Ormsson was now ordered, on pain of punishment, to substantiate various statements that he had apparently made in support of *síra* Jón's case against Þuríður. Evidently he was not able to do so, for in the fall of 1658 Þuríður was finally acquitted (in the local court at Mosvellir near Holt) of the charge of sorcery, on the basis of the *tylftareiður* of twelve women who asserted her innocence. This acquittal was apparently confirmed without opposition by the Althing in 1659.[94] At this point Þuríður (and her friends) turned the tables on *síra* Jón and brought charges against him for having groundlessly vilified and persecuted her.[95] Unfortunately there are no surviving records of the final outcome of her case.[96]

As I mentioned at the beginning of this Introduction, it was this reverse that provoked *síra* Jón, probably in the winter 1658–1659, to write the *Story of Sufferings* (Icel. *Píslarsaga*) which forms the substance of this book. Though autobiographical, it is not of course an autobiography, since it covers only the relatively short period of about three years (1655–1658) during which he grappled in court with the "forces of darkness." In it he graphically describes the torments that he and his household endured, his reasons for blaming them on sorceries practiced by the two Jón Jónssons and later by Þuríður, and his frantic efforts to bring the alleged culprits to justice. His book is both an apologia for his own proceedings, and a bitter attack on the negligence and indifference of most of the Icelandic magistrates of his day regarding the horrible realities of sorcery.[97] So monstrous a crime against God and man is sorcery, in his view, that in judging accusations of sorcery magistrates

Introduction 31

are duty bound to bypass the normal rules of legal procedure proper for lesser crimes, such as rules for the gathering of evidence.[98] In cases of sorcery the magistrate must act as judge and prosecutor in one; anything less is a breach of the 1617 edict of King Christian IV. Especially the acquittal of Þuríður in 1658 showed, in *síra* Jón's view, a complete disregard of this fundamental "truth."

Not much is known about the later years of *síra* Jón's tenure of the Eyri parish—apart from the fact that he did take steps to renovate and beautify the Eyrarkirkja. As far as we know, he wrote nothing substantial after the *Story of Sufferings* (and the supplementary tracts that accompanied it).[99] As he grew older his obsession with witchcraft seems to have abated, and we hear of no more disturbances in his parish due to this cause from about 1660 onward. (Even by 1658 the demonic attacks from which he suffered had become milder than before.[100]) The report of the official episcopal visitation of 1675 to the parish of Eyri in Skutulsfjörður states that *síra* Jón gave his parishioners an honorable report, and they gave him the same.[101] But there is also nothing to suggest that in his later years he changed his views on the reality of sorcery, or repented of his earlier persecution of the two Jón Jónssons and Þuríður. In 1675 the poverty of his family apparently led him to make a request to the synod of priests (meeting in conjunction with the Althing) for additional compensation for the losses he had suffered in earlier years from black magic.[102]

But the calming of his obsession with witchcraft as the years passed may also have been a matter of necessity. Times were changing. By 1680 the harassment of sorcerers, though not yet defunct, was flagging in Iceland[103] as well as throughout the rest of Europe. By then *síra* Jón would have had even more difficulty than in 1656–1658 in launching a witchcraft trial, even if he had wanted to. Besides, his champion Þorleifur Kortsson had stepped down from his position of authority in 1679.

In 1689 *síra* Jón, now infirm with age, resigned his parish, handing it over to another priest, and in 1690 he moved to Kirkjuból (the former home of the two Jón Jónssons), where his son Snorri Jónsson and the latter's wife were already living. By 1692 *síra* Jón was bedridden, though in full possession of his mental faculties. He died in 1696, at the age of about 86.[104]

§9. *Attitudes of Scholars Toward the* Story of Sufferings

It is interesting to trace the different attitudes that have been taken by scholars toward Jón Magnússon, his sickness, and his *Story of Sufferings*. The original manuscript of the work has long been lost. As I mentioned in §1, the only known copy of it was made in the eighteenth century and found its way into the manuscript collection of the Royal Library of Copenhagen, where it gathered dust until the last decade of the nineteenth century, when the Icelandic geographer, geologist, and cultural historian Þorvaldur Thoroddsen drew attention to it in his *Landfræðisaga Íslands*. He interpreted it in the light of the theory, current since the eighteenth century, that the witchcraft craze of the sixteenth and seventeenth centuries was an outbreak of mental illness—in fact a "mental epidemic," analogous to the great epidemics of physical disease, in which the disorder of one victim infects others, until the disease is raging throughout an entire population. He had nothing good to say of the work either from a literary or a religious point of view. He regarded it as the repulsive product of a crazed author, a relic of a dark, cruel, ignorant, superstitious age, in which the people lived in constant terror of devils and demons prowling around their homes.[105] In fact Þorvaldur Thoroddsen is thought to have played a large part in encouraging the attitude, current up to the present time, that regards the seventeenth century as a dark and tragic era.

The editors of the three editions of the *Píslarsaga* that have so far been published in the original Icelandic (in 1914, 1967, and 2001; see §1) give, in their Introductions, different analyses of Jón Magnússon's physical and spiritual state, each emphasizing an aspect of what is even now a difficult and not fully solved problem. They also differ greatly in the material which they include.

Sigfús Blöndal, editor of the first (1914) edition, includes all of the surviving manuscript of *síra* Jón's *Píslarsaga*, together with a few other short surviving documents relating to the decisions of the Althing in 1658 and Þuríður's charges against *síra* Jón. He declares with assurance that the symptoms from which *síra* Jón suffered all point to neurasthenia combined with hysteria, and adds that "for a while, one may say, the priest had a touch of insanity."[106] He does point out the literary excellences of the *Píslarsaga*. But apart from that he in general concurs with the view of Þorvaldur Thoroddsen—except that he allows the possibility that telepathy may have been the means by which sorcerers communicated sickness and mental disturbance to their victims.[107]

The second (1967) edition is the shortest of the three. Its editor, the outstanding literary scholar Sigurður Nordal, omits three of the four supplementary tracts that come at the end of the surviving manuscript, on the ground that they add little to the remaining one which he does include (our Chapter X). He also does not include any of the supporting letters and legal documents that are to be found in the 2001 edition. Though he gives high praise to the literary qualities of the *Píslarsaga*, he agrees with Sigfús Blöndal that *síra* Jón Magnússon was both mentally and physically sick.[108] But he certainly does not agree that the *Píslarsaga* gives a representative picture of the mental state of Icelanders in the seventeenth century. In his Introduction to the work, he summarizes the relevance of the *Píslarsaga* to the history of Iceland in its time as follows: it shows what *could* happen in the seventeenth century—as opposed, say, to the fifteenth or nineteenth centuries—when all the conditions specially prevalent in that century came together in one time and place.[109]

But Sigurður Nordal does not stop there. In his Introduction he brings out a vital facet of *síra* Jón's life to which little or no attention had previously been paid—the positive side of his religious or spiritual life. Instead of assuming that his fanatical Christian beliefs served only to exacerbate his mental imbalance, Sigurður Nordal asks whether in fact it was his Christianity that also prevented him from becoming totally insane. Later in this Introduction I will discuss this in greater depth.

The third and most recent (2001) edition of the *Píslarsaga* is, from a historical point of view, the most ambitious and satisfactory of the three. It includes not merely the complete *Píslarsaga*, but all the extant documents that concern *síra* Jón himself, his parish, his communications with his dean and fellow priests, and his prosecution of the Jón Jónssons and Þuríður. Moreover its editor, Matthías Viðar Sæmundsson, provides a lengthy and interesting discussion of the way in which people thought about mental disease and its relation to sorcery, both in the seventeenth century and later. He does not deny Sigfús Blöndal's statement that Jón Magnússon, during his sickness which he attributed to demonic assaults, was suffering from acute neurasthenia. But he sees a real danger in trying to understand seventeenth-century thinking and feeling by means of twentieth-century intellectual tools, as Sigfús Blöndal and many others have done.[110] He compares it to trying to undertan a seventeenth-century chess game in terms of twentieth-century rules of chess. He prefers to be guided by what thinkers of the seventeenth century, such as the English writer Robert Burton in his *Anatomy of Melancholy* (1621), have to say about mental disorders arising from improperly digested religious ideas. In particular he heartily rejects the notion, propounded by Þorvaldur Thoroddsen and many others since the eighteenth century, that the witchcraft craze was a sort of "madness epidemic." Such a notion, he feels, betrays an inability to put oneself into the mind-set of the sixteenth and seventeenth centuries.[111] Indeed, many of the resolute witch-burners of that era were men of solid intellect, who were acting rationally in their own light.[112]

In connection with Burton's analyses Matthías Viðar does give a general idea of the theological climate of seventeenth-century Protestant Europe. But, unlike Sigurður Nordal, he has little to say about *síra* Jón's specific religious practices or experiences or their relevance to his life as a whole. It seems to me that this is a serious omission; and in the remainder of this essay I shall try to rectify it from a Christian standpoint.

In making this attempt I shall bring out two points. In the first place I feel that too much has been made of *síra* Jón's mental illness. His insistence on the demonic origin of his physical symptoms, and his preoccupation with ferreting out the sorcerers supposedly responsible for them and having them cruelly punished, were not signs of insanity in themselves, but rather of the prevalent world view of his times, though the stress and intensity of his one-pointed absorption in these undoubtedly did bring on the neurotic symptoms that he describes in the *Story of Sufferings*.

Secondly, I shall follow Sigurður Nordal in placing an emphasis on *síra* Jón's strictly religious (indeed, mystical) experiences. Five of these are recorded in the *Story of Sufferings*, and will be briefly discussed in the following pages. The position will be taken here that these experiences, based as they were on an unshakeable Christian faith, were quite "disjoint" from whatever physical and psychological disorders afflicted him, and took place on a quite different "level" of his being.

§10. *The Nature of* Síra Jón's *Distresses*

In spite of the evidence of the *Story of Sufferings*, and various letters and court documents relating to his witchcraft prosecutions which have survived the passage of time, much is still unclear and controversial about the personality and sufferings of Jón Magnússon. Some things *are* clear: For example, he was a man of strong, unbending character, able and unafraid publicly to rebuke the misdemeanors of his parishioners (as was expected of a priest in those days), and undeterred by opposition in high places. He had strong feelings of responsibility for the welfare of his wife and children. His literary ability was indubitable. He had mastered the essence of Christianity as it was understood in his time, and, as the Latin quotations in his book show, he had had, like most if not all priests of his day, a good education in Latin language and literature. Most of the time he was able to function as an effective parish priest.

On the other hand, during the period when he thought himself a victim of sorcery he was clearly a sick man, subject to great torments both physical and mental, and unable for a while to do any work. Much of his suffering during this period was shared by almost all the other members of his household (though he himself seems to have suffered far more intensely than the rest). If we discount the objective reality of sorcery (including telepathy) as a possible cause, we must admit some medical basis, physical or psychological, for the collective sufferings of *síra* Jón and his household. Various possibilities have been conjectured by different authors in recent years.[113] Some emphasize specific physical causes, out of which the psychological disorders developed as a reaction. Ólína Þorvarðardóttir, for example, has suggested a virulent form of influenza;[114] and others have suggested ergot-poisoning.[115] Others have pointed to the cheerless environment in which *síra* Jón lived—the wretched

Introduction 35

living conditions, the pitiless landscape, the harsh climate, the darkness of winter, and the absence of healthy entertainment and of the congenial company of his own kind.[116] Another important factor was psychological, his own unquestioning belief in the objective reality of black magic, together with the fact that he "knew" that the Jón Jónssons (and later Þuríður) were practicing it on him. Magic, as modern anthropologists point out, can be "pragmatically efficacious": it can change the mental states, and thereby the physical acts, of those who are involved in it.[117] It can happen that a suggestible person takes steps leading to his own illness or even death if he becomes aware that his society, or others of superior power and knowledge, require it of him.[118]

At any rate, whatever the cause, *síra* Jón seems to have suffered at this time from acute neurosis, and perhaps other disorders as well. And a strong personality like *síra* Jón could well have transmitted his own nervous complaints to those around him, especially since he was the authority-figure whom many of the simple folk around him looked up to for guidance in belief and behavior. And his capacity to transmit his own strong feelings and emotions to others was much heightened by a characteristic of his, common among normal people of any era, that appears repeatedly in the *Story of Sufferings*, namely, his urge to dramatize his feelings, to express them in stark outward form so that there could be no mistaking them. Three examples of this come to mind: first, his kneeling, in the presence of others, before a destitute old woman of his parish, to beg a blessing of her;[119] secondly, his need, when in desperate straits, to pray to God not quietly and in secret but loudly in the hearing of his household;[120] and thirdly, his instructions to his household, if they saw him acting improperly, to tie him to two boards in the shape of a cross so that, seeing him thus, God would be reminded of the redemptive death of His Son Jesus.[121] Conversely, he is inclined to attribute sinful hardheartedness to those who, like Þuríður, do *not* make an outward display of their feelings.[122]

But neurosis is not insanity. Many students of the witchcraft craze have interpreted the behavior of *síra* Jón as indicative of more than nervous exhaustion, in fact of actual insanity. They support this view by pointing to his apparent hallucinations, his persecution complex, and the apparent irrationality of his relentless harassment of those who allegedly practiced sorcery against him, especially Þuríður. But I believe that a careful examination of his behavior in the light of the mind-set of his age will show that the diagnosis of insanity is not justified.

To begin with, it is vital to see *síra* Jón as a product of his own time and his own upbringing. Trained in the Skálholt school, under the supervision of his foster father Bishop Oddur Einarsson, he would have believed implicitly in the basic teachings of the Christian faith—the horrors of sin, and at the same time the final victory of God in Christ over all the powers of evil, sin, and death.[123] Foremost among the horrors of sin was the power of the devil to work havoc on human beings, and indeed on whole communities, through the practice of sorcery by those wretched men and women who had (knowingly or unknowingly) sold their souls to him in order to be able to manipulate supernatural powers for their own purposes. So it would be quite natural and indeed inevitable, when he himself and his household became afflicted with "unnatural" illnesses, for him to attribute his sufferings with complete assurance to the attacks of fiends and demons dispatched by sorcerers, and to try to find who these sorcerers might be so that they could be punished.

A modern reader of the *Story of Sufferings* is struck by the flimsiness of the circumstantial evidence adduced by *síra* Jón to support his charges of sorcery against the Jón Jónssons and Þuríður, and is apt to take the view that this reveals a morbid breakdown in *síra* Jón's powers of reasoning, an obsession which modern people would call paranoid.[124] But, given his background, I do not think that we need to assume any "breakdown of his reasoning powers" beyond the limitations that were imposed by the spirit of his times. If, as he believed, the a priori probability of *some* sorcerer being at the bottom of his afflictions was almost one hundred percent, so that the only problem was to discover *which* of his acquaintances might be the guilty one, then the flimsy circumstantial evidence adduced by *síra* Jón for pinning guilt on the Jón Jónssons and Þuríður would be logically much more telling than it would be if it were *first* necessary to establish that some sorcery was taking place.[125]

Another point to bear in mind in assessing *síra* Jón's mental condition is this: In his *Story of Sufferings* he repeatedly and confidently speaks of devils and demons visibly haunting his farmhouse and plaguing him and others, and visibly stalking the countryside in the very form of the presumed sorcerers (the Jón Jónssons, Þuríður, and also some presumed accomplices of the latter). Before using this as evidence that *síra* Jón was subject to hallucinations, one should notice that in almost every case[126] he attributes this awareness of demons not to his own perceptions but to the perceptions of others who are said to be second-sighted (clairvoyant). Here again we must remember that the conviction that some people had second sight, i.e., could perceive the spirit world, was almost universal in his day. So, since the a priori probability of the presence of devils was almost one hundred percent, why should he not place implicit faith in those who told him that they saw them?[127] At any rate, there seems to be little evidence that *síra* Jón himself was subject to visual hallucinations.

Even though *síra* Jón does not often claim to *see* demons around his sickbed, he often tells us that he *feels* them present in his sufferings. This may have been a verbalization of his physical and mental woes imposed on him by the spirit of the times in which he lived.

Another feature of his age that we see reflected in *síra* Jón is the willingness to inflict horrendous punishment, namely death by burning, for the crime of sorcery. Not only was he eager to have the Jón Jónssons and Þuríður burned to death, but he regretted that the former two had not been tortured prior to execution.[128] If this attitude seems to deprive *síra* Jón of every last vestige of our sympathy, we must remember that an intense literalistic sense of the reality of heaven and hell, and of the horror of sin, were part and parcel of the mental atmosphere of his age, and that from this sense flowed the conviction that anything, even an agonizing death, inflicted so as to induce last-minute repentance in a hardened criminal and thereby save him or her from everlasting torture in hell was an enormous kindness. *Síra* Jón declares in fact that he has no personal animosity against the Jón Jónssons. Certainly the *Story of Sufferings* describes them in very uncompromising terms—for example, as "blind slaves of the devil and their own perverted malignant natures, who are totally incapable of reform."[129] At the same time he asserts that he bore no ill will toward the father and son whom he was prosecuting for sorcery,[130] and that he rejoiced genuinely when he was told (falsely, as he later concluded) that they had sincerely repented before their death.[131] His final word about them was that they were so enslaved to the devil that they were no longer in control of their own behavior, so that anger toward them was as futile as anger at the biting of a poisonous snake.[132]

If the last several paragraphs were a *complete* statement of *síra* Jón's situation, his mental sufferings would have been no more than what would have been naturally induced in him by (a) the preconceptions and prejudices of the seventeenth-century culture in which he lived, (b) the sufferings due to whatever medical or psychological causes were afflicting him and his household, and (c) the fears and anxieties due to his own precarious medical, economic, and social situation—troubles very natural and predictable, and not requiring any assumption of insanity. What sensitive individual would not suffer mental agonies when so beset with fears for the outcome of his painful sickness, worries over the poverty of his family and household and his inability to work to support them, frustration over what he felt to be his inadequacy in the struggle for the extermination of sorcery, an acute dread of the enmity of the Jón Jónssons and Þuríður whose sorcery gave them such power over him, his isolation from kindred spirits, and resentment of the lethargy of the magistrates who to a large extent refused to take him seriously?[133]

But this is not the whole story, for it does not take into account his deep spiritual life, manifested in the mystical experiences of which he gives us an account in his *Story of Sufferings*. *Síra* Jón was a man not only of unusual forcefulness in secular affairs, but also of unusual sensitivity to the demands of what we may call "the spiritual life" or "spiritual values." There is little doubt that this sensitivity to spiritual values intensified the agonies brought on by his illnesses and the desperate circumstances of his life, by plunging him into an agonizing despair at his own weakness and sinfulness. The overarching spiritual sin that tormented him (much more grievously than it would have tormented less spiritually gifted individuals) and which resulted in a sense of total spiritual dryness and of being abandoned by God to the machinations of the devil, seems to have been his *inability to resign himself to the will of God*. Acceptance (even joyful acceptance) of the will of God—this has always been one of the cardinal Christian teachings.[134] But *síra* Jón's physical and mental agonies clearly seemed too horrible for him to practice this teaching while in the thick of them. Though his faith in God never wavered, there must have been times—even though he never says this in so many words—when he hated God for inflicting such sufferings on him. And does not hatred of God lead to eternal damnation?[135] It is this spiritual agony that forms the apex of *síra* Jón's sufferings, and takes them even beyond the naturalistic realm referred to in the preceding paragraph. It is because of this spiritual element in his struggles that one can truly say that his Christianity (that is, his sensitivity to the spiritual values embedded in Christianity) exacerbated his physical and mental disorders.

On the other hand, as we shall shortly see, his spiritual life was also his bulwark against total breakdown. In Sigurður Nordal's words, his unshakeable Christian faith was the one reason why he never went completely insane.[136]

The difference between his physical and "commonplace" mental sufferings, on the one hand, and his spiritual sufferings on the other, comes clearly to light when we consider the means which he adopts to alleviate them. To mitigate his more "commonplace" sufferings, he adopts commonplace means, such as moving from one place to another, protesting to the local magistrates, demanding justice and reparations. But to mitigate his spiritual sufferings he has no other than spiritual means—fervent prayer, most often the so-called Prayer of Jesus.[137]

In the next section I shall present to the reader the spiritual, or mystical, experiences of *síra* Jón as they are recorded by him in the *Story of Sufferings*. I see them, first, as confirmation of Sigurður Nordal's statement that the one reason why *síra* Jón never went completely insane lay in his unwavering Christian faith. Secondly, I believe that they place him within the tradition of Christian mysticism, especially his stumbling upon the Jesus Prayer, which is a foundation stone of Eastern Orthodox spiritual practice.

In the concluding section of this Introduction I shall tackle the difficult question of the relationship between the spiritual, "mystical" life and the tangible, church-related life of *síra* Jón. This question arises, of course, in the study of the lives of many mystics, but it is particularly urgent and obtrusive in the case of *síra* Jón because of the many (from a modern standpoint) discordant and unhappy features of the latter. The suggestion will be made that the "two lives" of *síra* Jón were lived on two different levels of his being, corresponding perhaps to St. Paul's distinction between the "flesh" and the "spirit."[138]

§11. Síra Jón's Spiritual Experiences

The first spiritual experience of which *síra* Jón tells us occurred long before the outbreak of sorcery at Eyri, in the year 1627, when he was a schoolboy of about seventeen. He was travelling on horseback along the shore of Hvalfjörður, in good physical health, when he was suddenly (for no apparent reason) struck with an intense despair, a sense that God had abandoned him. Let us hear what he himself says about it:

> I felt that all the well-being of my life and soul was taken away from me, as if I had been entirely abandoned by God, and that I was inexorably faced with but one course of action—to ride my horse at a gallop into the sea and commit suicide. ...... I would have given the whole world to be able to remember just one passage of consolation from God's word. But, however much I strained to do so, I could not for the life of me recollect anything except only the most holy name of Jesus, and this I repeated constantly. ...... I made up my mind that I would live or die—whichever the Lord willed for me—in the name of Jesus.[139]

How strange that this boy of seventeen should have thus, almost involuntarily, hit upon the repetition of the name of Jesus (a form of the Eastern Orthodox Jesus Prayer, of which he surely had no prior knowledge) as the one and only rock that he could cling to for survival in his great distress! This was a portent of the spiritual sufferings that were to assail him many years later—and perhaps even an advance training in the means of combating them.

Our next glimpse into *síra* Jón's spiritual life shows that his faith in the saving power of the name of Jesus had not left him twenty-eight years later, when he was in the thick of the attacks, both spiritual and physical, that he attributed to the demonic sorcery of the Jón Jónssons. He writes:

> I also asked my household to tell me if anything thoughtless or improper escaped my mouth. If such should happen, I intended either never to speak a word again or to beseech my people to sew my mouth shut. In all these severe attacks I felt I was drained of all my piety, and that my heart was harder than stone or steel. So I thought to myself that, since God could see the impotence of my heart, my tongue at least should not be inactive. I made up my mind that, as long as my tongue could move, it should never tire of calling and calling upon the Lord. I reckoned that, if it was the Lord's will that the devils should be the death of me, it might happen that I would find mercy at His hands if I died while praying and calling upon Him. Or even if the Lord willed to cast me out from His presence into hell and damnation, I should be the only one among all the damned to be calling upon Him, even though I had no further hope of grace. ...... The words that I chose most often to repeat constantly during these horrors were as follows: "O Lamb of God, Thou that sittest on the throne of my God, have mercy upon me!"[140]—and others too in the same vein.[141]

To many modern people (especially Protestants) it will seem strange that *síra* Jón was able to find spiritual relief and strength from a practice as apparently mechanical as constant repetition of a formula. This is self-hypnosis, they may say, or at best mere "work-righteousness," expecting to earn favor with God through works, whereas real religion is a matter of faith imparted through God's grace. This would be a valid criticism if his repetition of the prayer formula did not itself flow from faith. From what we read in his *Story of Sufferings* it is evident that, for *síra* Jón, his practice of the Jesus Prayer was no "bargaining tool" but an outlet for the strong and deep faith that was already within him—so deep in fact that it welled up from below the level of mere devout feeling, of which *síra* Jón was by his own admission completely drained at times, and so strong that Sigurður Nordal was able to write in his Introduction to the *Píslarsaga*:

> In spite of his intense neurasthenia, in spite of the epidemic of fanaticism that held him in its clutches, even in spite of the "sorcery" that reduced him to delirium and seemed about to deprive him of his wits, *síra* Jón never became completely insane. Though to some extent he is just as absorbed in thinking about himself and his own sufferings as we commonly find in neaurasthenic, deranged people, it never enters his head to condemn God for the maltreatment which He allows to afflict this poor minister of His word in Eyri on Skutulsfjörður. Nowhere in the *Story of Sufferings* is there any hint of a shadow of doubt regarding God's grace and righteousness.[142]

The following passage from the *Story of Sufferings* shows another important feature of *síra* Jón's *spiritual* sufferings—namely, that whatever his physical or mental lapses, he was given the ability to be aware of them, to stand apart from them and look upon them from outside. He remained able to look himself in the face as he was, with all the degradation into which his infirmities had cast him:

> Often the most repulsive thoughts besieged my heart—one might say, all the hellish filth and wickedness in which the devils wade and wallow—so violently stamped and pressed down into my heart and thoughts, that it seemed impossible for me to defy them or to shut out this depravity. On the other hand I felt that if even one part of all that was being thrust at me were to find entry into me, I could not (according to the judgment that remained to me) but be cast into the unquenchable flames of hell. So, whenever such thoughts came over me, I set myself with all my strength and willpower—and even beyond my own strength—to call and cry to the Lord that this evil should not be able to enter into my heart. When beset by such tempestuous attacks I could not sigh to the Lord quietly and in secret; I had to cry loudly and with the most earnest zeal. For that was the most critical juncture that a devout person can face, when God's Spirit seems totally withdrawn, and the devil with all his savagery has returned and entered the human heart.

> I was very frequently subjected to a great deal of abominable foulness in the spirit, so that—much to my own disgust—my mind perverted, crushed, and trampled God's holy word into blasphemy. Sometimes I was obliged to find different words with the same meaning, and to abandon those which my mind had already twisted and perverted, so as not to pile an excess of loathsomeness on my wretched soul.[143]

Because of this ability to stand apart from himself and perceive himself as he was, he retained an inner humility, in apparent contradiction to the aggressiveness with which the outside world saw him persecuting the Jón Jónssons and Þuríður. This humility is brought out in a touching episode recounted in the *Story of Sufferings*:

One day, as he was journeying home on horseback from a visit to Þuríður during which he had spoken to her very harshly, a friendly farm family, consisting of a farmer and his wife and children and mother-in-law, came out to greet him as he passed by their farm. A few moments before they met, *síra* Jón felt a message spoken in his heart: "You are not worthy to be riding on horseback when you meet this woman who is coming toward you on foot." He immediately understood that this referred to the mother-in-law. ..... The latter was an extremely devout woman who had gained the victory over unspecified "grievous, prolonged temptations and assaults of the devil." She and her husband, while he was living, had been known for their works of mercy. Now, she was an infirm destitute old widow supported by her children. *Síra* Jón dismounted and fell on his knees before her, and refused to stand up until he had received a blessing from the old woman. "In my eyes," he writes, "she was a person of great consequence. ..... In this person the Lord wanted to show me how precious in God's eyes are His saints, even though they are despised and considered worthless by ignorant people since they have no gold or silver or worldly finery to flaunt."[144]

Considering the spiritual difficulties in which he stood, it is no wonder that *síra* Jón sought a blessing from the old woman whom he regarded so highly. His torments had so increased his sense of his own worthlessness and need of blessing that elsewhere he writes:

> I know that this whole story reflects on me in the most wretched, ineffectual, and miserable manner. In all these trials I admit that in the presence of God I seemed to myself to be more like a dead worm than a living human being. This whole chronicle reflects little credit on me, only humiliation, disgust, and wretchedness. Many may well think that it would have been more decent of me to have kept quiet about it than to have revealed and broadcast it.[145]

If *síra* Jón's Christianity was the *cause* of his greatest torments and difficulties, it is equally true that his Christianity was their *cure*—or at least the means whereby he was able not to succumb to them completely. We have seen above that the practice of holding on to the Jesus Prayer, even in the midst of desolation and despair, was a "strong tower"[146] in which he found strength and comfort in his greatest distress. But *síra* Jón's spiritual experiences were not all sorrow, distress, and abandonment by God. The light of God's grace did occasionally shine into his heart, bringing an incomparable joy. On one occasion, after a violent attack (which he believed to be demonic), he tells us:

> I begged my heavenly Father to grant me love for Jesus, my Redeemer, from whom I felt cut off. At the same time that I was constraining my heart to pray for this boon, I heard this phrase clearly spoken to me: "I shall be victorious tomorrow!" .... I myself was in doubt whether it was a bad angel or a good one that had spoken this ...... The next night ..... such an ardent sense of devotion was infused into my heart, with such joy and rapture, that I cannot write about it or describe it. I lay, as it were, in a flood of rapturous tears, more than compensated for all my injuries, willing and eager to endure every load of misery that the Lord might see fit to heap on me, if I might hold on to this one thing, namely, the grace of the Lord in His only-begotten Son Jesus. ..... From the evidence of this experience I perceived and concluded that it was a holy angel of God that had given me this message for my comfort and restoration, not an evil spirit.[147]

Sometimes, in between storms of anguish, he felt the Lord consoling him with a great enlightenment regarding certain passages of scripture:

> It sometimes happened, when the great storms in my soul had abated, that some words of scripture which I recognized and knew perfectly well would enter my mind, and an interpretation of their meaning would be revealed to me which to my understanding was quite marvelous. I knew that no human being could have interpreted them in this way, no matter how learned he was. I was overcome with amazement at the wonder and glory of God, and I felt capable of conversing with even the greatest scholars (had I been in their presence) about the judgments and wonders of God.[148]

Conclusion

The outcome of the above discussion seems to be that *síra* Jón's mental life is divided into two compartments. First is his public life, in which he is ruled by the prejudices and dictates of the society in which he lives, in which he relentlessly persecutes supposed sorcerers, suffers mental and physical agonies, and is so obsessed with the justice of his cause that he becomes for a time mentally unbalanced. The second is his spiritual life, the core of which is his unshakeable faith in the glory and power and goodness of God, and which at times invades his feelings, bringing sometimes great pain and sometimes great joy. And this second compartment, his spiritual or mystical life, is on a quite different "level" from the superstition, prejudice, and mental imbalance of the first.[149] Sigurður Nordal has an insightful comment to make in this connection:

> Finally it should be emphasized that neither the means of deliverance to which *síra* Jón resorts, nor his periods of rapture, have essentially anything to do with his superstition or mental imbalance. Completely healthy persons can have similar experiences—and perhaps they are the healthiest of all people. And the parallel between them and him reaches further than would appear at first glance. It is not the least of the merits of the *Píslarsaga* that it familiarizes us with a sick man who on the brink of death resorts to the most desperate measures in order not to be destroyed. Healthier people, who have less to struggle against, may show more restraint in adopting these measures. But none the less they are similar to the practices that all must cultivate who want to dispel the fog that hides reality from them.[150]

Some will ask: assuming that such a division is justifiable, how are the two compartments related? Which one is dominant? Most crucial for the modern reader is the question: how can one take seriously the spiritual life of a man whose public life has features so repulsive by twentieth-century standards? The answer to these questions, I believe, is quite simple: *Even a genuine man of God is bound to show in his life the influence of the preconceptions and prejudices of the society in which he lives. No one is excluded from genuine spiritual life if he tries honestly to live up to what he believes to be the correct standards of his time. Síra Jón's life demonstrates to an unbelievably striking degree that the above two compartments can coexist.*

But *how* do they coexist? How can the same person be simultaneously both compassionate and cruel, so convinced of God's grace and goodness and yet so obsessed with the devil? This question must be faced. I believe that the two compartments can coexist in one and the same person *on two different levels.* Let me try to clarify this with an analogy. Suppose a young man, after a long courtship, has just been told by the girl he loves that she will marry him. He is walking home in an ecstasy of happiness. Not being too attentive to where he is stepping, he falls into a hole and breaks a leg. Now, with the agonizing pain of his broken bone, is he still happy or is he not? On a "deep" level he certainly is; but on a "superficial" level he certainly is not! In the same way, Jón Magnússon may have felt anger against sorcerers and had an obsession about sorcery on a tangible level, but on a "deeper" level known the peace of faith and detachment. Sooner or later the "deeper" level, where God's grace dwells, will break through and assert itself on the visible level, and it is on the "deeper" level that one's real Christianity lies.

It is my conclusion that Jón Magnússon's mental imbalance was a secondary aspect of his life—even though it is this aspect that has given him fame (or infamy!). The real substance of his life is to be found in his faith in

God and his devotion to what he saw as the will of God. One must admire the sincerity with which he sought to be faithful to God's will. Even though that sincerity seemed to lead him astray and cover him with suffering, shame, and the aversion of later generations, it was a mark of inner worth which in the long run deserves to overshadow the excesses of his conduct and the disgrace which has hitherto been his lot. His spiritual experiences described above, some of which led him to the practice of the Jesus Prayer, seem to show that, in spite of all, the grace of God did rest upon him, that his sincerity at least was pleasing in God's eyes.

The final judgment on his life must rest in the hands of Him who "shall not judge by what the eyes see, or decide by what the ears hear."[151]

Notes

1. The first to have given the manuscript this title seems to have been Þorvaldur Thoroddsen; see §§1 and 9 of this Introduction.
2. A French translation of the *Píslarsaga* has recently appeared, by Einar Már Jónsson, under the title *Histoire de Mes Souffrances*. See the Bibliography.
3. Another reason for the importance of the *Píslarsaga* for students of 17th-century Iceland is its candid revelations of the author's own feelings and religious experiences. The masters of Lutheran orthodoxy in 17th-century Iceland, *síra* Hallgrímur Pétursson and Bishop Jón Vídalín, do discuss religious experience in general in their great works (the *Passion Hymns* and the *Vídalínspostilla*), but seem deliberately to steer away from intimate revelations of their *own* personal spiritual experience. See Sigurður Nordal's Introduction to the *Píslarsaga* (1967 edn., p. 23).

    Another 17th-century Icelandic author who believed in the reality of sorcery, and who describes illnesses that he himself suffered and ascribed to the assaults of sorcery, was the annalist Pétur Einarsson (1597–1666), author of the *Ballarárannáll*. Quotations from his accounts of these illnesses will be found in Sigurjón Jónsson, *Sóttarfar og sjúkdomar á Íslandi 1400–1800*, pp. 220–223.

    Another autobiographical account, similar to the *Píslarsaga* in date, style, and exposition, is the short work *Contra Luranum*, written in 1660, by Petrus Simmingh, a Swedish priest in Altuna. See Strömback 1931, "Några drag ur äldre och nyare isländsk folktro," *Island. Bilder från gammal och ny tid*, 76. I owe this reference to Ólína Þorvarðardóttir, *Brennuöldin*, p. 101.
4. See the review of Matthías Viðar Sæmundsson's 2001 edn. of the *Píslarsaga* by Ruth C. Ellison, in *Saga-Book*, vol. 27, 2003, pp. 142–147, especially p. 143.
5. In all three editions, the 17th-century Icelandic spelling of the manuscript has been almost entirely replaced by modern Icelandic spelling.
6. These four supplementary apologetic tracts are titled (in the order in which they occur in the manuscript): (a) *Viðlit historíunnar þeirra seinni djöfuls kvalræða* (A Glance at the Story of the Later Devilish Torments); (b) *Íslenskra laga og réttar processus og framferð* (Due Process and Procedure in Icelandic Courts of Law); (c) *Rök og andmæli: Innlegg framlagt hér að Eyri (að ég meini) Þuríðar líkindi* (Arguments and

Objections: Deposition of Evidence Submitted Here at Eyri, as I Think, Against Þuríður); and (d) *Hugleiðingar mínar um uppspurn og eftirleitni galdramála* (My Thoughts on the Ferreting Out and Investigation of Sorcery Cases).
7. It is not clear at what stage the Icelandic texts of Chapters VI and VII were inserted into the original or surviving manuscript of the *Píslarsaga*.
8. The most important document representing this point of view is the *Canon Episcopi*, which first appeared at the beginning of the 10th century. In medieval times this document was considered to be highly authoritative, since it was held (wrongly, as it later turned out) to be one of the canons of the Council of Ancyra which took place in A.D. 314. The *Canon Episcopi* maintains that the spirits and supernatural events apparently evoked in the practice of witchcraft are delusions, like objects seen in dreams. They are fabricated by Satan in order to lead humans (mostly women) away from the true faith, seducing them, for example, into a false belief that they are being magically transported at dead of night over long distances to witches' sabbaths, there to engage in worship of the devil. The Canon orders bishops to make every effort to eradicate these delusions from their congregations. Those who persist in them are to be expelled from their parishes in disgrace.

Thomas Aquinas, in his teachings on witchcraft, does not deviate from the views of the *Canon Episcopi*.

(See for example Jeffrey B. Russell, *Witchcraft in the Middle Ages*, pp. 76, 77, 147.)
9. Other influential "authoritative" accounts of the Church's doctrines on demonology appeared during the centuries of the witchcraft craze. Prominent among these were: *Daemonolatreia*, published in 1595 by the scholarly French lawyer Nicolas Rémy; and *Demonomanie des Sorciers* by the great political philosopher Jean Bodin, which appeared in 1580.

For a vivid popular account in English of the growth, progress, and subsidence of the great European witchcraft craze, see Hugh R. Trevor-Roper, *The European Witch-craze of the Sixteenth and Seventeenth Centuries*.
10. See for example *Luther's Works*, vol. 41, p. 172.
11. See *Witchcraft in Europe 1100–1700*, p. 13.
12. See Hugh Trevor-Roper, *The European Witch-craze*, pp. 132–134 and 146–148. Opponents of the witch-craze in the 16th and 17th centuries who publicized their views were treading on dangerous ground. All of the four mentioned in the text here were in fact denounced by orthodox churchmen as accomplices of Satan, though none of these four were actually brought to trial. The most influential of them seems to have been Johann Weyer. His treatise *De praestigiis Daemonum* was denounced by Catholic and Protestant theologians alike.
13. This seems to have been Luther's position on witchcraft—at least at one period of the Reformer's life. For example, he tells (approvingly) the story of parents who brought their daughter to St. Macarius, and begged him to restore her to her proper human form, since—they said—"as you can see, she has been magically transformed into a cow." But St. Macarius, whose vision the devil was unable to pervert, saw not a cow but a normal girl, and complied with the parents' wish by praying, not that the girl should resume her human form, but that the parents' vision should be restored to its normal function. (See *Luther's Works*, vol. 26, pp. 190–191.)

For a discussion by Matthías V. Sæmundsson of this changed attitude toward the function of witchcraft, see "Galdur og geðveiki," *Píslarsaga*, 2001 edn., pp. 348–350.

14. For an analysis of the reasons for the decline of the witch-craze in Europe around 1700, see *Witchcraft and Magic in Europe: The Eighteenth and Nineteenth Centuries*, ed. by Bengt Ankarloo and Stuart Clark, Part I.

    Tambiah (*Magic, Science, Religion, and the Scope of Rationality*, pp. 89, 90), applying his anthropological approach to the work of Trevor-Roper, analyzes the reason for the persistence and the final decline of the witchcraft craze as follows:

    "Trevor-Roper's interpretation of the European witchcraze makes two major points. The first is that the witch beliefs of that time have to be placed in their general context and this requires our seeing them as an integral part of the whole cosmology of the time and as part of deep-seated social forms, rooted in permanent social attitudes. Hence it is unsound to detach the witchcraft beliefs from their total embedding, and to ask how these beliefs could have been taken to be true given their manifest absurdities as seen by the 'rational' standards of today. Trevor-Roper says it is misguided to regard the 'reason' and 'logic' of today as a self-contained, independent system of permanent validity. 'We recognize that even rationalism is relative; that it operates within a general philosophic context, and that it cannot properly be detached from this context.'

    "The corollary of this holistic perspective is that the witchcraft beliefs and practices and excesses of the 16th and 17th centuries could not be dissolved or eradicated in isolation, but only if the whole context of those views was revised. Unless there occurred a social transformation, the social basis of the belief would remain, and unless there was a critical change in the whole cosmology, the beliefs would continue. To destroy the myth, to drain away the poisoned pool, the whole intellectual and social structure that sustained it and had solidified around it had to be broken. When the change came, therefore, at the close of the 17th century, it was a total 'philosophical revolution which changed the whole concept of Nature and its operations,' initiating modern 'rationalism' and rejecting biblical fundamentalism. The final victory that liberated nature from biblical fundamentalism came on the one side from German Pietists and English Deists (the heirs of the Protestant heretics of the 17th century), and on the other from Descartes and his universal 'mechanical' laws of nature."
15. The word "assembly" will always be used in this book to translate the Icel. *þing*.
16. Or perhaps 999.
17. About a century later an amended version of the Church Ordinance was issued by King Christian IV, designed especially for use in Norway and Iceland. It differs from the 1537 Ordinance mostly in laying down more precise laws about marriage and moral behavior, especially for priests. Its prescriptions about worship, baptism, ordination of priests, etc., are unchanged. It was published in Icelandic translation at Hólar in 1635, not long before the events of this book. See Páll E. Ólason, *Saga Íslendinga*, vol. 5, p. 217; *Kristni á Íslandi*, vol. 3, p. 64.
18. See pp. 147, 148, 163.
19. See Helgi Þorláksson, *Saga Íslands VI*, p. 382.
20. At the time of the sorcery trials with which this book deals, the *lögmaður* for the northern and western quarters was Magnús Björnsson (who was responsible for the first burning of an alleged sorcerer in Iceland, in 1625), and a little later (1662–1679) Þorleifur Kortsson (see Appendix 1); the *lögmaður* for the southern and eastern quarters was Árni Oddsson (see Chap. X, Note 41).
21. See Einar Laxness, *Íslands saga*, vol. 2, pp. 140–145.

22. The procedure for the *tylftareiður* is laid down in the *Jónsbók* as follows:
"If a person is accused of treason by the king, he shall defend himself with the *tylftareiður*, and the same applies to all major crimes. Six persons shall be named to stand on either side of the defendant, of status equal to his before the law, neighbors of his, well-informed about the case but neither related to him nor implicated in the crime, adult, of blameless reputation, and never known to have perjured himself or borne false witness. Seven of these, and the defendant himself, [must swear the full oath of innocence,] and in addition there must be four witnesses (*fangavottar*) who are adult and never known to have borne false witness. All the others must confirm the defendant's oath, attesting before God that they know of nothing to hinder them from swearing the oath with a clear conscience." (*Jónsbók*, 1970 edn., p. 278)

The *Jónsbók*, adopted by the Althing as the basis for Icelandic law in 1281, was still considered authoritative in Jón Magnússon's time, though by the 17th century some procedures had undergone change. For example, in a *tylftareiður* the court rather than the accused would often nominate at least some of the compurgators, who then had to choose between swearing their oath for or against the innocence of the accused. For more details see Ruth C. Ellison, *The Kirkjuból Affair*, p. 221.

In our story, Þuríður Jónsdóttir and her supporters were able to muster 12 compurgators to swear that she was innocent of witchcraft, and she was acquitted. But her father and brother were not able to muster the required number, and were burned to death.

23. See Einar Laxness, *Íslands saga*, vol. 3, pp. 83–87.
24. Needless to say, the monopoly could not always be enforced, especially when (for example, because of war between Denmark and neighboring countries) the Danes were unable to send ships to supply their trading stations.

Not until 1787, in the wake of the disastrous Laki volcanic eruption of 1783, was this trade monopoly abolished, and the Icelandic trade made free to all Danish subjects. This last restriction was removed in 1854, when trade with Iceland was opened to nationals of all countries.

25. For a thorough exposition of the mode of construction of Icelandic turf farm buildings in past centuries see Hörður Ágústsson, "Íslenski torfbærinn," *Íslensk Þjóðmenning I. Uppruni og umhverfi*, pp. 228–344.
26. The poorest farms had earthen floors, which became pools of mud during heavy rains.
27. See Appendix 1 under: *Baðstofa* and *Skáli*.
28. See Arnheiður Sigurðardóttir, *Híbýlahættir á miðöldum*, p. 78.
29. As one example of white magic, it was thought helpful to a woman in labor to wrap around her belly a strip of skin on which some holy text had been written. See Helgi Þorláksson, *Saga Íslands VI*, pp. 364, 367, 370.
30. See Einar G. Pétursson, *Eddurit Jóns Guðmundssonar lærða*, in 2 vols.
31. See Helgi Þorláksson, *Saga Íslands VI*, pp. 367–370.
32. Quoted from Ólafur Davíðsson, *Galdur og galdramál á Íslandi*, p. 91. Since this is a pronouncement by an ecclesiastical body, the only punishment for sorcery prescribed here is an ecclesiastical one.
33. Translated in Appendix 2.
34. See Helgi Þorláksson, *Saga Íslands VI*, p. 366.
35. See for example Ólafur Davíðsson, *Galdur og galdramál á Íslandi*, pp. 39–42. Here Ólafur Davíðsson makes the point that the polemical tracts written in Iceland about

the wickedness of sorcery probably had the effect of making people, if anything, even more convinced and fearful of the reality of sorcery than they were before!

Not only such tangible disasters as sudden sicknesses of man and beast or violent storms, but also cases of insanity were apt to be attributed to demonic assaults. On p. 368 of his article "Galdur og geðveiki," *Píslarsaga*, 2001 edn., Matthías Viðar Sæmundsson cites a story vividly illustrating the tendency to attribute insanity to demonic possession: an insane man in the Vestmannaeyjar is said to have been fettered to a beam of the local parish church, on the theory that the evil spirit causing his insanity would not be able to endure the contact with a holy building. Evidently the treatment was not effective!

It is interesting to note that the ancient Icelandic lawbook *Grágás* (see §3 of this Introduction) shows a more enlightened attitude toward mental disease than the 17th-century tendency to attribute it to demonic possession. See Jón Steffensen, "Alþýðulækningar," *Íslensk þjóðmenning VII, Alþýðuvísindi*, pp. 123–125.

For original sources, see the passages from Ólafur Davíðsson, Matthías V. Sæmundsson, and Jón Steffensen quoted above.

36. See Ólafur Davíðsson, *Galdur og galdramál á Íslandi*, especially pp. 57 and 335–338. For the population figures in 1703 see *Manntalið á Íslandi 1703*. The West Fjords are here defined as consisting of Barðastrandarsýsla, Vestur- and Norður-Ísafjarðarsýsla, and Strandasýsla.

Why was the sex ratio of accused sorcerers so very different in Iceland from what it was on the continent of Europe? To this question, obvious and basic though it is for the understanding of the sociology of Icelandic witchcraft, a completely satisfactory answer has yet to be given, though suggestions have been made by scholars such as Helgi Þorláksson and Ruth C. Ellison. Both of these emphasize that the public perception of what it means to be a sorcerer or witch was different in Iceland from what it was on the continent. On the continent a witch, whether male or female, was a person who made a pact with the devil, and was magically transported to "witches' sabbaths" where he or she worshipped the devil and engaged in sexual orgies with demons; and these nefarious acts were of course carried on in secret. The "classical European witch" was female, old, ugly, poor, and lived alone at the edge of the village. But somehow this conception of witches never caught on in Iceland. Indeed, the "classical European witch" hardly existed there (Ruth Ellison). Pacts with the devil, witches' sabbaths, and sexual orgies are rarely mentioned in Icelandic court documents. (See Matthías V. Sæmundsson, "Galdur og geðveiki," *Píslarsaga*, 2001 edn., p. 382.) The typical Icelandic sorcerer is a literate male; he pores over manuals of magic, copies or carves conjurations and magical staves; and, like the Jón Jónssons of this book, he carries on his magical practices outside of his home. The average Icelandic woman of the 17th century would have been disqualified from this kind of activity. In the first place, few Icelandic women of that time were literate. (See Appendix 1 under: Literacy.) Because of the sparseness of the population in Iceland women were largely confined to their homes, where they were under the constant observation of the rest of the household, with little opportunity for clandestine behavior. (See Helgi Þorláksson, *Saga Íslands VI*, pp. 377, 378; Ruth C. Ellison, "The Kirkjuból Affair. A Seventeenth-Century Icelandic Witchcraft Case Analyzed," *Seventeenth Century*, vol. 8, 1993, pp. 219, 220.)

37. See *Kristni á Íslandi III*, p. 271. For the primary source, see Gísli Oddsson, *Íslensk annálabrot og Undur Íslands*, Akureyri, 1942, p. 124.

Introduction 49

38. See Matthías V. Sæmundsson, "Galdur og geðveiki," *Píslarsaga*, 2001 edn., pp. 368-374.
39. For more information on this interesting man see Appendix 1 under: Páll Björnsson. No written work on sorcery was printed in 17th-century Iceland. The tracts that were produced on the subject were only circulated in manuscript form—even *síra* Páll Björnsson's *Kennimark kölska*. An edition of this work came out in 1976, and was reviewed by Einar G. Pétursson in 1977 (see Bibliography).
40. See Matthías V. Sæmundsson, "Galdur og geðveiki," *Píslarsaga*, 2001 edn., p. 382.
41. *Kennimark kölska*, 1976 edn., Chap. 7, p. 17.
42. This is reminiscent of the story told by Luther; see Note 13 of this Introduction.
43. The work *De Spiritu et Anima* does not belong to the corpus of St. Augustine's writings but is a pseudo-Augustinian treatise compiled some time in the Middle Ages. It is printed in the series *Patrologia Latina*, vol. 40, pp. 779-842. The passage quoted here occurs at the beginning of Chapter 26, on p. 798 of that volume. I owe this reference to Dr. Phillip Cary.
44. *Kennimark kölska*, 1976 edn., Chap. 24, p. 82.
45. *Exodus* 7:11. See *Kennimark kölska*, Chap. 27.
46. *Kennimark kölska*, 1976 edn., Chap. 26, pp. 86, 87.
47. See *Kennimark kölska*, 1976 edn., Chap. 33.
48. The book from which this passage is taken is by Niels Hemmingsen, and is called *Antidotum*. It was published in Icelandic translation by Bishop Guðbrandur in 1597. See Matthías V. Sæmundsson, "Galdur og geðveiki," *Píslarsaga*, 2001 edn., pp. 383, 385.
49. See *Úr bréfabókum Brynjólfs biskups Sveinssonar*, p. 51.

    In his better moments *síra* Jón Magnússon also expresses the same profound conviction that the power of God far surpasses the power of Satan. See for example Note 4 of Chap. X.
50. Sigurður Nordal, in his article "Galdrarit" (see the Bibliography), recognizes that sorcery and sorcery trials were only a small part of the total Icelandic scene in the 17th century.

    The difference noted here between the northwestern part of the country on the one hand, and the southern and eastern parts on the other, has often been linked to personalities (Þorleifur Kortsson, *síra* Páll Björnsson, and *síra* Jón Magnússon in the West Fjords, for example), or to the particularly bleak climate and surroundings in the West Fjords (see Note 116), or sometimes to ergotism (see Note 115). But some scholars have attributed it to economic causes. There is evidence that there was much migration into the West Fjords in the latter part of the 17th century, and that farming land was in short supply there, leading to vigorous competition for available farms, especially among the poorer classes. This together with the general belief in the efficacy of sorcery may have provoked many accusations of sorcery when disputes and ill feeling arose over the right to occupy one farm or another. (See Helgi Þorláksson, *Saga Íslands VI*, pp. 375-378.)
51. Among the pioneers of this movement abroad were Tycho Brahe (1546-1601), Johannes Kepler (1571-1630), Galileo Galilei (1564-1642), and of course Isaac Newton (1642-1727).
52. See Appendix 1 under: Páll Björnsson.
53. For an elaboration of this theme see Helgi Þorláksson, "Aldarfarið á sautjándu öld," *Hallgrímsstefna*, pp. 15-28.

54. See Ólafur Davíðsson, *Galdur og galdramál á Íslandi*, pp. 312–331.
55. See §3 of this Introduction.
56. This index is to be found in *Úr bréfabókum Brynjólfs biskups Sveinssonar*, pp. 166–168. See also Matthías Viðar Sæmundsson, *Galdrar á Íslandi*, pp. 451–453.
57. For more detailed conjectures regarding the genesis of the *Íslensk galdrabók*, see Matthías Viðar Sæmundsson, *Galdrar á Íslandi*, p. 10.
58. See the Bibliography, under these three editors, for more precise references.
59. Another interesting Icelandic manual of magic from the 17th century is found in manuscript Lbs 143 8vo in the National Library of Iceland. It is supposed to have been written about 1670. It was first printed in full in the year 2004 under the title *Galdrakver, Ráð til varnar gegn illum öflum þessa og annars heims* (A Manual of Magic, Containing Means of Protection Against Evil Powers of This World and the Next). See the Bibliography. As the title indicates, it differs from the *Skálholt Manual* and the *Íslensk galdrabók* in that it describes only "white" magic.
60. See Ólína Þorvarðardóttir, *Brennuöldin*, pp. 198–209.
61. Here I rely on Flowers, *The Galdrabók: An Icelandic Grimoire*, pp. 53–54.
62. See Flowers, *The Galdrabók: An Icelandic Grimoire*, pp. 47–48. See also our Appendix 1 under: Magical Spells and Staves, [3].

  For a more detailed discussion of the Ægishjálmur see Matthías V. Sæmundsson, *Galdrar á Íslandi*, pp. 284–286.
63. For some examples of the spells contained in the *Íslensk galdrabók* that are directly or indirectly relevant to the *Story of Sufferings*, see Appendix 1 under: Magical Spells and Staves.
64. See Matthías V. Sæmundsson, *Galdur á brennuöld*, pp. 33–46.

  In the old Scandinavian mythology the great expert in sorcery is the god Óðinn, from whom the art of magic, both white and black, has descended through the ages. He is said to be the ultimate author of the runes and conjurations through which magic is practiced. See *Hávamál*, vs. 138–145. See also *Ynglinga saga*, chap. 7 (in the *Heimskringla*, Íslensk fornrit, vol. XXVI, pp. 18–20).
65. Stephen Flowers, *The Galdrabók: An Icelandic Grimoire*, p. 53. This interpretation by Flowers is of course a modernized assessment of ancient ways of thinking, and so should be treated with caution. I suspect it contains a large grain of truth, though other scholars may disagree.
66. See Matthías V. Sæmundsson, *Galdrar á Íslandi*, p. 51.

  Icelandic folk-magic was, as I have mentioned, based on the traditions of heathenism. In the pre-Christian Eddic poems we find references to at least one legendary hero (Sigurður, slayer of Fáfnir) who is well aware that the mind (*hugur*) is the all-important factor in a warrior's exploits, more important even than his physical prowess and his sword. (See Matthías V. Sæmundsson, *Galdrar á Íslandi*, p. 51; *Eddukvæði*, ed. by Ólafur Briem, Skálholt 1968, pp. 329–335.)
67. See Páll Björnsson, *Kennimark kölska*, 1976, p. 20; quoted in Matthías V. Sæmundsson, *Galdrar á Íslandi*, 1992, p. 42.

  In this connection we read in Páll Björnsson, *Kennimark kölska*, 1976 edn., p. 48: "According to a recent statement by an Icelandic sorcerer, if a person wants to learn the art of sorcery he must at the outset abandon all thought of God; instead, he must pray to the devil to enter into him and make himself familiar to him."

  Almost a century later, Jón Steingrímsson, in his schoolboy days at the Hólar school, observes that the same tradition persists among his fellow students: "I too

| Introduction | | 51 |

was allured by this [practice of sorcery]. But the rules were that for this practice one had to abandon all thoughts of piety, along with other things that I could not stomach. So, fortunately, I had no success, and very quickly abandoned the black art!" (Jón Steingrímsson, *A Very Present Help in Trouble: The Autobiography of the Fire-Priest*, trans. by Michael Fell, p. 60).

Síra Jón himself is well aware that proficiency in the magical arts requires a positive, concentrated state of mind. He writes (see pp. 79): "I think that sorcerers are at their most efficacious when they are single-minded and unafraid in their evildoing. But if they become full of fear, they will prove inept in the devil's work too."

68. Dr. Einar Már Jónsson informs me that this spit is considered to be a moraine left behind by a former ice age.

69. In fact, at that time there were no towns—or even villages, except perhaps for the diocesan seats of Skálholt and Hólar—anywhere in Iceland. There was only a scattered farming population, numbering altogether around 50,000 in the whole country.

70. Most farm properties in Iceland have a history that extends far back in time, and each is identified by a name which has persisted over the centuries.

71. See §4 for the Danish Trade Monopoly.

None of the buildings that stood on the Eyri spit in Jón Magnússon's time—neither the church, the rectory, nor the Danish trading station—have survived to the present. The Danish trading station is now a museum; but its buildings, that the tourist now visits, date from the 18th century.

72. For many centuries it was customary for Icelandic bishops to maintain an inventory (Icel. *máldagi*) of the officially recognized belongings of each church in his diocese. With such an inventory the priest or bishop could keep track of church property and prevent it from being misappropriated.

The best known Icelandic church inventory was that compiled for all the churches of his diocese by Bishop Vilchin of Skálholt in 1397. This inventory for Eyrarkirkja is the last extant inventory for that church from pre-Reformation times. Previous extant inventories for this church are listed on p. 183 of Margaret Cormack, *The Saints in Iceland*.

73. For the source of this information about the Eyrarkirkja in the 17th century see *Píslarsaga*, 2001 edn., pp. 11–13, 21, and 269–271 (where we also find a description of the dilapidated rectory in which Jón Magnússon and his family had to live). The image of the Virgin and Child is mentioned in the *Píslarsaga*, 2001 edn., pp. 21, 42, 266, 275.

74. See Jón P. Þór, *Saga Ísafjarðar* ....., vol. 1, p. 50.

For the geographical positions of most of the 12 farms listed here, see the map on p. 8 of Matthías V. Sæmundsson's 2001 edn. of the *Píslarsaga*. See also the map of Skutulsfjörður in this book.

75. See Jón P. Þór, *Saga Ísafjarðar* ....., vol. 1, pp. 50–54.

The 1703 census, conducted only seven years after Jón Magnússon's death, was the first complete census (Icel. *manntal*) of the population of Iceland. It was carried out, at the behest of the Danish government, by a committtee consisting of two of the most distinguished Icelanders of the time, Árni Magnússon and Páll Vídalín. It listed every Icelander living at that time, with his or her name, age, and residence—the first such complete census of an entire nation ever carried out anywhere in the world.

76. The same committee that compiled the 1703 census also compiled a Farm Register (Icel. *jarðabók*), listing all the farms and crofts together with the value and amenities

of each. A farm like Kirkjuból which had a church attached to it (see below) was generally more valuable than other farms.
77. There was a good reason why siblings were sometimes given identical names: because of the very high mortality among babies and children in 17th-century Iceland, this was the way to increase the likelihood that a particular baptismal name (here Jón) would survive into the next generation of the family.
78. See p. 167.
79. For a brief account of the intellectual background and convictions of Bishop Oddur Einarsson see §3 of this Introduction. For a more extended account of his episcopate see Páll E. Ólason, *Saga Íslendinga*, vol. 5, pp. 26–40 and 71–78.
80. See *Píslarsaga*, 2001 edn., p. 19.
81. See pp. 107–108.
82. See p. 106.
83. At their trial, both the Jón Jónssons admitted to having practiced sorcery against *síra* Jón, with the intent of inflicting illness on him. See p. 110.
84. See pp. 85, 86.
85. At this time Magnús Magnússon was only 25 years old, and had held the office of *sýslumaður* for only about two years. See *Píslarsaga*, 2001 edn., p. 332.
86. See Appendix 3.
87. The time limit that was set for the Jón Jónssons to assemble their compurgators was apparently left somewhat indefinite; see Note 6 of Chapter VI.
88. This is pointed out on p. 31 of the Introduction to Einar Már Jónsson's French translation of the *Píslarsaga*.
89. See Appendix 1 under: Erlendur Ormsson.

In the Introduction to his French translation of the *Píslarsaga*, Einar Már Jónsson conjectures a reconstruction of the train of circumstances that led up to the critical August 29th meeting between *síra* Jón, Erlendur Ormsson, and Þuríður at Kirkjuból. His reconstruction is as follows: Erlendur arrived at Eyri (presumably for the first time) only a few days before August 29th. At the time of his arrival, *síra* Jón and his household had recovered from the previous torments, and there seemed to be no evidence of any continuing sorcery. But Erlendur was not content to let matters rest. To impress the credulous *síra* Jón with his "prophetic gifts," he announced to him that Þuríður was surely the heir of her father's and brother's diabolism, and ought to be investigated. *Síra* Jón agreed, and arranged to call on her at Kirkjuból in the company of Erlendur, who would presumably try to extract a confession from her. In order that his visit should not have the appearance of a "put-up job," *síra* Jón states in the *Story of Sufferings* that the purpose of his visit was to transact some parish business with Sturli Bjarnason, one of the farmers who lived at Kirkjuból. But his real purpose was to join with Erlendur in exhorting Þuríður to repent and confess. When Þuríður showed herself entirely unresponsive to the pressure put upon her by the two men, *síra* Jón concluded that she was a woman of wicked hardheartedness—which was to be expected from a confirmed disciple of the devil. At this point, as we read in the *Story of Sufferings*, the second round of *síra* Jón's torments begins.
90. See p. 139.
91. See p. 216.
92. She was the sister of the *lögsagnari* Gísli Jónsson and the aunt of the *sýslumaður* Magnús Magnússon.
93. See *Píslarsaga*, 2001 edn., p. 30; also the last document in our Appendix 4.

94. See Appendix 5.

One notices a striking difference between Icelandic public opinion regarding the witchcraft trial of the two Jón Jónssons in 1656 on the one hand, and that of Þuríður Jónsdóttir in 1658 on the other. In 1656 the tide of public opinion seems to have been running against the Jón Jónssons, both locally in the West Fjords (see Chapter VI and the beginning of Chapter VIII) and at the Althing (see Appendix 5, for the year 1656). But very shortly afterwards, in 1657–59, public opinion ran heavily in favor of Þuríður, both in the West Fjords (see for example the last document of Appendix 4) and at the Althing (see Appendix 5, for the years 1658 and 1659). Even Þorleifur Kortsson showed himself unenthusiastic about convicting Þuríður, though he knew the "evidence" against her (see *Píslarsaga*, 2001 edn., p. 395).

What was the reason for this?

One factor was undoubtedly the behavior of *síra* Jón Magnússon's chief witness against Þuríður, namely Erlendur Ormsson (see Appendix 1 under: Erlendur Ormsson). The entry in Appendix 5 for the year 1658 makes it crystal clear that his evidence presented that year at the Althing was regarded as practically worthless. Another perhaps even more important factor was the public perception of the personalities of the defendants. Most people in *síra* Jón's parish had heard rumors to the effect that the two Jón Jónssons had been practicing magic for years (see Chapter VI, Item IV), and presumably that they hated their priest. Þuríður, on the other hand, seems to have been generally perceived as an attractive, intelligent, and well-behaved young woman (see p. 128, and the last document of Appendix 4)— the kind of person likely to arouse the sympathies of an exclusively male court, and surely not apt to be a witch!

95. See Appendix 6.
96. It would be interesting to know what became of Þuríður after her court case against *síra* Jón. We have no sure information about her subsequent life, but the following fact suggests a reasonable conjecture: the 1703 Census records that in that year there lived on one of the rental farms of Núpur, on Dýrafjörður in the West Fjords, a 65-year-old woman named Þuríður Jónsdóttir, the mother of the farmer's wife. This Þuríður Jónsdóttir would have been 18 years old in 1656 when the two Jón Jónssons were burned, and so might well have been their daughter and sister. See *Manntal á Íslandi 1703*, p. 201. See also *Píslarsaga*, 2001 edn., p. 31.
97. Why did *síra* Jón undertake to compose his *Story of Sufferings* (together with the supplementary apologetic texts) toward the end of 1658, after Þuríður had been acquitted at Mosvellir and the whole affair seemed closed? Einar Már Jónsson has suggested that *síra* Jón may have intended to carry the case to an even higher court of appeal than the Althing, namely to the Danish king himself in Copenhagen. But this intention was apparently never realized. (See p. 45 of the Introduction to Einar Már's French translation of the *Píslarsaga*.)
98. The necessity of bypassing normal rules of legal procedure in order to condemn witches to the flames was one of the pervasive features of the European witchcraft craze. It was stressed from the very beginning, in the *Malleus Maleficarum*.
99. Apart from the *Story of Sufferings* and the supplementary tracts, there survive three letters written by *síra* Jón. The first, written in 1653, refuses the request of dean Jón Sveinsson (father of dean Jón Jónsson) to be allowed to hire *síra* Jón's stepdaughter Rannveig as his housekeeper. The second, written in 1657 to dean Jón Jónsson demanding the prosecution of Þuríður Jónsdóttir, is translated in our Appendix 4.

The last letter, written in 1669 to dean Jón Jónsson, is a humble request for the pardoning of *síra* Jón's son Snorri, who by then was a priest but had been dismissed from his priestly office for fathering an illegitimate child. The first and last of these letters are not given in this book, but are printed (in the original Icelandic, of course) in the 2001 edn. of the *Píslarsaga*, pp. 238–239 and 244–245.

100. See p. 102.
101. See *Píslarsaga*, 2001 edn., p. 278.
102. See Matthías V. Sæmundsson, "Ævi séra Jóns Magnússonar," *Píslarsaga*, 2001 edn., p. 36.
103. For the final period of witchcraft persecution in Iceland, see the end of §5.
104. See Matthías V. Sæmundsson, "Ævi séra Jóns Magnússonar," *Píslarsaga*, 2001 edn., pp. 39, 40.
105. See Þorvaldur Thoroddsen, *Landfræðisaga Íslands*, vol. 2, p. 35–42. On p. 36 we read:
    "…. This book is a very remarkable source of material on the belief in magic, the fear, the stupidity, and the apathy current in the 17th century. It shows clearly how the human nervous system was debilitated by superstition and the terror of demons—an infection that gripped the population like a plague. From the description of his persecutions given by the priest it is clear that he himself was a sick, half-crazy man. So potent was the germ of the disease that his whole household became half-crazy too. The sensations that he describes give evidence of a high degree of neurasthenia and hysteria."
106. According to Sigfús Blöndal, the tingling sensations, the stabs of pain, the "globulus hystericus," and the "mouches volantes," which *síra* Jón by his own account suffered from, are recognized symptoms of neurasthenia. See *Píslarsaga*, 1914 edn., pp. IV, V. Neurasthenic patients are often convinced that they are suffering from illnesses and experiencing symptoms (such as paralysis, blindness, suffocation) for which no organic causes can be found.
107. Matthías V. Sæmundsson, "Galdur og geðveiki," *Píslarsaga*, 2001 edn., p. 362.
108. See *Píslarsaga*, 1967 edn., p. 25.
    The present translator's point of view regarding the mental condition of *síra* Jón is generally closer to that of Sigurður Nordal than to that of the other editors of the *Píslarsaga*. However, Sigurður Nordal gives more emphasis to the mental sickness of *síra* Jón than is given here.
109. See *Píslarsaga*, 1967 edn., pp. 16, 17.
110. He even questions whether the emotion of *fear*, as felt today, can be automatically equated with that felt in the 17th century! See Matthías V. Sæmundsson, "Galdur og geðveiki," *Píslarsaga*, 2001 edn., pp. 412, 413.
111. "Such insensitivity to the faith and experience of former centuries means that we no longer share a common language with them, and that our connection with the past is restricted to the general medical diagnoses of our own times." (See Matthías V. Sæmundsson, "Galdur og geðveiki," *Píslarsaga*, 2001 edn., pp. 361)
112. "The magistrates who sentenced men to be burned made their decisions in full consciousness. Their actions were based on what they thought to be both reasonable and necessary." (Matthías V. Sæmundsson, "Galdur og geðveiki," *Píslarsaga*, 2001 edn., p. 361)
113. See for example Matthías Viðar Sæmundsson, *Galdrar á Íslandi*, pp. 278–283.
114. See Ólína Þorvarðardóttir, *Brennuöldin*, p. 101.

For the evidence adduced by Ólína in favor of an influenza epidemic, see Chapter I, Note 16; also Chapter II, Note 4.
115. See for example Margrét Þorvaldsdóttir, "Myrkrahöfðingjar fyrr og nú," *Lesbók Morgunblaðsins*, March 18th, 2000. Ergot-poisoning is a serious complaint which can cause death, and is also known to give rise to hallucinations, which according to the evidence of the *Píslarsaga* assailed many members of *síra* Jón's household. It is not contagious, but arises from a fungus which can lodge in rye bread. The latter, being cheaper than other kinds of bread, may have been commonly consumed in *síra* Jón's district.

Compare Linda Caporael, "Ergotism: The Satan Loosed in Salem?", *Science*, vol. 192 (2 April 1976). In this article the author presents evidence suggesting that the physiological source of the outbreak of witchcraft delusion in Salem, Massachusetts, in the years 1691–1692, was ergot-poisoning.

I should however mention that, according to a personal communication from Einar Már Jónsson based on a conversation of his with the historian Gísli Gunnarsson, there is evidence to show that the average Icelander of the 17th century consumed little bread.
116. Eggert Ólafsson (1726–1768), poet, scholar, and pioneer of the Icelandic Enlightenment, wrote as follows from his own observations of life in the West Fjords in the 18th century:

"In this country, as elsewhere, it is believed that evil spirits dwell in desolate, dark places, in mountains, valleys, churchyards and so forth; so it is hardly surprising that people claim to have perceived ghosts in the remotest parts up here in the north. In the more populous southern parts of the country, on the other hand, where only a few foreigners live (apart from the merchants who come there in the summer), one hears much less about ghosts. To my understanding, the causes of this superstition are as follows: The long winters and the long, dark nights, and especially the loneliness of these remote places up north, have combined to create fear and unhealthy fantasies in the people there, who are naturally taciturn and inclined to depression. And these influences gather even greater strength from the fact that these same people are aware of the well-being that the nation enjoyed in former times, in contrast to the present when they are tormented by poverty and every sort of wretchedness, and have no means of recreation or rational enjoyment to divert their thoughts. ...... An honest life, lived in the simple fear of God or, to put it briefly, intelligent thinking and living, are the surest guard against ghosts and sorcery. The fact is that some of the so-called master magicians in Iceland have been obliged to admit that there were certain individuals and families who could not be injured by sorcery since, as they observed, these were intelligent people free of all superstition and fantasies, and moreover bold, resolute, and physically healthy." (*Ferðabók Eggerts Ólafssonar og Bjarna Pálssonar um ferðir þeirra á Íslandi árin 1752–1757*. Reykjavík, 1943; vol. 1, p. 334, 335)
117. See for example Tambiah, *Magic, Science, Religion, and the Scope of Rationality*, p. 81.
118. Compare Harry D. Eastwell, *Voodoo Death and the Mechanism for Dispatch of the Dying in East Arnhem, Australia*.
119. See p. 141.
120. See p. 93.
121. See p. 91.

122. Thus, Þuríður is dry-eyed when she prays, and does not respond when upbraided by *síra* Jón and Erlendur Ormsson. See Matthías V. Sæmundsson, "Galdur og geðveiki," *Píslarsaga*, 2001 edn., pp. 365, 366.
123. To those who look on the 17th and early 18th centuries as a time of exclusive concentration on the horrors of sin and suffering, one should point out that the greatest Icelandic expositors of Lutheran doctrine in that period, namely Hallgrímur Pétursson and Jón Vídalín, maintained a sound balance between emphasis on sin and emphasis on redemption, faith, and joy.
124. Little study has been made in modern times by psychiatrists regarding the mental condition of *síra* Jón. The only such study of which this translator is aware is an article by the Icelandic psychiatrist Óttar Guðmundsson, who has argued on the basis of available evidence that it is most unlikely that *síra* Jón was a schizophrenic (see his article "Schizophrenian og Píslarsaga sr. Jóns Magnússonar," *Pressan*, 17 May 1990). His argument is twofold: First, schizophrenics lose the ability to carry on normal social intercourse with other people; and this does not seem to have been the case with *síra* Jón. Secondly, *síra* Jón seems to have returned to a normal state of mind during the last 20 years or more of his life; and such a long remission is very rare among schizophrenics.

    In a much earlier work, Sigurjón Jónsson, a doctor, considers it a certainty that he was a victim of both schizophrenia and hysteria (*móðursýki*) (*Sóttarfar og sjúkdómar á Íslandi 1400–1800*, p. 211).
125. The sentence "To my mind they associate Þuríður .... and other devilry," on p. 163, indicates that *síra* Jón is aware that the plausibility of his arguments for Þuríður's guilt depends on the correctness of his a priori conviction that *someone's* sorcery must be at work.
126. The only place in the *Story of Sufferings* where *síra* Jón states that he himself saw a demonic form is on p. 142.
127. *Síra* Jón was clearly a credulous person; and it probably would not have occurred to him to suspect that clairvoyant persons might, consciously or unconsciously, be tailoring their visions to what they knew that *síra* Jón expected!
128. See p. 129.
129. See p. 84.
130. See p. 95.
131. See p. 95 and p. 126.
132. See p. 95.
133. Could it be that *síra* Jón's complaint to Bishop Gísli Oddsson many years before, that the stress of his priestly duties was more than he could bear (see §8), foreshadowed a hypersensitivity to stress which may have accentuated the mental distress that he now suffered?
134. "Saying 'yes' to the will of God deprives suffering of its power." This teaching is beautifully expressed by *síra* Jón's Icelandic contemporary Hallgrímur Pétursson in his Passion Hymn 44.
135. In the Introduction to his 1967 edn. of the *Píslarsaga* (p. 31), Sigurður Nordal mentions a remarkable 18th-century Lutheran priest who was sometimes overcome with hatred of God and of His word, so that he felt himself to be irretrievably damned. This was Hans Egede, the Danish "apostle of Greenland," who in 1721 led a very arduous but ultimately successful mission to Greenland for the conversion of

Introduction   57

its Inuit inhabitants to Christianity. Sigurður Nordal's source is the diary kept by Egede; see Harry Fett, *Vort nationale enevælde*, Oslo 1925, pp. 104–105.
136. *Píslarsaga*, 1967 edn., p. 40.
137. See Appendix 1 under: Prayer of Jesus.
138. See for example *Romans* 8:5–8.
139. See pp. 99, 100.
140. This version of the Jesus Prayer seems to be a composite of more than one biblical passage. In *John* 1:29 Jesus is called the Lamb of God; in *Revelation* 22:1, 3 the Lamb is said to share the throne of God; and in *Luke* 18:38, 39 the blind man calls out desperately to Jesus for help.
141. See p. 92.

Síra Jón's heroic determination to be "the only one among the damned to be calling upon Him" reminds us of a similar resolve by his French contemporary Brother Lawrence (see Lawrence of the Resurrection, *The Practice of the Presence of God*, 2nd Conversation).
142. *Píslarsaga*, 1967 edn., p. 40.
143. See pp. 92, 93.
144. See pp. 140, 141. See also Appendix 1 under: Randíður Ólafsdóttir.
145. See p. 94.
146. See *Proverbs* 18:10.
147. See p. 131.
148. See p. 101.
149. This distinction between the two "compartments" of *síra* Jón's mental life reminds one of St. Paul's antithesis between life in the flesh and life in the Spirit; see *Romans* 8:5–8. Luther explains this in his exposition of *Romans* 8:5:

"*For those who live according to the flesh*, in the native state, not yet born again in the Spirit through baptism or repentance, *set their minds on the things of the flesh*, that is, the good things of creation; that is, such things are pleasing to them and seem good to them, and therefore they do not 'agree that the Law of God is good' (*Romans* 7:16), but set their minds and feelings on other things. *But those who live according to the Spirit*, men who are born of the Spirit and of God to become new creatures, *set their minds on the things of the Spirit*, that is, on the good things that are uncreated, that are God Himself." (*Luther's Works*, vol. 25, p. 68).

It is clear from *Romans* 8:5–8 that these two "compartments," the Spirit and the flesh, are "disjoint" from each other, even though they may both be present and, as it were, struggling for mastery in the life of a single individual.
150. *Píslarsaga*, 1967 edn., p. 45.
151. *Isaiah* 11:3.

PART I

The First Part of the Story of the Sufferings of Síra Jón Magnússon

I. The Antecedents and Beginnings of the Attacks on Síra Jón At and After the End of October 1655[1]

A Summary and Short Account of the Frightful Injuries and Sufferings that Have Afflicted Me, JÓN MAGNÚSSON, Called to Serve in the Holy Office of Preacher in the Little Parish Church at Eyri at Skutulsfjörður, Through the Witchcraft and Demonic Attacks to Which Two of My Parishioners, a Father and Son Living at Kirkjuból, Both Named Jón Jónsson, Have Publicly Confessed at the Assembly, Being Subsequently, in Virtue of Their Confession and the Sentence Passed by a Court of Twelve Men, Burned to Death According to the Laws of the Land. This Came About in the Following Manner:

On 20 October 1655,[2] the Saturday just before the Nineteenth Sunday after Trinity, I was visited here, along with other people, by Snæbjörn Pálsson, one of the three householders who lived at Kirkjuból. He expressed the wish that I should conduct a service there in the chapel,[3] since the members of the household were in the habit of receiving the sacrament there. It was an old custom that the farmers at Kirkjuból should take turns in informing me when the people there were eager for a celebration of the mass in their chapel, both on his own and the others' behalf. But because there was bad weather with a snowfall that Saturday, and for other reasons too, the man and I agreed to postpone the service until the following weekend in hope of better weather. When we had together reached this decision, I left Snæbjörn and went out of the church alone and walked home, giving the matter no further thought at that time. But when I was halfway between the church and the farmhouse, near a stone that stands on the spot, these words came strangely into my mind: "It will be of no advantage to you to postpone what is to befall you rather than going there right away." Heeding these words I resolved not to defer the matter, and so I went with the man to Kirkjuból without delay. I was less anxious about what might happen to me there than I was about the painstaking performance of my duty as a priest, since I felt sure that this was God's word and inspiration. I had no fear of being harmed by sorcery. Twice already I had experienced the Lord's mighty and merciful aid in such matters, as I came to know after the event from the lips of those very people who knew best, and who praised me highly, saying that it was impossible to overcome my good fortune. In such matters [I knew of no better recourse][4] than to take refuge in the compassion of the Most High; and this enabled me more than once to be brave and intrepid, having no fear of any devilish sorcery, since I had already experienced the mighty protection of the Lord's grace and mercy. That very same week, before I went with Snæbjörn to Kirkjubó1, something peculiar had happened at my home: those who were second-sighted became aware of an apparition in the form of a dog, running up to the window of the room where I and my household were seated indoors, and then running back by the same path leading to where these men lived. We were astonished at this unusual happening, for which we could see no cause. However, this event was in keeping with the confession of the men who were put on trial. For on the very days when these ghostly visitations took place at my home, the father, the elder Jón, had dispatched demonic sorcery against me here—sorcery which had at first assailed his own younger daughter Þorgerður, whom his son, Jón the younger, confessed to having healed by his knowledge of magic.

Having arrived at Kirkjubó1 with the aforementioned Snæbjörn, I lodged with him on that occasion, it being his turn according to our custom. But after midnight, when I had retired and gone to sleep, a satanic spirit assailed me in bed, tormenting me even after I awoke. I could feel it on my feet, like a mouse or a rat, and could not by any means get to sleep again. The same devilry had happened to me seven or eight years earlier. At that time it bothered me only at night, and not even every night, but only once in a while, and kept this up in my home for five or six weeks. One night, when I could not get to sleep, I became annoyed with this unclean spirit and ordered it in the name of the Lord to leave me, which it did, whereupon my entire household was rid of all these scourges. Jón the elder himself, in his cups and half-drunk, spoke to me in confidence about this same spirit that he had dispatched,[5] promising not to do anything like that again, and he kept his promise for a year thereafter. This was the same kind of thing that befell me at Kirkjubó1 that night. But as soon as I got up, I suffered no distress at all. So I felt no anxiety about it, though I knew what source it came from.

I then went to the church. I had noticed that at times there had been enmity, quarrels, wrangling, and foul language among some of the people on this farm. So, when the people who wished to make their confession had assembled, I gave them a warning that this enmity, wrangling, and other accompanying evils must cease. I said I would make every effort to that end if there was no other remedy, provided someone would tell me the situation.

But the elder Jón repudiated my plea and called on witnesses—which however did not do him any good, since his witnesses stuck to the truth and testified quite differently from the way he had expected. Another exhortation of mine to the people was that they should not neglect God's word or His parish church. Indeed, the younger Jón had been down at the store on Sunday at the hour of mass, and had not come even that short distance to church, occupying himself instead with drink and making purchases. The next Sunday, at the time when churchgoers were on their way home, the younger Jón was setting out from home by boat to the Danish ship to amuse himself on board, having had no wish to attend church. On the third Sunday he stayed at home. This was the day on which, according to a complaint made against him in the hearing of the congregation by Ásta Narfadóttir, a servant-woman of his father, he had punched her on the head with his fist, so that she fell down. The father and son had talked in a very unseemly way about this, and wanted to make out that her complaint was a lie. The father especially spoke and behaved in an outlandish and unchristian fashion—or so it seemed to me—so that I was on the point of excluding him on this occasion from the Lord's table. I was just about to tell him this; the words were almost on my mouth, so sickened was I by the unseemliness of it. But then the thought came to me: "You do not know this man any better than the Lord knew the traitor Judas, and yet He permitted him to share in the holy sacrament of the Lord's Supper just as He did the other apostles." So I restrained myself from putting him under any ban. I left the church and spoke privately with his son Jón the younger, requesting him to tell me what had passed between him and the girl. He admitted the truth of her accusation, but made various excuses which seemed to me mere evasion and empty words. I advised him to go and be reconciled to the girl in a Christian spirit, so that he might receive the sacrament worthily. As a result of my mediation they were reconciled, and he received the sacrament along with a public admonition. After I had spoken with the younger Jón outside, I went back into the church, where I noticed that the old man was fuming over this squabble. I took him aside, into the chancel and away from the others, and informed him what had passed between his son and the girl. I told him that my only desire was that they should both reach an accord in a spirit of Christian love, as befitted those who desired to partake of the Lord's Supper. But he refused to listen, and turning away angrily went back into the nave of the church.

Such were the reasons that these wretched men had for setting on me with their sorcery and making attempts on my life in the ghastly way described in the account that follows. That the father had set out on this course even before I had spoken to either of them or done my priestly duty by admonishing them, was generally thought to be due to the aforementioned girl: she had threatened the younger Jón that she would tell the priest or other good men what he had done to her, in view of the fact that he refused to speak to her in a seemly manner. The older Jón afterwards, when he was in custody, admitted to some good people that he had asked another man, called Jón Pétursson, to help him do away with me by sorcery, but that this man had refused to be a party to the plan. This turned out to be true; but in fact he had made this request of him some years earlier than the events now being described. And yet both of these men, judging from their speech and behavior, had been on excellent, godly terms with me, as if they had been my good friends. Anyone can see from this how useful it is to keep company with people of this sort, exhorting them to walk in God's ways, piety and Christian virtue, and to get them to *revocare gradum superasque evadere ad auras!*[6]

That same Sunday evening I rode back home in the company of the aforementioned Snæbjörn Pálsson. On the following Monday, about midday, there came over me an extraordinarily oppressive and unnatural sleep, so that from noon until darkness I could hardly wake up.[7] That same evening, when I sat at my little table, I felt as if a cat were rustling at my feet under the table, causing me a singularly nauseating and repulsive sensation. I was quite unable to endure it, and had no choice but to go to bed. But when I got into bed that night, I was unable to sleep for a long time. At the same time I was assailed with weird, impure, and evil thoughts. At first I forgot to struggle against them, as I should have, with prayer and sighs to the Lord, until I received a warning. (The fact is that the aforementioned previous warning had completely slipped my memory.) Now, in the midst of these evil fancies, the thought struck me: "You had better put your mind on something else rather than these wicked thoughts." Right away I assented to these words and began to pray to the Lord for his assistance and grace that I might be rid of this evil poison. At the same time that I started turning my heart to God in prayer, it was as if a dog jumped onto my bed, first onto my legs and then over my whole body, striking me with a cruel horror and panic, and digging his claws, which felt like red-hot needles, into my neck so horribly that I could not tell whether I would survive or perish. No description of mine can depict this onslaught as it was in reality. I think it lasted for about an hour. In the midst of this fiendish torment I could think of no other recourse or remedy than to put every ounce of my strength into calling on the Lord with prayers and groans, as best I could during such an assault. Afterwards I was weak and ill. But as usual I was out of bed by midday, by then feeling somewhat better. But when evening came the same devilry started up again and continued to torment me all that week, though not quite so horribly as at the first attack.

I now perceived that this was unadulterated witchcraft. I was well aware of what had happened to me before (as related above), and since matters were not improving, I concluded that there was no point in keeping silent about it. So next Sunday I described what had happened to me from the pulpit. However I did not name any individual, but phrased my comments so as to make it seem incredible that anyone in my parish should be guilty of such shameful behavior. But, if there were any such, I admonished them to come to their senses and mend their ways. At every word the aforementioned father and son looked strangely, and the expression of their faces changed—as I heard some upright people mention with surprise. They took it personally, just as if they had been mentioned by name. (This kind of behavior is, I believe, the strongest evidence of guilt, for here conscience demonstrates a person's evildoing in the clearest possible way. However, these signs are not taken very seriously by some superior court judges in witchcraft cases, as I have had occasion to find out.) I also entreated all upright and devout people to join me in offering communal prayer to God for my sake, that this kind of diabolical harassment might be averted and brought to an end, and I could see that many of the people did so.

On the following Sunday the younger Jón from Kirkjuból, the son, came to church along with some others. At the close of the service, when he left the choir (he and his father were both choir deacons[8]), he shook hands with me according to custom. Immediately I felt a burning sensation in the palm of my hand (*tanquam torpedine tactus*[9]). This struck me as peculiar, and it occurred to me that it was the outcome of diabolical expertise. For where his hand had touched mine, on the inner side of each finger, there was a smarting sensation as if from a burn, though there was no heat and no severe pain. In regard to this he admitted at the end, along with other confessions, that he had put a magical stave on his hand and transmitted the sorcery to me by the handshake. When I realized this I was at a loss to know what to do. It occurred to me to rub my hand against the altarpiece where I was standing, and I did so until the burning sensation abated.

A few days later I felt a weakness in the same right hand, with pain in the wrist. Sometimes spasms of pain went up the outside of my arm so that I could hardly use my hand. Then I had to take food with my left hand—a fact that my household could not help noticing. But by God's grace this infirmity gradually passed away.

One Sunday after that event the elder Jón Jónsson came to church along with others. On his way home after the reading of God's word he was observed to stop for a while outside the window in the roof of the [my] *baðstofa* and look up at the window. We noticed this because we had never before known him to be in the habit of taking such detours or pausing when he was here on his trips to church. As it happened, that same Sunday evening some of the people of my household, as they now recall and can testify, noticed that I found it less agreeable to be there [near that window] than at any other place indoors, and that sometimes, going there, it seemed as if I could hardly sit down, least of all in my usual seat next to the window. Moreover, [the elder Jón Jónsson] was seen standing still and staring in the same way in front of the side-alcove[10] in the church adjacent to the south side of the choir. In the choir, on the same side as the little alcove, while I lay flat on the floor in prayer, I was trampled upon by the devil; I felt as if some frenzied man [were pounding me] with knees and fists. Another time, as I was similarly lying prostrate in prayer, the devil blew into my right ear, which was turned toward the same little alcove, with such terrible hissing that it was no longer any use my praying in that place, and so I had to betake myself sometimes to the nave of the church and sometimes outside the church to say my prayers.

And now these devilish practices were intensified more and more, most of all when these wretched men attended church, since I did not relax my admonitions and warnings on the subject as long as I was able to carry on church services. The more these fiendish assaults increased and became apparent—both inside the farmhouse and outside, and also in church—the more the troop of fiends multiplied, both in number and in the variety of their shapes. Whereas on the first occasion only one fiend was seen, in the shape of a dog, there was now such a multitude of them that not only were they visible in each separate nook and corner of the *baðstofa*, wherever there was shadow and darkness, but in the *skáli* and corridors too there swarmed a countless multitude of fiends of various shapes and forms, so that the farmhouse and every outbuilding was full of them. This is what those with second sight told us. According to their perceptions, those who were not clairvoyant walked right through these fiendish forms when they were tightly packed together. I was able to verify the same fact as long as I could get dressed and move around. Whenever the clairvoyants warned me not to go into spots that were in shadow I felt and experienced the very things that they saw. Moreover they were able to tell me almost every night whether the attacks on me would be milder or more severe, and I do not remember their predictions ever failing when I was able to speak to them about it. Finally the devil walked in the very size, shape, and appearance of those men who were responsible for the whole business. Even some who were not clairvoyant saw them, and people from other farms in the district gave the same reports about these apparitions as those who were of my household, when these devilish harassments spread to the other farms.

Moreover, on my farm light-colored insects like butterflies were clearly seen fluttering in circles above me and elsewhere in the rooms. Everybody saw these insects and butterflies throughout the whole winter season. Some people also saw insects of other forms, with long tails or with distended claws and legs, which it would take too long to record.

Because of these phenomena and the palpable daily experience that I had in confirmation of them, I am totally unable to acquiesce in the judgment of those, whoever they may be, who ignore these visions as insignificant, either because they have not investigated the case properly or through stupidity and irresolution. Nevertheless, I do admit that a first-rate judge is needed in order to rule out factors that should be excluded, so that no errors may slip into the verdict and the final determination of the truth. For this purpose, other circumstances surrounding the affair can be very helpful.

And so these devilish prodigies multiplied, most of all at times when I gave admonishments. I made every effort to deliver these not in my own words but in those supplied by the gospels, [that is,] the lectionary texts in each of the gospels, where any attentive person will find a wealth of material for admonishments of this sort if he looks up the gospel texts from the Nineteenth Sunday after Trinity to Advent of the year 1655. I have learned not only from these but also from the exhortations that I myself composed and addressed subsequently to those who would be shown to have been reared in a nest of witchcraft if they had been investigated with a documented, reasonable, and godly moderation and zeal[11]—I have learned how wholesome it would be to exhort these sorcerers, who are no better than the devil himself, to repent and return to the kingdom of God![12] I have more material to write on this matter than can be put in this tract, if it should be necessary to do so.

So I think I can draw a plain conclusion from the elder Jón's standing and staring which led to such consequences: he must have been muttering some magical text or *incantamentum*[13] over the window in the roof of the *baðstofa* and over the side-alcove of the church, just as his son, Jón the younger, admitted having done over the *baðstofa*. I am drawing this example to the attention of those who are content with finding witnesses to the actual deeds of sorcery, but are unwilling to follow any other line of investigation in these matters. I shall have a little more to write about this in due course, in another place.

But let me not distract the reader from the plain narrative of these crimes. It so happened one evening that I was lying on the *pallur*[14] among the people of my household, pondering on these things. As usual I felt the presence of a demonic spirit under the boards of the *pallur* on which I was lying, and it occurred to me to try to find out by natural means whether these demonic spirits originated from human magic and witchcraft or not. So I devised a plan: I had an iron pipe broken off a bolt, jammed into a piece of wood, and loaded with gunpowder (but nothing more). I had it aimed at the place where I knew the demonic spirit to be, and then fired. As soon as the blast struck the fiend, he assaulted me, and even more violently the man who had fired this gun. The latter was hardly able to withstand the assault, as we both observed. From this experience I felt convinced on natural grounds that this demon was no independent adventitious spirit, but a spirit bound fast, constrained by the pythonic arts and the power to command evil spirits—as indeed the nature of fire would indicate.[15]

And so these devilish abominations and attacks on our farm were constantly on the increase. In the evenings the people of my household could not even sit or stand in peace without feeling them. One would say to another: "Look, it's here! It's got hold of my foot, my side, my head!" Everyone who suffered these pains sought relief by moving away from the place where he was, either to wander around or to sit or stand in another place. And the harassments that the people complained of were sometimes accompanied by itching, numbness, or a horrible sense of heat or cold, now more and now less. Some complained of a burning sensation in the chest, or back, or in the ribs; some of piercing cold; some of blows on the head or chest; some of nasty lumps in the throat that often passed down to the chest. Some individuals were knocked unconscious, others almost so. And more: at night there were terrifying creatures abroad, and our beds quivered and shook.[16] And devils crawled all over our people, who felt as if they were mice. Though all this affected me more grievously than anyone else, there were several of the household who experienced the same. Lights burned from dusk to daybreak in every room where there were any people. In addition to everything else mentioned above, loud and frightening cracking noises were heard in the boards and ends of the beds.

Notes

1. This Chapter I covers the following material from the three printed Icelandic editions of the *Píslarsaga*:
    1914 edn., p. 1 (line 1) to p. 11 (line 9);
    1967 edn., p. 49 (line 1) to p. 60 (line 9);
    2001 edn., p. 59 (line 1) to p. 67 (line 12).
2. See Appendix 1 under: Calendar.
3. For the three householders and the chapel at Kirkjubòl, see §7 of the Introduction.
4. In the Icelandic manuscript some words have clearly been omitted at this point. The words in square brackets are conjectured in order to make sense of the sentence.
5. See Appendix 1 under: *Sending*.
6. This Latin phrase is quoted from Virgil's *Aeneid*, Book 6, line 128, and means "to recall one's steps and pass out to the upper air" (see the Loeb Classical Library edn. of the *Aeneid*, translated by H. R. Fairclough and revised by G. P. Goold, vol. 1, p. 541). It occurs in a passage where Virgil is describing the feat of returning to the upper world of light after having once descended into Hades. In *síra* Jón's context it means "to give up one's evil ways and gain the kingdom of heaven." The sentence is clearly ironic.
7. See Appendix 1 under: Magical Spells and Staves, [1].
8. See Appendix 1 under: Deacon.
9. That is: "as if I had been touched by a torpedo fish."
    A torpedo fish, also called a crampfish or electric ray, is a fish which is capable of giving powerful electric shocks either for defense or to kill prey.
10. See Appendix 1 under: Side-alcove.

11. This is an oblique reference to Þuríður Jónsdóttir, daughter and sister of the two Jón Jónssons. Though the main subject of Part II of the *Story of Sufferings*, she is hardly mentioned in Part I. One of the principal circumstantial evidences against her was that she was brought up in a "nest of witchcraft" (see p. 159).
12. This sentence is ironic, implying that admonitions directed at such depraved people are almost useless. Compare Note 6.
13. Latin for "conjuration."
14. A *pallur* is a platform or raised section of the floor; see §4 of the Introduction.
15. This incident requires some comment. *Síra* Jón is here distinguishing between two kinds of evil spirits: One is the ghost (Icel. *draugur*) of a dead person, whom a sorcerer raises and dispatches to work harm on his enemy. Such a *draugur* is called in Icelandic a *sending* (see under this word in Appendix 1); it is physical in nature, can be made to be localized in one place, and can attack its victim physically and be wrestled with by the latter. Shooting at a *draugur* of this sort was a common way of attempting to get rid of it. (I owe this information to a personal communication by Einar G. Pétursson.) The reference to the "nature of fire" is perhaps explained by the fact that in Icelandic folktales a *sending* is often perceived in the form of a ball of fire (Icel. *eldhnöttur*) (see the references given under *eldur* in the Index Volume VI of Jón Árnason, *Íslenskar þjóðsögur og ævintýri*).

    The sorcerer's art by which a *sending* can be bound to one locality is specified here as the "pythonic" art. The Greek word *python* means a spirit of divination (see *Acts* 16:16). According to *síra* Páll Björnsson it refers especially to an evil spirit who utters oracles through the secret parts of the human body (see his *Kennimark kölska*, Chapter 2).

    The other kind of evil spirit is the genuine satanic fiend—the "independent, adventitious kind"—over whom the human sorcerer has no direct control.

    It was *síra* Jón's aim, through this experiment, to determine which of the two sorts of fiends was responsible for his sufferings. He concluded that it was the first sort, dispatched against him by human sorcerers.
16. This passage, from "and the harassments ....." to ".... and our beds quivered and shook," has been quoted as evidence that *síra* Jón's household was suffering from an influenza epidemic. See Introduction, Note 114.

II. Síra Jón Accuses the Kirkjuból Father and Son Before Magnús Magnússon the Sýslumaður. At an Assembly at Eyri in Skutulsfjörður, They are Required to Produce the Oaths of Twelve Persons. A Fruitless Search for Texts on Witchcraft at Kirkjuból[1]

Through all this I waited, delaying and taking no positive action, until I saw matters had come to such a pass that the people of my household would be obliged to abandon the farm and flee. Indeed, the witchcraft had induced such torpor and witlessness in most of them that they could not even make up their minds to seek sustenance by fishing. But I could see that every single one of them would leave, since their well-being and their very lives were at stake and in the utmost danger. So I had myself ferried across the fjord,[2] and then went from Arnardalur to Súðavík in Álftafjörður. At that place there lived an upright, high-minded man, a very good friend of mine, named Þorlákur Arason. He gave me and my companions a friendly reception. But it was a matter of no little vexation to me that the devils went along with me even there, and made their presence evident to the Súðavík people. There I met the district *sýslumaður*, Magnús Magnússon, and described to him the witchcraft and horrible demonic attacks that had plagued me and my household. He lost no time in excusing himself, giving various reasons for his excuses. But when people had gone to bed, and the same sufferings as usual were harassing me, I approached the *sýslumaður* again, and asked him—in fact demanded of him—that he should do the duty of his office in regard to this business. I threatened him that if he refused, and if I survived, I would bring a complaint against him before his superiors. Þorlákur Arason, who was a *lögréttumaður*, took my part very effectively and advised the *sýslumaður* to follow up the matter. Through his advice the latter dispatched a letter and message westward the very next morning to his uncle, Gísli Jónsson, who lived in Barðastrandarsýsla, the next district to the west. Gísli Jónsson was the deputy for his (Gísli's) wife's sister's husband Þorleifur Kortsson, who lived in Hrútafjörður to the north[3] and was appointed *sýslumaður* in half of this *sýsla*, Magnús Magnússon having the other half. At this point I set off homeward. When I came to Arnardalur I learned that one of my parishioners, Jón Ólafsson by name, had taken the trouble to go from Arnardalur to Kirkjuból and inform the two warlocks (whose friend he was) about my trip to see the *sýslumaður*. I was told that the same man had, during those very days, composed for their gratification a versified curse against their enemies.

On the Saturday just before the First Sunday in Advent Björn Bjarnason, then the farmer at Arnardalur, ferried me home across the fjord. I went first to the church, intending to say prayers there, as is customary. I had formerly been in the habit of saying them in the choir by the alcove outside of which the elder Jón had stopped for a while, as I related above. But when I had prostrated myself, a strong, biting wind from the alcove assailed my right ear, coming as it were from a gaping dog, spewing such a disgusting sound into my face and the inside of my ear, and putting me into such a horrible and extreme state of dread, that I realized that this was the work of the vicious fiend.[4] In spite of this I intended to continue my prayers, but it was impossible. I had to get up and leave the place.

On the First Sunday in Advent I conducted the divine service, though, as was often the case, I felt great weakness. But when I stood up in the pulpit to speak the word of God to the congregation, I became aware of a [diabolical] scheme to rob me of my reason and judgment by means of so-called *æðigaldur* (madness magic), so that I should lose my wits entirely. When I realized this I shortened my sermon as much as I could, so as to make my exit from the pulpit without giving offence to God or scandalizing the congregation. But when I came before the altar, I was barely able to stand there, with my chest and arms resting on it while the *exitus*[5] was being sung. After I had taken off my surplice, I found it impossible for me to say the customary prayers before the altar. So then and there I went from the altar to the chancel entrance, intending to go out of the church in the hope that I would feel somewhat better in the open air. But when I saw the sky through the church doors I was afraid to look on it with these eyes of mine. So, seeing no recourse or remedy, I turned back toward the altar. As I stood at the chancel entrance, I threw myself down on the floor with my arms stretched out before the Lord. But my heart was cold beyond measure, and I could neither feel any devotion nor shed the least tear. However much I tried to feel [my eyes] wet with *devotion*,[6] it was completely out of my reach, so dry and hard was my heart, like a stone. I did manage, though, to open my mouth in grievous complaint and wailing before God. The people in the church who saw this were terrified, and during the time of prayer many wept at the sight. But I then felt somewhat better, so that I stood up and then sat down in the church while the people took leave of me, many with tears and sighs. And so they all departed home. But shortly thereafter one girl, who had attended church and lived at Seljaland, was found struck down and speechless on her way home, only a short distance from the farm. She was supported and carried back here again, repeatedly fainting when she came inside the farmhouse.

When my poor wife learned of this and realized what a bad condition I was in, she asked Björn Bjarnason of Arnardalur, who with people of his household had brought me home from his farm the previous evening, to stay for a while until they saw what turn my condition would take. He generously agreed to do so. At this point I felt that I recognized the consequences brought upon me by Jón Ólafsson's trip to the two Jón Jónssons to inform them of my journey to Súðavík. From this journey of mine both he and they would easily have hit upon the purpose of my meeting with the *sýslumaður*—though I kept quiet about it when I was at Arnardalur, so that it could not have reached their ears from my own words. So it proves true that evil men are not caught off guard! And now the facts of experience bore witness how these vicious men sought to destroy me by their sorcery and devilish arts.

That same night, when the evening was far advanced, the same loathsomeness came upon me that I had experienced previously in the church. I lay on the *pallur*, with my own household and that of Björn around me. I wanted very much to go outside, thinking that it might relieve me and so that I could gaze up to heaven and pray for help and grace. But Björn Bjarnason had made up his mind, and said that it was perfectly clear to him that I could not tolerate being at home, and invited me to his own house in the hope that I might find relief there. I accepted his invitation and took leave of my own people and my poor wife, who stayed behind lying on the beach in an excess of grief and lamentation, as devout people will easily imagine. It was on the First Sunday in Advent that these calamities befell me, which I understood and recognized to be *aðigaldur*—the work of those same evil men, heaped on top of all the other evil spirits that they had dispatched against me[7] and that I have already described.

The next morning, Monday, was calm and windless, and the men of my household decided to go out fishing. But when they came to bait the fishing-lines at the boathouse they had a strong sense of something foul. They boarded the boat and rowed out seaward by the usual course, but still had the sense of demonic presence on board until they reached Hnífsdalsvík.[8] All this time they were distinctly aware of the demonic spirit on board the boat, and finally one of them, Guðmundur Ísleiksson, was struck by it and lay speechless. The other crew members therefore decided to put in to the nearest land, at Hnífsdalur. There they put the man to bed, but when he did not get better they wrapped him in a sail and took him home, where he lay sick for nearly five days between life and death. On the same day that this happened, those of my household who were still on the move brought my wife and our little boy to me at Arnardalur; for these demonic infestations had reduced people to such a state of distress and danger that, as far as we could tell, everyone on my farm would be struck dead along with all the livestock. Such was the fate looming plainly before us, judging from what our people were seeing and experiencing in themselves and others. As they parted from the three of us on the beach at Arnardalur, our words and attitudes showed that neither party knew whether they would ever see the others alive again. Among other matters I was grieved in no small measure by what I heard from home about my man[9] and what he was reported to have said when he was able to draw breath. He had repeatedly asked to be allowed to join me, and said that I had fled my home and abandoned the souls living there to be lacerated and terrorized by devils, whereas I should have shown myself ready to live and die with them. Thereby, he said, I had shown the qualities of a hireling.[10] However, the decision was taken and we three stayed at Arnardalur for a good week. Throughout that whole week I was subjected most of the time to brutal, violent batterings and onslaughts by devils. I had been especially afraid that the two Jón Jónssons might hear of my arrival at Arnardalur, and this is in fact what happened. At that point the violence of the demonic attacks and batterings was intensified, and that comparison [between me and the hireling] became a real distress to me. Indeed, after the father and son had heard of my move, the most vicious afflictions continued unabated. Those of my parishioners who had seen me in church on the Sunday before, and who now came over the fjord from Hnífsdalur to Arnardalur and saw me lying in the *skáli* there, were hardly able to recognize me.

The letter of summons, addressed to the Jón Jónssons father and son, which was to accompany the prior summons that had been sent throughout the district in preparation for the first assembly session,[11] had been dispatched by the *sýslumenn*. I had been on the point of preventing the sending of both the summons and the letter, for I was worried about the satanic attacks that would befall me in the wake of such a foolish procedure—as I found to my cost both then and at other times. When the summons and the letter reached them, I suffered a most vicious assault, so that I lay as one dead and thought that I would not survive. The message which I then dictated and which was first presented to the *sýslumenn* at Arnardalur testifies to this. In my opinion, their procedures, which some—perhaps even most—of the lawyers and judges of our country would consider to be a Christian and praiseworthy legal maneuver, became to me as I was then situated, and to my household too, means of homicide, the equivalent of murder weapons. This was irrefutably displayed in the actual outcome, for the *sýslumaður*, Magnús Magnússon, refused to accept any of the advice that I gave him when I spoke to him in Súðavík, let alone carry it out. I and my lawsuit had to pay the price of his refusal. It caused us even more serious difficulties, and even greater tortures to myself and others.

I had now returned home from Arnardalur, for I saw that I got no more relief there than at home, especially since the time that those evil men came to know of my sojourn there. Also a second assembly summons had gone out a day before the assembly session took place, since the authorities (as their verdict indicates) made obstacles with respect to the first one. But I felt no more free from the fiendish witchcraft than I had been at Arnardalur, when the first summons had gone out with the accompanying foolish letter. These developments are, I hope and trust, still not entirely forgotten by that pious man Jón Ólafsson, known for his travels to the East Indies.[12] He came and lay down above me with the people of my household when I, finding no benefit from lying in my accustomed bed, lay instead on the hard boards of the *pallur*. He and the people around me restrained me with their hands. What almost everybody felt now became completely clear to them. The aforementioned Jón Ólafsson was on the point of nausea, for the devils were crawling up over him, as he himself described it.[13] But what I myself was suffering then was probably beyond the power of anyone to comprehend.

The workings and *processes*[14] of Icelandic law, at the time of preparation for this witchcraft lawsuit, were so gentle and affable toward me,[15] that I did not then know whom I should blame most for my terrible torments. Should I blame the *sýslumenn* themselves, whose proceedings were so stupid that they seemed like whips and spurs designed to inflame and set on these devil's tools against my life and the life of those souls who lived on the farm here, since Jón the elder had been known as a warlock for a good thirty years—or even longer, from the time when he became acquainted with the late Þorleifur Þórðarson? These men both knew each other at that time. In this regard we shall see later how good and profitable to me was the legal process of Icelandic law! No one who had anything to do with the case was much to be envied, however much more important he might have been than a poor fellow like me.

After one nocturnal attack the Lord gave me some relief, so that I was able to drag myself to the church, where those attending the assembly would decide the case. What took place on that occasion is attested by the judgment[16] itself, apart from the following incident that seemed to me surprising: When I had struggled down from the farm and reached the church doors, I wanted to speak to one of my parishioners, Björn Jónsson, who lived at Engidalur, near Kirkjuból.[17] I thought he would not be entirely unacquainted with the two Jón Jónssons. But when the father and son, who at that juncture were inside the church with others attending the session, realized that I was talking with Björn, the younger Jón ran out of the church and pulled me away from Björn, jerking me so that I nearly fell. But at that point Bjarni Snorrason[18] ran up and stood between the two of us. Not all of those inside the church are likely to forget the reaction of the elder Jón: he was also on the point of bursting out of the church after his son, the younger Jón, to where Björn and I were standing. But people stood in his way to prevent him, since they must have thought this reaction of his peculiar. At that point he blurted out publicly that they ought to let him go out and look Björn in the eyes.[19] To this Gísli Jónsson, the deputy of Þorleifur Kortsson, replied that Jón ought not to talk too much, and at the same time Gísli Jónsson forbade me to say anything privately to Björn. On this occasion I complied with his prohibition, though I thought it strange that he should apply it to me.

Another thing that struck me as strange at that assembly session was that the authorities and judges were able to listen inattentively while the younger Jón Jónsson openly damned and cursed me in church as I lay in the pew, repeating his curses over and over again and saying that misfortune would be the lot of all those who imputed witchcraft to him or his family. I kept quiet for a while, anxious to know whether any of the members of the assembly or judges would be willing to answer or take note of these curses. But when I grew tired of listening to all this, I answered Jón and asked him why he did not curse those who were responsible for the witchcraft. At that he moderated his words. One of those present answered him with the same question as mine, and with that he finally ceased his execrations.

Something which I thought noteworthy happened when deputy Gísli Jónsson went to Kirkjuból to uncover any telltale vestiges of this sorcery. He told of a peculiar pain in his foot that he said he had felt on the way, and of some fresh delusions that came over him by the bed of the younger Jón. But Gísli's journey was not fruitless; for it was then that he got hold of those texts and leaves which, he declared, he had found and extracted from the breast of Snæbjörn Pálsson, and which were opened and exhibited before the court. Some people thought them offensive, and very likely to be pages of magic. One was a calfskin parchment that had contained large, plain characters and letters. Gísli also declared before the court that he had left other material behind under the man's arm which he had been unwilling to take from him by force. He said he shrank from upsetting the man, since the latter had been lying sick in bed, and his wife had begged him to show mercy. He said that he had promised her that her husband would not be penalized for [possession of this material]. Moreover Gísli declared that he was going to keep his promise, and in fact he has done so up to the present day, so that Snæbjörn has never been investigated or punished for his possession of these leaves. Magnús Magnússon the *sýslumaður* was also present at these proceedings.

In addition to all this, an event happened on the very evening of the day of the assembly session, after the discovery and disclosure of these leaves, that will probably remain in the memory of men of worth. To pious people it appeared very distinctly that the older Jón was overcome and as it were condemned to death by his own conscience, for, to the surprise of those present, he hung his head and all words failed him. After the oaths had been administered in regard to one section of the evidence, Gísli Jónsson openly spoke of imprisonment in irons, whereupon some made for the church doors. When the younger Jón saw this, he stood up and began to pronounce curses on himself, abjuring God should he have been the author of the sorcery in question. He called down upon himself the wrath of God and damnation in this world and the next, with such a frightful and unequivocal oath that it seemed to me that no oath sworn by anyone upon the Bible could effect a more powerful conjuration than the words that he spoke, anathematizing himself and renouncing on his own behalf both God and all good things. His father, the older Jón, repeated the same words after him.

Most of the people present were quite dumbfounded when they heard this oath and these fearful curses. It really was a most shocking thing to hear. People were numb with astonishment at the outburst. But it produced no effect beyond what the court itself concluded. This stemmed largely from the haste and bustle of the members of the assembly. I think this incident may well have acted as a cloak and pretext for the practice of obliging sorcerers to collect sworn testimony, since nowadays experienced lawyers are eager to prescribe the swearing of oaths in cases of sorcery. This was certainly the case in this assembly. For on top of the above obnoxious oaths, these men were also ordered to testify on oath, in spite of all the evidence amassed [against them], and this led to the judgment that the court pronounced. As far as I can tell, foul cursing of that sort is an indication of an evil conscience and points to an awareness of one's own guiltiness. Countless examples testify to this, including, as it turned out, the example of these wretched men.

After these terrible oaths had been sworn, Gísli Jónsson and Brynjólfur Bjarnason composed and wrote the decision of the court, requiring the father and the son to present sworn testimony by twelve persons [*tylftareiður*], though it was contrary to all likelihood, as well as to the selfsame oaths and perjuries that the accused had just sworn in the hearing of all present, which it reported in its perfunctory and pedestrian style.[20] When the Jón Jónssons, father and son, realized this, they started importuning the local people to give them sworn testimony. At this the noise and clamor of conversation increased so much in the church that people could hardly understand each other. The aforementioned Gísli and Brynjólfur had to talk into each other's ears because of the commotion and clamor inside the church, so brazenly did the father and son hammer at people to give them sworn testimony. But the people shrank away from them, like sheep before wolves, and retreated as best they could. In fact their proceedings were totally inappropriate to the behavior and manners of innocent men, whose habit is always to let God and the truth have a share in their affairs and necessities.

When sworn testimonies turned out not to be so ready to hand for the father and son, Jón Ólafsson, who lived at Arnardalur and was one of the court-appointed compurgators, started insistently and zealously urging and cajoling people to testify on oath in their favor. He was the man who had previously done them the favor of telling them about my journey to Súðavík, as I have already mentioned, and as a result of whose talebearing I sustained the most violent attacks. Now he persistently maintained their innocence. The noise of his protestations out in the churchyard reached me where I lay, throughout all this, on the pew in front of the choir. As far as I could tell, nobody took note of this, or forbade him to be so forceful and zealous in such an evil cause. Nor did anyone prevent the father and son from speaking to any person, either quietly or in loud tones, as I had been prohibited from speaking to Björn of Engidalur. So there I lay on the pew, weighed down by these sorcerers' spells, and had to watch and listen to this *spectaculum* as if with an eyeglass. And so the leading men completed their work, as set forth in the judgment. They did however have some sense of the truth of the matter, and excused themselves to me that they could not take any further steps because of the expected proceedings and decisions at the Althing. They felt they could not overstep these decisions—for which I had to pity them insofar as I knew that many of the members of the court felt compassion for me, and would have helped me if they had been able to discern a good, reasonable method of doing so. Both I and many others had to pay the price of this so-called process of law, and would have had to pay inestimably more if the Lord God had not sent His holy angels to protect and preserve us, with the result that this whole district, and perhaps an even larger portion of our country, was saved from perishing utterly. But I shall say more about this in another place.

When the assembly adjourned, and the father and son started homeward, I heard it said by clairvoyant people that there were visible signs that the activity of the fiends had converged toward the bottom of the fjord. It was also observed that the spit leading inward along the fjord, along which the demonic activity passed, and likewise the sea [next to it], had been as it were churned into waves and shaken violently, as if an earthquake had gone over it from one end to the other. This was what Björn of Engidalur and other clairvoyant people related to me, especially those whose homeward journey lay toward the bottom of the fjord. I mention this coming and going of fiends but will not enlarge upon it, since it is too much to write what each individual reported to me.

That same night our experience with these visions was consistent with what happened at other times, for neither I nor anyone else on this farm were aware of any fiendish goings-on after the two Jón Jónssons had departed home. To find out the cause of this one must look into the mind and soul of man, and there one will see what role fear and anxiety play. I think that sorcerers are at their most efficacious when they are single-minded and unafraid in their evildoing. But if they become full of fear, they will prove inept in the devil's work too. For this reason they ought not to be handled any more gently than the devil himself; for whatever treatment befits the devil befits them also, since they are joined and bound up with him in the closest of relationships—as we can irrefutably deduce from God's own word.

On the very day of the assembly four men were either stricken or [at least] affected. One of them, Sigmundur Guðmundsson by name, was a member of the court, and was led out of the church supported by others and put to bed. He had not been present when the court made its decision, though he was enrolled in it and no one had been appointed to replace him. For the proceedings took place hastily and precipitately—a fact that I will not enlarge upon here in this account. The others who were affected were Björn Jónsson, Jón of Fossar, and Ásmundur G.[21]

Besides what has been recounted above, I think I should not omit an occurrence that happened to Jón Sveinsson the executioner,[22] who was sent for and brought from Barðastrandarsýsla (for there is no executioner here in this district to strike fear into any gang of rascals). This man arrived ahead of the members of the assembly. But when he got to Eyri he was attacked and seriously beaten by fiends, and was carried from the yard into the farm, more dead than alive, and put to bed in the *skáli*. There he suffered many vicious and crippling assaults, so that it scarcely seemed that he would survive. When he regained consciousness, he was in a state of panic and seemed about to become helpless, not least because of the visions of devils that he complained of. Both he and other clairvoyants who were with him saw devils hovering over him in his bed. He also saw the forms of the Jón Jónssons, father and son, whose appearance and attire he described so that people recognized his description, though, as he declared, he had never seen either of them before in his life. After that the people of my household moved him into the *baðstofa* where I was already lying, and arranged for him to stay there since they did not feel capable of keeping him in the front room. On one occasion when he awoke from sleep he related plainly what he had dreamed, in my hearing and that of my household. He said that in his dream he had seen a man who spoke to him as follows: "You have come here to get my father into trouble, but I can frustrate your journey as I can everybody else's!" Then in his dream the man stabbed him in the chest with a knife having a brass handle, which he had been holding in his hand. (At this point my people recognized that the younger Jón did have a knife with a brass handle. Such a knife was confiscated from him at the Danish houses[23] when he was imprisoned. He had greatly desired to get it back, and asked to have it lent to him at the last session of the court. It was the general opinion that Jón the younger had used the knife for carving and bloodletting.) Then Jón Sveinsson pointed with his finger to the place on his chest where he claimed that the man had stabbed him and the knife had entered his chest, and where he said he felt the greatest pain. All this became known to the *sýslumenn*, and indeed to the members of the assembly. But I had no wish to adduce these happenings as evidence before the men who are called learned, for I knew that they would attach little significance to them. But now that everything has come to light, it can be clearly seen, after the event and when their truthfulness has been verified, whether such dreams are significant or not.

The following night, after Magnús Magnússon the *sýslumaður* and all the assembly people had departed from Eyri, I was again haunted by a riotous multitude of demons. The previous night had been peaceful and quiet for me and others, while the assembly people had not all departed. But now I had no benefit at all from staying in bed, since I was not yet completely deprived of strength in between devilish assaults. At this point I saw myself forsaken by the authorities, and abandoned to the assaults and terrors of those devilish men as before—with this addition, that I felt that the court had plunged me into the pains of hell and death by refusing, in spite of the signs and evidences that were clear and tangible to all eyes, to take the slightest step to restrain these men or prevent this devilry, which not only touched the life of one person but put the well-being of an entire district and jurisdiction[24] in jeopardy. In this tempest of demonic aggression I decided to take a boat that very night to Arnardalur, where the *sýslumaður* Magnús Magnússon had gone with his retinue. I had now seen how the court had decided the case and concluded the affair, and knew that I would not get any reexamination. So I demanded there of the *sýslumaður* that, since the documents that had been read in public before the court at this assembly had been found in the house of a man who shared the same farm as the Jón Jónssons, a search should be made among the household goods of the latter, to whom the evidence also pointed, to see whether any indications or telltale items could be found among their possessions likewise. I had talked to Magnús about this at my former meeting with him at Súðavík, but at that time, when I first requested his help, he paid no attention whatever. Now, at Arnardalur, I made the same demand of him. While completely refusing to go to their house at nighttime as if they were thieves, he did accede to my demand in so far as he agreed to take the trouble to go back to Kirkjuból and make the required search. But because the search was conducted in broad daylight, the other men, when they saw people coming, had time to rummage among their belongings and open and close their chests. So, as might be expected, no manuals of sorcery were discovered. Still, the journey was not without its repercussions. For when Magnús Magnússon's party had gone far enough toward Kirkjuból to be easily seen from there, the *sýslumaður* was racked with a frightful pain in one foot, so that he felt unable to proceed to the farm. He took off his sock, and rubbed the staff that he walked with against his bare flesh. I have heard it said that, after the search was over, the aforementioned *sýslumaður* asked the younger Jón of Kirkjuból to take hold of his foot, and that the latter stroked his bare foot and ran his hands over it there in the Kirkjuból church. This makes me think that Jón the younger would have been quite likely to have handled small ailments—indeed, felt obligated to heal them—on occasions when he himself had been responsible for the [original] pain.

Notes

1. This Chapter II covers the following material from the three printed Icelandic editions of the *Píslarsaga*:
   1914 edn., p. 11 (line 10) to p. 24 (line 13);
   1967 edn., p. 60 (line 10) to p. 74 (line 6 from bottom);
   2001 edn., p. 67 (line 13) to p. 77 (line 12 from bottom).
2. This would of course have been Skutulsfjörður, on the west side of which Eyri was located. Having crossed the fjord to Arnardalur, a farm on the east side of Skutulsfjörður, he would have travelled by land around the peninsula separating Skutulsfjörður from the next fjord to the east, namely Álftafjörður, on which the farm (now village) of Súðavík lay.
3. Actually Hrútafjörður lies to the southeast of Skutulsfjörður and Álftafjörður. See the map.
4. This passage, from "but when I had prostrated myself ...." to "... vicious fiend," has been quoted as evidence of ear infection associated with an influenza epidemic. See Introduction, Note 114.
5. *Exitus* is Latin for "exit" or "departure." In the present context it means the last hymn sung in the mass.
6. The Latin word *devotio* appears here.
7. Icel. *galdrasendingar* (plural of *galdrasending*). See Appendix 1 under: *Sending*.
8. A small bay in the Djúp, a short distance to the west of the mouth of Skutulsfjörður.
9. I.e., Guðmundur Ísleiksson.
10. See the *Gospel of John* 10:12: "But he that is an hireling, and not the shepherd, whose own the sheep are not, seeth the wolf coming, and leaveth the sheep and fleeth; and the wolf catcheth them and scattereth the sheep" (King James version).
11. The reader may recall (see Introduction, §8) that in December 1655 an assembly was convened at Eyri to decide what should be done about *síra* Jón's accusations of sorcery against the two Jón Jónssons. This is the assembly whose report is translated in our Appendix 3. In it the Jón Jónssons were told that, to establish their innocence, they would have to muster twelve compurgators willing to swear an oath (*tylftareiður*) affirming their innocence. According to the report of this assembly (see pp. 195, 196), a prior assembly session had been scheduled, but was cancelled because of exceptionally bad weather. This cancelled session is the "first assembly session" referred to in the text.

12. See Appendix 1 under: Jón Ólafsson *Indíafari*.
13. This incident is not confirmed in any other source. Even the Third Part of the *Reisubók* (Travel Book) of Jón Ólafsson *Indíafari*, which describes the life of the famous traveller after he returned to Iceland in 1626, makes no mention of it—indeed, no mention of Jón Magnússon at all. Sigfús Blöndal (the first editor of the *Reisubók* in 1908) conjectured that the Third Part was written by the *sýslumaður* Magnús Magnússon himself. This, if true, would explain its silence regarding *síra* Jón's sufferings.
14. Latin for "legal proceedings."
15. This is of course sarcasm. *Síra* Jón means that the processes of law were so ineffectual that they actually assisted the nefarious conspiracy of the warlocks.
16. I.e., the judgment translated in Appendix 3. See Note 11.
17. Björn Jónsson of Engidalur was evidently on *síra* Jón's side in these legal wranglings over sorcery, and against his neighbors the Jón Jónssons of Kirkjuból. So the hostility of the Jón Jónssons toward Björn is hardly surprising.
18. Bjarni Snorrason was the stepson of *síra* Jón Magnússon.
19. This incident, showing the elder Jón Jónsson in a hurry to look Björn in the eyes, is noteworthy because it illustrates the belief of 17th-century Icelandic sorcerers that, if one looks intently at another individual before the latter has a chance to return the gaze, one gains a mysterious power over the other. See Appendix 1 under: Magical Spells and Staves, [2] and [3]. See also Matthías V. Sæmundsson, *Galdrar á Íslandi*, p. 290.
20. The Icelandic translated here as "in its perfunctory and pedestrian style" means literally "with bags and utensils," i.e., with common articles needed on a farm. *Síra* Jón uses this sarcastic metaphor to imply that the court's judgment (namely, Appendix 3) was written in a routine and thoughtless manner.
21. Ásmundur's patronymic, except for the letter G, is left blank in the manuscript. He is probably the Ásmundur Guðmundsson mentioned in p. 108.
22. "Executioner," which here translates the Icel. *böðull*, means an official who carries out corporal punishment, whether capital or not.
23. Presumably the "Danish houses" are the stores of the Danish merchants at Eyri. For the Danish trade monopoly in Iceland see §4 of the Introduction.
24. The "jurisdiction" referred to here is the region under the jurisdiction of the court at Eyri.

III. The Attacks Continue into the Year 1656, but Magnús the Sýslumaður Refuses to Take any Action. Síra Jón Sends a Message to the Other Sýslumaður, Þorleifur Kortsson, at Bær in Hrútafjörður[1]

As a postscript to the business of the assembly I will cite what I call the plaintiff in the case, namely, the scorched consciences of the father and son. From the time that I first publicly announced in church what had befallen me and my household, these two men applied my suspicions and exhortations to themselves, bringing suspicion upon themselves by their various disjointed expressions. That honest man Jón Ólafsson [*Indíafari*] of Eyrardalur, and likewise Árni Jónsson and others, will testify what they inferred regarding the matter from the Jón Jónssons when they were their overnight guests. I consider this kind of testimony to be the most truthful and significant, for who can have clearer knowledge than one's own conscience?

From what I have recounted above it is apparent how far the measures taken in this case fell short of what was right and proper—especially in view of the additional evidence that came to light when God Himself laid bare the truth of the case by opening the mouths of the parties involved, so that of their own accord, under no compulsion, they confessed their guilt. There was now no lack of evidence, since everyone was now free to report things that he had heard and noticed, things that had been shrouded in secrecy during my time of anguish—a fact which can hardly be condemned, the legal system of this country being what it is, and being practiced as it is by nearly everyone. But I do not think it likely to be praised by those of our countrymen whose lives are being battered by the murderous assaults of sorcerers. It is surely my duty to protest against the system on behalf of those persons, however little effect my efforts may have. *Eventum trado Jehovae.*[2]

As I have already related, the civil judges and magistrates now departed, leaving me and the farm in the grip of this murderous assault. But the other [two] were allowed to go free. If they had managed to repeat their perjuries and round up men to swear oaths in their favor, Icelandic law might well have had *me* burned to death—an outcome for which I would have given them thanks! As for my dean,[3] from whom I expected some protection, he was nowhere to be found during this whole period. To my knowledge not a peep was heard out of him at this time regarding any of my troubles, let alone any words in my favor or support for the manifest truth of my case. But I did not blame him much for this, good man that he is—though in the subsequent summer months something else arose to divide us, about which I had better restrain my tongue for the time being. If only God's holy word and the shining examples of the erstwhile love for it[4] were pondered over; if the laws of our country were correctly considered and their intent extracted by dissection and gutting;[5] if the duty imposed on us as Christians, to which we have sworn obedience, were carefully observed; if His royal Majesty's many missives and decrees addressed to this country were properly attended to! Then I think that any perceptive, intelligent, and healthy-minded man would notice and recognize a flaw in all these proceedings, and would surely pity me, and others like me who are tortured by witchcraft, for being heavy-hearted and grieving—no less over the authorities who are appointed to be our protectors here in God's stead and who act as they do, than over the wretched sorcerers themselves, blind slaves of the devil and their own perverted malignant natures, who are totally incapable of reform.

But let me not interrupt the story.

After I had returned home from my aforementioned journey to Arnardalur and Kirkjuból, I lay down, worn out and exhausted after all that had passed, on my little four-poster bed that I sometimes used to rest on. But on this occasion it was of no help. So my bed and I were moved [from the *pallur*] down to the floor, and my household sat or lay on the floor all around me. But my sufferings in bed were still the same; so, not knowing where to turn for relief, I lay down on the bare floor. On that very day, while I was away from home, my poor wife, Þorkatla Bjarnadóttir, was so afflicted by the onslaught of demons that she could find no peace in any room, and had to go out to the cowshed to seek relief. For the people who were so afflicted had no other resort than to be on the move from one place to another—that is, while they could still move. Prior to that time I had tried going around from one bed and one room to another. We had also attempted to get rest and sleep on the pantry floor. But the time came, after these meanderings from one room or bed to another had been tried out, that I had to resign myself to all that should befall me by God's will until the last ounce of strength was drained out of my bones. Indeed, during the first part of the period of these attacks, some strength was restored to me after each bludgeoning, each attack. For the Lord allowed each attack to subside, so that I could drag myself around and be out of bed at intervals. But the intensity and ferocity of these fiendish torments that tortured me increased so greatly that, after the first assembly that I have already written about, I could not get myself out of bed more than twice before Christmas, and during and after Christmas I could not get up at all. For days and nights on end I lay continuously crushed and bruised by this demonic burden as if under an unbearable load, and I could not tell when I would give up the ghost. But after the feast of Christmas I seemed to experience breathing-spells of some days between the attacks—sometimes for a full day, sometimes more or less—until the month of *porri*.[6]

I do not think I can describe these tortures or express them in words so as to make them understood. I find no way to portray them by the spoken or written word, no correct or proper depiction of what I suffered that will make it comprehensible. The reason is that these torments were neither human nor within the bounds of human understanding. They were not like natural diseases, which I have often experienced in my lifetime, both as a youth and as an older man, and some of which have pushed me to the brink of death. Compared to these devilish tortures, human sicknesses are nothing but chaff and trifles. I would rather lie sick for ten years with the most grievous illness, even if I had to cry out day and night in excruciating pains, than spend one day in these devilish torments and tortures. I know of nothing that bears any comparison with these fiendish agonies. The torments that I experienced were not all of one kind or inflicted with the same mode of torture. They were widely different at different times, and each had to be endured in its own season. Sometimes it was as if I were being squeezed and squashed under an enormously heavy weight, as when a worm is squashed or cheese is compressed, so that every ounce of strength was drained out of me; and along with the crushing weight I felt as if my body were being jabbed with small red-hot glowing needles, so densely spread over my flesh that it seemed comparable to the feeling of pins and needles. Sometimes I felt as if I were being transfixed through the side that I was lying on with a spike which seemed to pierce through the body between my ribs, so that I expected it would be the death of me. Sometimes I lay in a blazing fire, struggling for breath. I felt sure that the flames from the fire were leaping through my entire body, especially my chest, and flashes of fire seemed to erupt from my fingers, so that I felt convinced that I was going to burn to ashes. So what was my surprise to find my flesh unharmed! At times I was gripped with piercing cold. At times the half of my body that lay upward might be freezing, while the half that lay downward might be in the grip of fiery heat. There were times when that freezing cold passed from my feet upwards along the body, as when the movement of clouds waxes and wanes in the sky. At times the flesh on my bones felt as if it were crawling with a mass of worms, seething and twisting in a most ghastly and abhorrent manner. And yet all this was but a trifle compared with the interior tortures that assailed me, starting especially from the First Sunday in Advent and far surpassing all torments that can be expressed in words. I cannot doubt that I have tested and proved the words spoken by divine revelation to a certain pious man in our district: "Because it touched him, it has become for him a hellish chastisement" (*Patefactio*[7] 5). More about these afflictions will come to light later in my story.

When Christmas was past, my sufferings abated somewhat, and I reflected on the investigation that had taken place—how hasty it had been and how little clemency had been shown toward me. Most of the manifest evidences for witchcraft had not been taken up. I knew that those sorcerers would never desist from their devilish practices until they had discharged all the bolts of their witchcraft.[8] This, as far as I could tell, would mean that this farm of mine, indeed the whole district, would be ruined, along with every single human being in it. I saw at that first assembly that the whole burden of proof was placed on me alone—in spite of my condition that was patent to all—and that there was no one to support my cause. So I dictated an open letter to the *sýslumaður*, Magnús Magnússon, in which I requested, indeed demanded, that a new assembly should be convened to deal with those evidences that had been disregarded and left uninvestigated at the first assembly. I delivered this letter personally to Magnús Magnússon when he was sitting here on the *pallur* of the *baðstofa* by the bed where I was lying. (At that time he was looking in on the Danish shops, since the Danes had given him the key and the task of keeping watch on them that year.[9]) But he did not take my demand to heart. Instead, as I understood it, and as the facts bore out, he upheld the judgment of the court. When I discovered that this was the attitude of the *sýslumaður*, the aforementioned Magnús Magnússon, I sent my foster son Bjarni Snorrason north to Hrútafjörður on a mission to the other *sýslumaður* Þorleifur Kortsson (though I missed my foster son grievously, because of the urgent needs of my household). I sent him an account of the progress of the case and a copy of the judgment, and asked that at this stage he also should convene an assembly and conduct an investigation, as appears from the excuses in the letter which he sent back to me by my aforementioned messenger.[10] But the distances to the other men in authority, namely the bishop and the *lögmaður*, were so great that, what with the additional obstacle of my own poverty and lack of means, I was obliged to swallow all this, along with the sufferings that oppressed me. Indeed, during that time everything [that happened] had the same savor for me. So I waited for what the Lord's will should bring. But what justice was done to me then will be easily seen by anyone who carefully considers the legal proceedings that took place.

Notes

1. This Chapter III covers the following material from the three printed Icelandic editions of the *Píslarsaga*:
   1914 edn., p. 24 (line 14) to p. 29 (line 6);
   1967 edn., p. 74 (line 5 from bottom) to p. 80 (line 4);
   2001 edn., p. 77 (line 11 from bottom) to p. 81 (line 23).
2. The Latin phrase means: I leave the outcome in the hands of God.
3. The dean in whose jurisdiction *síra* Jón Magnússon's parish lay was *síra* Jón Jónsson, priest at Holt. See Appendix 1 under: Dean, and also under: Jón Jónsson, priest and dean at Holt.
4. "Examples of the erstwhile love for it." Is *síra* Jón thinking of *Revelation* 2:4?
5. As Einar Már Jónsson points out in a note to his French translation here, *síra* Jón's wording compares the elucidation of the intent of the law somewhat quaintly to the process of dissecting and gutting a fish (which of course would have been familiar to all West Fjord people).
6. The month of *þorri* ran from the latter part of January to the latter part of February. See Appendix 1 under: Calendar.
7. *Patefactio* = Revelation (in Latin). The source of this quotation is not clear.
8. "Discharged all the bolts ...." *Síra* Jón here adds a Latin phrase, *exhausta pharetra* (i.e., emptied the quivers), to round out the metaphor. This phrase seems to have its source in Ovid, *Metamorphoses* 1. 443.
9. In Jón Magnússon's time the Danish government did not allow the Danish merchants who traded in Iceland to spend the winters in Iceland. Thus their shops there were empty during the winter season. See Introduction, §4.
10. Evidently Þorleifur Kortsson at first sent his apologies but declined *síra* Jón's request.

IV. The Father and Son at Kirkjuból Solicit Sworn Testimony. The Bodily and Spiritual Agonies of Síra Jón are Further Described, as well as his Admonitions to the Authorities[1]

Next I must relate how the younger Jón journeyed out past here to Bolungarvík and Hnífsdalur in order to collect witnesses to swear on behalf of himself and his father. On his way back he spent the night at Neðri-Hnífsdalur, biding his time there and not leaving the place until dusk the next day. From hindsight one concludes that he did this with a definite purpose. As he acknowledged later, his idea was to stop at my house as he passed by. The people in the *baðstofa* here did think they heard someone climbing up on the roof during the evening wake,[2] and it was verified by his own [later] admission that it was indeed he, reciting spells or practicing sorcery over the *baðstofa* where I was lying. This piece of his magic caused in me such a reaction that, in addition to the other diabolical pains to which I was subjected, on the following evening I seemed to hear a recurrent blowing of whales coming from inside or under my pillow through the ear that was turned downwards. This put me in terror of continuing to lie on that pillow, so I shifted my head up and along the bedhead, having no strength to do more. But however I shifted my head, the blowing still assaulted me from under my ear, for I was totally powerless to sit up. So I put my left hand under my ear and spoke to that devil to the effect that the Lord God would lend me His hand to crush and smash his devilish power. After I had spoken these words I withdrew my hand from under my head and lay as before with my head still. Though the whale-blowing vanished at these words, it returned in the form of fiery embers that bade fair to burn my head, especially that part of it that was turned toward the pillow. I then made up my mind to have the Bible opened at the page that separates the two Testaments, and laid my head on the open page, affirming my will to lay down my life on the strength of the words contained in the two parts of the book. At this the flames subsided, except that some fire struck my cheek now and then, here and there, where it lay against the book. But the relief that I got from the book was of little help to me; for while I was lying on it, I felt as if all the veins of my neck were becoming swollen, and my chest too, with a headache so intense that I felt I could not bear it. So I had the book removed, and lay down again in the same flames as before, whatever might come of it. No description of mine will convey any idea of what I then suffered or the quality of it. That stabbing flame, or worm,[3] lasted longest of those torments, though even in that the Lord brought about some alleviation, sometimes more, sometimes less. When in a somewhat more comfortable state I made the experiment of asking some of my household to put their hands under my head, they felt, as it were, twitching heat spells underneath it.

In these trials, as in others, I believe I had a taste of the results of the wonderful provisions of Icelandic law as they applied to me! Evil men, of the sort depicted in the foregoing account, were set at liberty to hound me and my household. Thus, with splendid foresight, long-acknowledged, publicly documented practitioners of magic are ordered to collect oath-witnesses—as in the clear case of Jón the younger, for example, who practiced this magic on me on the very same journey when he was collecting witnesses! I have also heard of another example: a man is said to have carried a booklet of magic in his trousers at the very time that he was supposed to swear an oath denying the practice of magic. More current examples of this sort would undoubtedly come to light if they were carefully searched out. The consequences of this will be apparent to those who have some knowledge of God.

Another thing that I heard while lying in the torments described above was this: most of those who were requested by the younger Jón to give sworn testimony and who refused experienced a taste of the same diabolical attacks. Some of those who did not wish to testify on oath were threatened by the devil in dreams, as people in our district know. I have also heard that even some people in faraway districts who prayed to God on my behalf received warnings in dreams from the devil, with intimidations and threats. Þórarinn of Borg in Skötufjörður told me of an example of this. It seems that a strange insect flew onto the face of *síra* Tómas of Snæfjöll when he had been praying for me from the pulpit—and much more besides. This shows that the devil is mighty, well armed for battle, keeping watch at his gates that nothing should go amiss.

These are the torments that I suffered in the flesh, for which I think there is no better name than the fleshly torments of hell. Everyone will clearly recognize this who considers, weighs, and sifts the matter under the following heads:[4] 1) *causae*, the ground or causes of injuries of this kind; 2) *instrumenta*, the tools or instruments; 3) *organa adjuvantia vel efficientia* [the subsidiary agents who assist or carry them out], those diabolical men who are confederate with the devil; and 4) *forma*, the mode and whole manner of these sufferings, regarding which one could speak at great length. But though they are just as described here, these bodily tortures were not merely bodily in nature. Mingled with these agonies were hellish torments of the soul, which were more cruel than any burden [of the flesh]. I rate the physical torments described here as nothing compared to those that harrowed the soul and the inner man in a most excruciating manner, and always accompanied the bodily assaults. This was especially the case beginning with Advent Sunday, as I have already mentioned, when not only did my heart become desiccated and drained of all the dew of God's grace but hardened like steel, so that however much I attempted to pray with sighs and groans, not the least comfort or relief was granted to me. The more completely I was rejected by God and cast out from His presence, the more did all creation seem to be utterly hostile to me. The devil wanted to bring me to the point of worshiping him and blaspheming God, since He gave me no help at all. No one can understand this except those who have experienced it. I think that no living person is capable of enduring this condition unless he is granted some support. (I have set forth separately elsewhere[5] the means of support that were granted to me, for those who want to learn more of this matter.)

Another thing that I remember is the misery that oppressed my soul when I had, in contempt, spat at one of those devilish insects or butterflies that flew fluttering over me (which happened persistently, equally by day and by night when the witchcraft was at its height, in full view of all my household without exception). What then happened was that the insect that had fluttered over me and flown at my face, so that I spat at it, immediately disappeared from my sight, and I felt what I can only describe as a whelp, or some such creature, crawling up and down in my belly and internal parts. This lasted for a large part of the day. During that time I felt as if I were lying like a dead piece of turf or clod of earth subjected to kicks and batterings—I cannot describe it. As regards what I usually experienced from the devils that crawled about like mice or whelps on the outside of my body, I did not set much store by that. Several persons on this farm experienced this both by day and by night, especially in the early part of the winter.

Also, I recall a terrible ordeal that came over me on one or more occasions. I thought I was aware of having lost proper control of my mouth, hands, joints, and limbs. So I instructed the people of my household in advance what they should do with me if they saw this happening by the Lord's consent. I told them I wanted to be tied to two boards in the shape of a cross, for by God's grace I imagined that, if my Father in heaven saw me fastened in this manner, He would remember the passion and crucifixion of His blessed Son Jesus and have mercy on me in His name.

I also asked my household to tell me if anything thoughtless or improper escaped my mouth. If such should happen, I intended either never to speak a word again or to beseech my people to sew my mouth shut. In all these severe attacks I felt I was drained of all my piety and that my heart was harder than stone or steel. So I thought to myself that, since God could see the impotence of my heart, my tongue at least should not be inactive. I made up my mind that, as long as my tongue could move, it should never tire of calling and calling [upon the Lord]. I reckoned that, if it were the Lord's will that the devils should be the death of me, it might happen that I would find mercy at His hands if I died while praying and calling upon Him. Or even if the Lord willed to cast me out from His presence into hell and damnation, I should be the only one among all the damned to be calling upon Him, even though I had no further hope of grace.[6] This sort of *conceptus*, thoughts, came over me in these *luctis et fluctibus*, in these waves of lamentation.[7] As a result, everyone in the room where I lay was obliged to refrain from speaking, unless it were in whispers or into each others' ears. I asked them to do this when I found out how it was with me when these great storms burst upon me. For I knew that I would be totally abandoned were I to let go this practice of prayer and calling upon God, or were I to fail to keep in my mouth and memory those words that I was constantly repeating, clinging to them more firmly than to life itself. The words that I chose most often to repeat constantly during these horrors were as follows: "O Lamb of God, Thou that sittest on the throne of my God, have mercy on me!"[8]—and others too in the same vein. It was my wish to remind the Lord both of the humiliation of Jesus and of His rising up in glory—both of which I desired to present to Him as the occasion of my wailing. At intervals, when the storms subsided, I endeavored to give admonitions to my household, according as I was able to reflect.

These and suchlike storms and tempests of the soul were so numerous that I had no desire to have them recorded, for on each occasion I expected to be called away from this world. Each morning I considered whether that day would be the day of my departure, and each evening I dreaded the terrors of the night. Each day that these great storms came over me felt to me longer than many other [normal] days. Often my mouth felt as if it were screwed up and squeezed over to one cheek, so that I thought my face was being distorted and that I would no longer be able to call on the Lord or pray to Him. The devils were tangible and palpable to me; I even felt as if I saw them. After the spell cast by the younger Jón, a snake was usually visible on the raised floorboards under my bed, sometimes coiling and writhing around me as I lay in bed. But I will not write much about this.

Often the most repulsive thoughts besieged my heart—one might say, all the hellish filth and wickedness in which the devils wade and wallow—so violently stamped and pressed down into my heart and thoughts, that it seemed impossible for me to defy them or to shut out this depravity. On the other hand I felt that if even one part of all that was being thrust at me were to find entry into me, I could not (according to the judgment that remained to me) but be cast into the unquenchable flames of hell. So, whenever such thoughts came over me, I set myself with all my strength and will power—and even beyond my own strength—to call and cry to the Lord that this evil should not be able to enter into my heart. When beset by such tempestuous attacks I could not sigh to the Lord quietly and in secret. I had to cry loudly and with the most earnest zeal, for that was the most critical juncture that a devout person can face, when God's Spirit seems totally withdrawn, and the devil with all his savagery has returned and entered the human heart.

I was very frequently subjected to a great deal of abominable foulness in the spirit, so that—much to my own disgust—my mind perverted, crushed, and trampled God's holy word into blasphemy. Sometimes I was obliged to find different words of the same meaning, and to abandon those which my mind had already twisted and perverted, so as not to pile an excess of loathsomeness on my wretched soul. O how much I could write here about all that I suffered from these spiritual torments, both in sleep and awake! Often my hours of sleep were ten times more painful and disgusting for me than the waking hours. In my dreams I felt as if I were being cast into a bottomless abyss. Sometimes I was shot up high into the air, and sometimes cast down head first into infinite depths. Many were the malicious pranks of this sort that the devil played on me, too numerous to count. I was exposed to all the darts of Satan and of those evil men who were scheming with all their diabolical arts and stratagems to destroy me, body and soul. So it is hardly surprising that those who were aware of all the tricks of sorcery employed by the [Jón Jónssons] father and son thought it strange, indeed utterly amazing, that I had not already lost my life or at least my wits—to quote the words of their daughter and sister Þuríður.[9]

How often have I wished, if I had the choice and if the whole undivided world were my own possession, that I could give it all in payment and choose to have inflicted upon me every torture that human brain or hand could invent or impose, if I might only be set free from these inner agonies of the soul. The torments that afflicted my flesh I considered to be petty and inconsequential like straw compared to those that racked my soul.

These afflictions I consider to be the very torments of the soul in hell. I think I could easily adduce good arguments and proofs, some taken from God's word, in confirmation of this opinion. But I will pass over them here so as at least to avoid being accused of long-windedness.

For these reasons I claim that all the pains that beset me for such a long time, especially the spiritual pains, are unintelligible to people at large. I know of no living person so wise and perceptive that he can measure or assess them by the standard of anything earthly. Indeed, if earthly things stumble by comparison with heavenly things, how much wider is the chasm between God's grace and the tortures of hell! I know of no man greedy enough to be willing to endure even for one day the pains that I have endured for many, many nights and days under the lethal attacks of the devil—pains that left me at the borderline of life and death—even though he were to acquire the whole wide world thereby. Moreover I know of no creature in all God's creation—the damned only excepted—no, not even a poisonous snake or adder, for whom I bear such hatred that I would wish on it even half an hour of those agonies that have assaulted me, especially the internal onslaughts. Should there be anyone who feels no dread of the wrath of almighty God, the righteous Judge, who has power and authority to cast men body and soul into the eternal torment of the damned whose fire is never quenched and whose worm never dies[10]—should there be such, let him come and talk to me if to no one else!

I have presented here a short summary, picture, and overview of the sorcery that beset my household and especially myself, starting from the Nineteenth Sunday after Trinity in the year 1655, until those miserable men were burned in Easter week *anno sequenti*[11] 1656. But I who suffered them find myself unable to depict in their full reality the bones, sinews, and nerves of these torments or their full-blown body. I did not write up the day-by-day events as they occurred, since both I and others thought it most unlikely that I would be granted any temporal relief from these sufferings. On the contrary, I often had to face up to a fate worse than death, so that my poor wife was sometimes oppressed with much grief. But I recorded at the time just a very few of my many sufferings, the most significant of them, manifested and corroborated by the signs on my body. Indeed, my bones and my joints could be clearly counted, and it was a shock to me to look at my eyes and my face in a mirror even after I had recuperated somewhat. Prior to that I had not the least desire to look at myself in a mirror.

I know that this whole story reflects on me in the most wretched, ineffectual, and miserable manner. In all these trials I admit that in the presence of God I seemed to myself to be more like a dead worm than a living human being. This whole chronicle reflects little credit on me, only humiliation, disgust, and wretchedness. Many may well think that it would have been more decent of me to have kept quiet about it than to have revealed and broadcast it. But even though some may think that I ought to hold back and leave out some aspects of my case, especially after careful consideration of the state of this present age, still there is more to a man's face than just his nostrils which he cleans by blowing his nose. So I have put aside the shame that might have kept me silent. For intelligent, worthy men will surely think it likely that the prophet Jonah too must have had to wash and change his clothes after rotting for three days in the belly of the whale, before appearing in the city of Nineveh.

Also—though the comparison[12] is irrelevant unless one wants to juxtapose Rome with Mantua, the greatest personality with the most insignificant—it can be truly said of me that this foulness [that I have suffered] is too precious for me to be mortified by it, whether before the great or the small of this world. The fact is that my Lord God knew that the place where I should rot was no better than the belly of a whale. So now there has been a turning point, and a sweetness has come out of all this bitter distress, so overwhelming that now I would not change places with the wealthiest people in our miserable country. I do not envy them or their possessions, for out of all my miseries and temptations I have reaped one advantage: I know that the Lord alone is God, and that His word is eternal life and eternal truth. Therefore let the ungodly tremble, but let those who fear God be filled with joy. So much for that.

Likewise I make it known boldly to all men that in all the supernatural assaults that I have suffered and described above, I never entertained any bitterness toward those wretched men whom I clearly recognized as the source of this evil witchcraft. This was demonstrated at the end, when they had acknowledged their guilt. For when I was told that they had sincerely repented I was overjoyed, had myself carried outside by the main door, and stretched out my arms and my hands to them. If God permits I shall write a little more about this. Moreover, my household is well aware that I forbade them to speak of those men in hatred. For I saw that their malice had blinded them, and that they had no more control over their actions than the rider of an unruly horse that gallops off against the will of its rider because he lacks the strength to rein it in. Of all creatures I call snakes and vipers most similar to men who practice witchcraft—and who is going to arraign one of these for biting or killing?

Most of all, on the other hand, I was vexed in spirit by the carelessness, irresolution, and stupidity of the authorities and magistrates of our country, who by their easygoing, not to say indulgent, attitude have allowed, and are allowing, magic and witchcraft to be studied, practiced, and carried on in this country. Even apart from this most vile of all major crimes, our land is already burdened enough with other serious criminal offenses. In my judgment and opinion this proves, even though no one speaks out, that the carelessness, irresolution, and pernicious neglect [shown by our authorities] is—*tanquam causa remotior*[13]— at least as responsible for the agonies endured by me and other souls tormented by magic as the unbridled malevolence of those who without any thought of the consequences have dared to plunge ahead into such terrible wickedness. These evil men now find fun and amusement in their behavior, since they are not only suffered to act thus in opposition to God's prohibition but even have a large following to defend them. And this I can prove very quickly and easily, even before authorities higher than those we have in this country.[14]

Another thing I bring to the attention of those willing to listen: if the Lord had willed that I should die as a result of these demonic and murderous torments, my blood would certainly have called down a harsher vengeance from the living God upon those judges in this land who are given authority and are native here, than upon the practitioners of magic themselves. For the authorities and judges of our country have eyes to see and also have God's word available to them, and moreover have the support of the excellent system of laws established here. If these laws had not been perverted but had been rightly understood and complied with, along with God's holy word, I and my peers would not have had to bear the brunt of this wickedness. But those others [the sorcerers themselves] were blind and given over to the devil and had entered into an alliance with him. So, even if they had wanted to, they could not control themselves, as the last chapter of their life history clearly demonstrates. In view of this I can perceive, as clear as daylight, the frightful vengeance and wrath of the living God that is already kindled against our country, which has heaped up such a mass of bloodguilt through this neglect. Who can tell me how many secret murders have been committed through sorcerers' magic[15]— murders that have never been investigated or even spoken of? Then there are the tears and sighs of those who are still alive, living a life worse than death, crushed under the weight of secret acts of murder. *Their* sighs and tears will be just as potent in the eyes of the living God and most righteous Judge as the blood of those who have been struck down! If anyone wants documentary evidence of this, let him take counsel with God's truth and His holy word. The Lord Himself has also communicated similar warnings on this matter through His holy angels to men now living. On this score I can adduce some true facts, if anybody wants to listen—though I know that these things are not only disregarded nowadays but held up to mockery and laughter by some, on whom the sentence of damnation is liable to break in waves before they know it.

I now take leave of this section, which has dealt with the agonies that came over me during the period that ended with the death of the sorcerers by burning. It is time now for a breathing spell.

Notes

1. This Chapter IV covers the following material from the three printed Icelandic editions of the *Píslarsaga*:
    1914 edn., p. 29 (line 7) to p. 39 (line 9 from bottom);
    1967 edn., p. 80 (line 5) to p. 91 (line 9 from bottom);
    2001 edn., p. 81 (line 24) to p. 89 (bottom).
2. See Appendix 1 under: Evening Wake.
3. See *Isaiah* 66:24: "Their worm will never die nor their fire be put out...."
4. Here *síra* Jón is referring to the fourfold Aristotelian classification of causes (Aristotle, *Physics*, 198a, 20–25), which was taken up into medieval scholastic philosophy: 1) The final cause, 2) the material cause, 3) the efficient cause, and 4) the formal cause. See for example the *Catholic Encyclopedia*, under the heading: Causality.

5. See Chapter V.
6. See Introduction, Note 141.
7. Here, as often elsewhere, *síra* Jón himself provides the (Icelandic) translation of the Latin words that he uses.
8. See Introduction, Note 140.
9. This is the first explicit mention of Þuríður, daughter of the elder and sister of the younger Jón Jónsson, who is to play the leading role in the Second Part of the *Story of Sufferings* (Chapters VIII to X).
10. See Note 3.
11. This is Latin for "of the following year."
12. The double comparison involving Mantua, Rome, *síra* Jón, and the prophet Jonah, though a little farfetched, can be understood as follows: Mantua and Rome, though the former was a relatively insignificant town and the latter the great metropolis of the ancient world, are bound together by the association of both with the life of the great Latin poet Virgil (the former having been his birthplace and the latter a place of his residence as an adult). Similarly, *síra* Jón and Jonah, though representing (according to *síra* Jón) the extremes of insignificance and importance respectively, show parallel features in their lives: Jonah's cleansing of himself from the filth of the whale's belly was parallel to *síra* Jón's public confession of the foulness that he had suffered from the witchery of his enemies; and both, by God's will, led ultimately to a spiritual enlightenment.
13. Latin for "as a remoter cause."
14. Is this a hint of *síra* Jón's intention (which was never realized) to carry his unsuccessful prosecution of Þuríður to an even higher court than the Althing, namely the Danish king himself? See the Introduction, Note 97.
15. The Icelandic word for "magic" used here is *phýtonsskapur*. Cf. Chap. I, Note 15.

V. Influences that Came to his Aid During his Trials[1]

Since it is the allotted duty that we owe to our Lord God—to whom alone belongs glory, honor, and all thanksgiving, for His is the kingdom, the power, and the glory for ever and ever—I do not want to conceal from those who, with a good will, may wish to hear it told, what were the things which sustained me in my wretchedness, and gave me strength through all the past horrors, calamities, and deluges of demonic tempests and temptations that I have been describing, and that poured over me not only throughout the period chronicled above but also later on. I want to tell of the means that sustained me and brought me over all those perilous and hellish torments, like a ferry bringing me to life and salvation. Others too, should they be plunged into a similar plight, may experience the same if they use the same remedies faithfully. These are as follows:

I. First, I drew strength and a certain power of resistance from the recollection of a serious temptation, lasting one or two hours, that came over me in my youth while I was on a journey. It was in that summer when Turkish pirates ravaged the Vestmannaeyjar,[2] and I was travelling with Jón Steinþórsson by Hvalfjörður. As we were riding along the shore and mud flats in front of the mountain called Þyrill, there came a horror upon me (though I was physically healthy), and I felt that all the well-being of my life and soul was taken away from me, as if I had been entirely abandoned by God, and that I was inexorably faced with but one [course of action]—to ride my horse at a gallop into the sea and commit suicide. In this fit, everything that I had ever heard or learned of God's word was completely wiped out of my memory. I would have given the whole world to be able to remember just one passage of consolation from God's word. But, however much I strained to do so, I could not for the life of me recollect anything except only the most holy name of Jesus, and this I repeated constantly. I thought I could not even cease from repeating my Redeemer's name long enough to ask my fellow traveller to remind me of some consoling passage from God's word for my peace of mind. For I felt that if I were to allow my mouth to let go that blessed name I would not be able to remember it again, any more than other words which in my previous unimpeded state had been completely familiar to me and riveted in my memory. And so I made up my mind that I would live or die—whichever the Lord willed for me—in the name of Jesus.[3] All my well-being of body and soul hung on this weakest of threads (so I thought)—on nothing but the power of this one word. If I lost that, I felt I would be completely defeated and destroyed. And so it was that, while the temptation lasted with greatest intensity, I could not give any answer to the good man who was travelling with me, though he spoke to me, but remained bent over the saddlebow, letting the horse go as it willed, until this grievous condition passed. Then I started thinking about what must have been the cause of this experience of temptation—namely my stupidity, combined with overconfidence in my ability to resist temptation because of all the instruction in God's word that I had received both in church and in the Skálholt school, and of all the beautiful and precious teachings imparted regularly to me and my contemporaries there. Then I thought about my stupidity, how God must have wanted to get rid of it in this manner, that I might testify to the unspeakable redemptive power of Jesus. This experience was my first schooling in temptation,[4] and it prompted me to apply the same method again, as I have already mentioned.[5] I taught this same method of doing battle to a woman whom I was asked to visit. She was greatly tormented by violent attacks of the devil, which must have befallen her through the art of sorcery, as I concluded from the evidence and signs described to me in that connection. But she too obtained the victory through the might of Jesus' redemption. Indeed, no one that I know of ever put up a better fight under Jesus' harsh discipline. She is a widow named Ólöf Bjarnardóttir, and is now in 1658 living at Hóll in Bolungarvík.

II. Next I found sustenance for body and soul in God's holy word, which was never taken from me so completely that I did not remember at least something to cling to, even if at times only very feebly. It was the story of our Lord's Passion in particular that I was most inclined to dwell on. I determined that, no matter if the Lord and His holy angels, along with heaven and earth, looked out and beheld my weakness, at least the righteous Judge would see that I was trying to crawl in the footsteps of my Lord. So in every horror that came over me, though for all I knew it might have been my death-struggle, I endeavored to cry to God and to pray for grace and assistance, and to call on every ounce of strength and zeal that I could command, for in the most singular and terrible of my sufferings I had no other refuge or recourse than this constant calling on God. Though I felt easier in the intervals between these violent attacks, and even when sometimes I felt my mouth and tongue so exhausted by this work of prayer and constant repetition that I had to seek relief by resting my lips, still I made these words of prayer, that were in my heart, keep my tongue in motion. For I thought that I should make this practice a habit to which I could resort whenever these attacks came over me, whether in waking or in sleep. But very often it happened that there was an extremely strong element of constraint in this practice, and I had to force myself to it against my obdurate will. Again it sometimes happened, when the great storms [in my soul] had abated, that some of God's words which I recognized and knew perfectly well would enter my mind, and an interpretation of their meaning would be revealed to me which to my understanding was quite marvelous. I knew that no human being could have interpreted them in this way, no matter how learned he was. I was overcome with amazement at the wonder and glory of God, and I felt capable of conversing even with the greatest scholars (had I been in their presence) about the judgments and wonders of God. From this any clear-sighted person can see how great a God our Lord is, who rules wonderfully even in the midst of His enemies, and has wisdom and power to give effortless aid, even in their greatest need, to those whom he fosters and cherishes.

III. In the third place I experienced no little consolation, in the intervals between these violent attacks, from the nearness and protection of God's holy angels, especially as the time of the torments dragged on. On one occasion a devout and honest girl of my household told me that she had seen a man in broad daylight, clothed in a long linen robe, move from the door of the *baðstofa* to the *pallur* where I lay at the point of death in the midst of one of my most violent attacks. At his presence I had experienced a lightening and a relief. Likewise I well remember one night when I lay awake suffering tortures, and my poor wife and her servant girls were on the *pallur* around the bed where I lay. I saw a man standing on the *pallur* in front of my bed, partly bent and leaning toward me, and praying over me. He was clothed in white and looked like a white cloud in the sky, unsubstantial and as if transparent. I distinctly heard the last words of the prayer that he uttered, since he was very near to me. They were these: "May God help us all by the protection of His holy angels!" As soon as he disappeared from my sight I took up these words onto my lips and repeated them over and over for some time, thinking to myself that God evidently wishes us to beseech Him for the protection and aid of His holy angels. Another such matter arose later that I think worth remembering, to which I shall return in its proper place.

IV. In the fourth place, I have found myself pondering the words that I knew God's Spirit had spoken to me in my heart for my instruction, and which I have already written down in this history of my sufferings. I have often called them to mind in my past distresses, and experienced their truth within a short space of time. This has caused me to wonder whether God had some special purpose in mind, since by His grace I, poor wretch, have been vouchsafed these insights. Much else of this sort has happened to me in the second phase of my torments, which I shall not fail to record at the appropriate place—though I am well aware that to thoughtless and selfish people accounts of this sort will give more cause for amusement and mockery than for benefit and profit. But I shall disregard their judgment. I will not let their folly make me so foolish as to set aside the glory of God and leave untold the truth and wonder of those works that He is performing even in our day. Indeed, I am delighted to be of service to people in distress who are content with very little in the way of comforts and consolations, but are gladdened by small things and saddened likewise.

V. Lastly, I derived no little peace of mind from the wonderful visions, dreams, and revelations that many devout and honest people related to me, and which I found remarkably apt for musing over. These visions and dreams, though coming from many different sources, were consistent with each other when I recollected and compared them. And many of them came true and were verified as regards definite times and hours. I should mention particularly one poor, quite inconsequential man whom I knew from my youth. His name was Sigurður Jónsson, and he was a devout man, indifferent to the stupid ways and vanities that many common people are inclined to. His father for some years had his fixed abode on my farm, and in all respects was one of the most devout and conscientious men that I have ever come across. It was revealed to this poor man Sigurður, both in his dreams and when he was awake, what was to be the fate of the wretched men who have been put to death, even before it happened. This man related other things to me as well, and whatever seemed particularly noteworthy I have written up. I can give no other name to these things than divine revelations made known by God through His holy angels. For this reason I have also read out some of these dreams here before the congregation of the Eyri church. But in fact it was ordained that these visions and dreams [of his] should be of no little consolation to me at a later time,[6] in the demonic attacks which began distinctly on the day commemorating the beheading of John the Baptist[7] in the fall of 1656 and have continued since then with onslaughts at various times, especially in the next two years. But now, during this summer of 1658 and the part of the winter that is past, the attacks have been milder than anything that I have previously had to experience, with the exception of one assault and apart from a *sending* from the devil which came here (and also made itself apparent at Tunga, as I have been told) and afterwards was heard of on the other side of Breiðadalsheiði.[8]

Notes

1. This Chapter V covers the following material from the three printed Icelandic editions of the *Píslarsaga*:
    1914 edn., p. 39 (line 8 from bottom) to p. 44 (line 8 from bottom);

1967 edn., p. 91 (line 8 from bottom) to p. 97 (line 7);
2001 edn., p. 90 (line 1) to p. 94 (line 2).
2. In the summer of the year 1627 about 300 pirates from North Africa, in three ships, descended on the almost defenseless Icelandic fishing community of Vestmannaeyjar, located on an island off the south coast of Iceland. Many of the inhabitants were massacred, and most of the rest, about 240 in number, were herded on board the ships and taken to Algiers in North Africa where they were sold in the slave market there. Many died there, and some converted to the Islamic faith. Nine years later, in 1636, money was collected and 35 of the captives were ransomed, of whom 27 finally returned to Iceland in 1637. Among the latter was Guðríður Símonardóttir, who later became famous as the wife of the poet-priest Hallgrímur Pétursson.

    These North African pirates were generally referred to by Icelanders as "Turks" (Icel. *Tyrkir*), since most of North Africa was then part of the Turkish (Ottoman) Empire.

    In the year 1627 Jón Magnússon would have been about 17 years old.
3. Compare the last verse of Hallgrímur Pétursson's well-known funeral hymn *On Death's Uncertain Hour*: "I live in the name of Jesus; in the name of Jesus I die."
4. This first experience by Jón Magnússon of apparent abandonment by God, as a seventeen-year-old boy riding along the shores of Hvalfjörður, had been preceded by years of study in the Skálholt school. His reference here to "the instruction in God's word that I had received both in church and in the Skálholt school, and the beautiful and precious teachings imparted equally to me and my contemporaries there" suggests that those teachings had awakened in him a fervent and intense desire for devotional practices. It may well be that his sensitive nervous constitution, overstrained by these intense practices, broke down momentarily and reduced him to the sense of total spiritual desolation which he describes here.

    It is worth observing that at this stage of his life it seems not to occur to Jón Magnússon to attribute his temporary sense of spiritual desolation to the work of demons or sorcerers.
5. See p. 92.
6. Sigurður Jónsson appears twice in the second Part of the *Story of Sufferings* as a source of visions pointing to the guilt of Þuríður Jónsdóttir. See p. 144 (*Píslarsaga*, 1967 edn., p. 138); and p. 163 (*Píslarsaga*, 1967 edn., p. 162).
7. 29th August.
8. Breiðadalsheiði is the high mountain pass that separates Eyri from Önundarfjörður to the south. See the map.

VI. The Verdict on the Jón Jónssons, Father and Son, that They Should be Burned to Death[1]

On 9 April 1656, at Eyri in Skutulsfjörður, at a formally convened assembly of three *hreppar*[2] and at the proper place of assembly,[3] the following men were appointed to serve as a court by His Royal Majesty's honorable *sýslumenn* Þorleifur Kortsson and Magnús Magnússon of the Þorskafjörður assembly: Þorlákur Arason *lögréttumaður*, Gísli Jónsson, Snæbjörn Torfason, Brynjólfur Bjarnason, Guðmundur Þorsteinsson, Jón Ólafsson, Jón Þórðarson, Bjarni Þorgeirsson, Jón Guðmundsson, Andrés Hallsson, Jón Jónsson, and Þorkell Árnason. They were to consider, investigate, and weigh carefully the case brought this winter by *síra* Jón Magnússon before Magnús Magnússon, *sýslumaður*, and Gísli Jónsson, deputy of Þorleifur Kortsson, regarding an examination of his (*síra* Jón's) illness which he believed to have been caused and brought about by a human agency. He had specified the two Jón Jónssons, father and son, of Kirkjuból, and gave certain evidence (which this verdict presents) showing, in his opinion, that they were responsible for his illness. On that occasion,[4] at the close of the deliberations on the material recorded and set forth there as evidence, the father and son were required to present a *tylftareiður*, sworn testimonies from twelve named witnesses under oath. These oaths they should swear by the time of the coming spring assembly.[5] Out of considerations of prudence the latter was not completely settled as the time limit, as the letter of the law would require, since it was the intent of the honorable high court judges, expressed before this court, that the accused should not thereby be alerted to take defensive action.[6]

However, stories spread more and more and evidence was constantly accumulating, along with earnest requests and insistent demands on the part of the priest, who expressed himself volubly on the matter, as did other good men who shared his opinion, as is shown by his and their written testimony which we shall present below. They claimed that according to royal law the *sýslumaður* Magnús Magnússon should rightly arrest the father and son and put them in irons until the case should be investigated and a decision arrived at by the present assembly. This demand of the priest, supported by the opinion of good men, was complied with by Magnús the *sýslumaður*, who arrested them and put them in irons, and since then has kept them in custody by royal authority. And we, the aforementioned members of the court, along with the others who have previously approved it, consider that the abovementioned father and son were lawfully arrested and held at that time according to the provisions of the twentieth [paragraph of the section of the Lawbook on] Personal Rights and the Amendments of King Hákon [to the Lawbook],[7] and various other laws. Also because in the past this has been the practice in our country in cases of serious and dangerous crime, and likewise among other Christian nations according to the laws and constitutions of each. And the evidence in this case, as well as the condition of the priest, has been constantly growing more and more grave. These indications and circumstances will now be presented as follows:

I. To begin with, according to *síra* Jón's account, the onset of the whole affair took place at Kirkjuból, where an incident occurred involving the younger Jón and one of the girls there, Ásta by name. Jón says that he pushed her, but Ásta claimed he punched her with his fist. The younger Jón disputed this and stoutly denied [her story], but later on he asked forgiveness of the girl in the presence of the congregation, and received a public admonition. In this affair, according to the priest's account, the elder Jón zealously supported his son and showed scorn and resentment toward the priest. Among the things he said were remarks like the following, reported by two men who said their wives had overheard them: "You're laughing at it now, but it's not a laughing matter, and [in a while] you won't be laughing so much!" The only thing that the elder Jón admitted to having said was: "You needn't laugh at it!" But the men were willing to validate their story with an oath and confirm it with a handshake. The aforesaid words, along with other spiteful and angry expressions directed at the priest by the elder Jón in support of his son, were spoken on a Sunday between holy absolution and the reception of the sacrament.

II. In the second place: Next, on the day after this event the priest believes that he fell into an unnatural sleep, and that on the following night, while awake, he was subjected to agonizing attacks of the devil, so that he had light fetched and took other measures. For verification of this he calls on the members of his household, who confirm that this happened.

III. In the third place: When the elder Jón was trying to push his way out of the church at the earlier assembly this winter,[8] he saw *síra* Jón intending to tell a certain man the main points of what he had heard. To this the elder Jón, being about to break his way through the crowd, reacted with the words: "Let me look into his eyes!" But the deputy Gísli Jónsson protested against this.

IV. The priest questioned all those attending the assembly (Icel. *þingsóknarmenn*) whether or not they had heard an old rumor linking the elder Jón to the practice of sorcery in times past or for a long period of time, and the scandalous reports that he had been carrying on with it long ago, many years before. Most of them signified by raising their hands in assent that they could not deny it. Later on it became public knowledge through the confession of the elder Jón himself, and will be inserted [in this document]. In view of this we now take up and consider the former judgment of the court,[9] with the evidence included in it, and also the court's decision that those who testify under oath are obliged to do one of two things—to declare [the two defendants] in their opinion either guilty or innocent, and the required oaths either fit or not fit to be sworn by both the older and the younger [Jón]. All those named to testify under oath were now present.

V. Here in addition we shall include the following verbatim accusation of the priest, *síra* Jón Magnússon:

> I the undersigned, appointed to be a servant of God's word, still lie bedridden in torment due to vicious acts of witchcraft, by the permissive will of God, because of my zeal for the duties laid upon me by my office, as the evidence for the antecedents and the beginning of this affair indicate. I publicly declare that I consider the father and son, Jón the elder and Jón Jónsson the younger of Kirkjuból, to be fully responsible for the sorcery and acts of witchcraft which this winter have befallen this parish, my household, and above all my own person, from the Nineteenth Sunday after Trinity up to the present. I make this declaration in the light of all those happenings, confirmations, arguments, and relevant antecedent events that may and will be adduced as pertinent to this affair, and that may be granted to me to give consistently with truthfulness and the law. In token of this I hereby sign my name by my own hand below, on 12 March 1656.
> (signed) Jón Magnússon (by his own hand)

We, the aforementioned members of the court, believe that the witnesses who are under oath are swearing these oaths that are now before them as conscientiously as they are able. They were transmitted anew to the aforementioned *sýslumenn* with a handshake.

This is the evidence for the guilt of Jón the elder. We shall now take up the case of Jón the younger.

In the second place, as regards the case of the younger Jón, the priest adduces the following evidence against him:

I. Firstly, a rumor has been current to the effect that it was his ambition to learn and practice the forbidden art of magic. The fact of this rumor was verified for the priest by [the testimony of] the persons assembled at the court session (Icel. *þingsóknendur*).

II. Next, it is well known and has been asserted by the priest, that the ill will shown by the Jón Jónssons father and son had mainly taken shape and intensified since the time that the younger Jón was unable to obtain his will in his suit for the priest's stepdaughter. This was later completely proved by his own subsequent admission, especially the first point.[10]

III. Thirdly, the priest affirms that Jón the younger took him by the hand while greeting him after a service in the Eyri church, and that when he let go his hand a pain spread over the palm of the priest's hand up to the base of the fingers. As evidence for the truth of his story he said he rubbed the palm of his hand on the beam of one pew, and Jón Þorsteinsson of Tunga and Stefán Brandsson said they watched him do this.

IV. Fourthly, he said that the devil had frequently appeared, both at home and away from home, in the form of both Jón Jónssons, father and son, and that this was established by witnesses. But at the present juncture it seems that this and other assertions adduced by witnesses do not need to be sworn to, because of the confessions of father and son which will follow and will, it is to be hoped, reveal the truth of the matter.

So our conclusion is the same as the verdict already pronounced about his father on this and other evidence too. The truth of the said collective testimony of the aforementioned jurors will be fully established by the swearing of one oath, to which they have previously committed themselves by a conclusive handclasp with the *sýslumaður* Magnús Magnússon, as formerly stated in this judgment. This oath, which they swore simultaneously, runs as follows:

"You, Jón Þorsteinsson, Sigmundur Guðmundsson, Gunnlaugur Skeggjason, Sigmundur Jónsson, Jón Jónsson, Egill Pálsson, Guðmundur Þorleifsson, Ásmundur Guðmundsson, Thumás Þorvaldsson, Sturli Bjarnason, Björn Jónsson, and Einar Arnórsson, lay your hand upon this sacred book and declare to God almighty the following: The oath that last winter, on 14 December 1655, was required on behalf of the Jón Jónssons father and son of Kirkjuból—regarding that oath you believe and declare with a pure and clear conscience that it could not be sworn truthfully but only falsely on behalf of that father and son; and moreover that these men are guilty, not innocent, of the acts of black magic which have been directed against *síra* Jón Magnússon throughout this past winter. And this oath you now swear neither out of favor nor friendship, hatred nor fear, but purely for the sake of God and the truth, and for no other cause. And now that this oath has been taken, may God be gracious to you if you are telling the truth, and angry at you if you are lying."

This oath having now been taken by the aforesaid witnesses under oath, and corroborated by them as the laws and the court require, we, the aforementioned members of the court, believe, in accord with the former decision, that both they and the *sýslumenn* have proceeded correctly, with the assent of the public at large. Now that all these steps have been taken, on the basis of evident and indisputable reason, we, the above members of the court along with the *sýslumenn* and other leading men from these parts, have carefully examined and interrogated these defendants, who are now in irons in royal custody. Earlier, when they were arrested, they confessed—each of them separately—the elder Jón that he had many years before borrowed a book of magical rites, and the younger Jón that he had borrowed sheets of magical rites which we could very easily recognize. So now once again the elder Jón made the following confessions in the hearing of us, the *sýslumenn*, and others:

I. That he had had among his belongings an old calfskin book, borrowed from a certain Thumás Jörundarson for longer or shorter periods.

II. The elder Jón also said that he had in his possession a small paper book of the same sort, that he had acquired from Jón Pétursson. These two facts were corroborated by Jón the younger.

III. Thirdly, Jón the elder said that a year and a half before he had requested the same Jón Pétursson to practice magical tricks on the priest. But Jón Pétursson had refused to do so, according to the statement of the accused.

IV. Fourthly, the elder Jón confessed and admitted that he had caused the death of a cow belonging to Björn of Engidalur, by means of imprecations that worked their effect on her.

V. Fifthly, he said he had tried practicing [witchcraft] on a fox, but it had not worked.

VI. Sixthly, he gave names to the magical staves that had been sketched by his son Jón the younger, which will be referred to later.

VII. Seventhly, he said that an explanatory document[11] would be found.

VIII. Eighthly, he says that he burned the above-mentioned books of witchcraft, but kept the Christmas register[12] from the calfskin book. This was found as stated.

IX. Ninthly, and finally, the elder Jón acknowledged that he had been guilty of causing the priest's sickness at first, though he had for a long time denied responsibility for it, adding to his disavowal curses and execrations. This was the clearest possible advertisement of his wicked act. So we should be content with what is presented above regarding the elder Jón. Though a few other pranks of his could be mentioned, they are not worth including here.

Since the beginning and onset of this affair was due to Jón Jónsson the younger, as the first article above suggests, we now return to him again and shall add to it his own unconstrained confession before the court as follows. This confession was confirmed by him both before and after the swearing of the oath required by the court, and will be presented in the following several articles:

I. He says that to begin with he tried out his arts on a half-grown puppy. To this end he carved two magical staves and threw them on the animal, but they had no effect except to cause some disorientation.

II. He said he had cast a spell on Ólafur, a cook for the Danes, by reciting aloud a certain verse and enhancing it with magical staves, which he laid on the ground at a place where Ólafur would walk over them. He thought it must have had some effect on him, since he [Ólafur] had fallen down and hurt himself in the chest.

III. He said he had taken care of a calf of his which, according to him, had been harassed by the devil. For this purpose he had used the [magical stave called] Solomon's Seal,[13] which he had clipped onto the calf's hide and also written on a sheet of paper, then torn the paper up and thrown it at the calf. Later, he said, the devil came to him that night and asked him why he had done that, but he answered: "Damn you, you won't cheat me!" That very night the devil dragged a cow belonging to his father down off a mountain, obeying his [Jón's] order to him to fulfill his [the devil's] wishes somewhere else.

IV. He acknowledged that he had carved runes that cause farting,[14] intending them for a certain girl whom he named.

V. He said that he had wanted to cause harm to Markús [Brandsson],[15] and had carved [runes] on a cylinder and sung over it the appropriate incantations. But his scheme miscarried, since Markús had managed to avoid it.

VI. He said he had given Markús two magical staves. One of them Markús was to put into the bed of the girl [whom he wanted] in order to change her mind and incline her to marry him (and this he drew while we watched). The other was to prevent him from drowning at sea.

VII. He described various forms of "wrestling magic"[16] and magical staves for colic, and how to cause a flow of blood into the incisions of the runic symbols, naming some such explicitly, for example: Golnisþey, Urnir, Hagallinn blá, Augnaþuss.[17]

VIII. He acknowledged being responsible for *síra* Jón Magnússon's illness, though not for the onset of it, for which his father admitted responsibility, as we have mentioned earlier.

IX. He admits that he scratched a magical stave (which his father called *Fjölnir*[18]) into the palm of his hand before he shook hands with the priest in church, from which the priest suffered a burning pain in his palm.[19]

X. He says that he recited the following lines:

> May the accursed fire blaze forth
> And suddenly assail you because of [your] hatred.
> And may all the evil that you intend for me
> Turn back on you and pursue you,

and to this end he had carved a magical stave on a piece of wood or whalebone and thrown it to the winds—which is consistent with the priest's story about the terrible metamorphosis of his sufferings.[20] Likewise, the younger

Jón Jónsson recited some lines that he had previously intended to take effect on the cook Ólafur, as follows:

> I bring you beer,
> Fine fellow,
> Mightily compounded
> By potent magic—
> The magic that Óðinn,
> Lord of the Æsir,
> And evil Gyða
> Have made as potent as can be.[21]

XI. He recited the beginning of an explanatory document[22] (as he called it) couched in a variety of words from other languages. He said it was good for healing and expelling evil influences, and acknowledged that he had used it on his sister[23] when she was said to have been taken ill a few days before the priest came to Kirkjuból.

XII. Lastly, he told various dubious, nonsensical stories about his correspondence with Jón Pétursson and other things, which it is pointless to detail here.

Having now presented this and other material, treated it, investigated it, pondered on it, and analyzed it thoroughly, and in all points compared the evidence regarding each of these two wretched men with the divine word of God, and also with our own code of laws and with those of all other civilized Christian peoples, we are unable to see cause for showing them mercy or leniency. Nor ought we in any way to do so because of the imminent dangers that threaten us and our district by the righteous arm of the Lord God. For He has been most horribly and fearfully provoked and His fiery anger aroused at the upsurge of the study of this diabolical art, as one hears and learns regarding many people and from many sources here and there. For the Lord abominates it, and also all those who cherish, study, practice, tolerate, approve, or work at it. Here is the word of the Lord regarding this:

I. *Exodus* 20[:3]: "I am the Lord your God, you shall have no other gods before me."—*Exodus* 22[:18]: "You shall not permit a sorceress to live."—*Leviticus* 20[:27]: "If any man or woman practices magic, soothsaying, or the interpretation of signs, they shall be stoned to death and killed. Their blood be upon them."—*item* [*Leviticus* 20:6]: "If a person turns to spirits of soothsaying or to those who interpret signs, and goes whoring after them, I will set my face against that person and eradicate him from among his people."—*Deuteronomy* 18[:10–12]: "There shall not be found among you anyone who practices divination, or an astrologer, or one who reflects on the sounds of birds, or a sorcerer, or a caster of spells, or a foreteller of pythonic spirits,[24] or an interpreter of signs, or a necromancer. For whoever does these things is an abomination to the Lord, and because of these abominable practices the Lord your God is driving them out before you."—*Isaiah* 47[:9]: "Suddenly, in one day, these things shall come upon you; you shall become both a widow and childless. Yes, they shall come upon you in full measure, because of the great multitude of sorcerers and spell-casters that are among you."—*Malachi* 3[:5]: "Thus says the Lord: I will come to you and punish, and I will be a swift witness against the sorcerers, the adulterers, and the perjurers."

II. Next comes the book of the laws of our country, the second section of the *Personal Rights* (Icel. *Mannhelgi*), where we read: "Those who are executed for murder, black magic, sorcery, any form of soothsaying, or outdoor vigils for the purpose of conjuring up trolls or practicing heathen rites—these are criminals without rights, whose death is not to be compensated."[25]

III. In the third place, the open letter of His Royal Majesty, in the year 1617,[26] declares and testifies concerning people of this sort, that some are to be exiled from all the king's lands and dominions, while men such as these here are to be put to death in accordance with God's word and the laws and ordinances—by fire or sword according to the actions of each, as is laid out in the aforementioned letter of His Royal Majesty. For the wickedness that is most widespread and rages most destructively must be punished most harshly. And evil deeds are to be so detested, that the man who is appointed to condemn and punish the wicked but does not do so—he is deserving of the same verdict that should have been passed on the guilty man. This is sufficiently proved by the words and examples in holy scripture, and also by the secular legal code.

IV. In the ancient laws of our country it is stated (see the tenth section of the *Kristinréttur*): If a man practices black magic, indicated by its being the cause of sickness or death to human beings or their cattle, his crime is punishable by death, which in this passage is the same thing as a sentence of full outlawry.[27]

V. It is the law among other Christian peoples and their worthy nobles, that any Christian man or woman who practices magic, or by its means inflicts injury on other men or their livestock, no matter who he may be, shall if he is convicted thereof be burned in fire.

VI. Lastly, in the whole legal procedure that has been applied to these individuals, the sworn witnesses whose testimony has been used have been appointed from this same district. They live closest [to the case] and are most knowledgeable about it. None of them were brought in from outside or from other parts. Everything has been carried out according to the laws and ordinances of our country, Danish law, and good wholesome customs tested in practice, and in addition we have the final confession of the men themselves.

Wherefore, in view of these articles and others too that support our verdict, and by virtue of the grace of the Holy Spirit invoked on us who sit in the seats of judgment, in the name of our Lord Jesus Christ to whom all authority is given in heaven and on earth and who will come again to judge the living and the dead, we, the aforementioned members of the court, do pronounce with the full force of the law that these oft-mentioned Jón Jónssons, the elder and younger, father and son, have both forfeited their lives and are hereby condemned to death. The death to be inflicted on them is that they shall be burned to ashes in a blazing fire, according to the practice in this and other countries, since in view of all their aforesaid evildoing they are proven criminals without any rights before the law.

It should be added that these unhappy creatures, at the session of the court, confessed that everything written above was true and correct, and accordingly received holy absolution along with the body and blood of our dear Redeemer Jesus Christ.

The aforementioned men in authority have concurred with us in this our verdict and have written their names here below along with the signatures of the members of the court named above. This verdict was pronounced at the Eyri assembly, and was rewritten at Kirkjuból in Langidalur[28] on 11 May of the aforenamed year.[29]

Magnús Magnússon
Snæbjörn Torfason

Notes

1. This Chapter VI covers the following material from the three printed Icelandic editions of the *Píslarsaga*:
   1914 edn., p. 44 (line 7 from bottom) to p. 54 (bottom);
   1967 edn., p. 98 (line 1) to p. 109 (line 16);
   2001 edn., p. 205 (line 1) to p. 214 (bottom).
2. See Appendix 1 under: *Hreppur*.
3. Icel. *þing*. See Introduction, Note 15.
4. The "occasion" referred to here is the session of the local court convened at Eyri on 14 December 1655 (see Appendix 3).
5. Presumably the "coming spring assembly" means the court session of 9 April 1656, whose verdict is here being presented. It is not clear whether the accused named all the witnesses who were to swear the *tylftareiður*, or whether the court named some of them.
6. The judges' procedure in declining to set an exact time limit within which to muster their compurgators was strictly speaking unfair to the Jón Jónssons father and son. It was dictated by the policy laid down in the 1617 decree of King Christian IV (see Appendix 2), and by the vehemence of *síra* Jón's fear of the consequences of giving the Jón Jónssons a definite period of liberty in which to practice their magic.
7. The Lawbook referred to here is the *Jónsbók*. An important part of the *Jónsbók* was the section on Personal Rights (Icel. *Mannhelgi*), the rights of persons injured or arrested.

The 20th paragraph of the *Mannhelgi* runs as follows:
"*If one man binds another.*
If a man binds a free man for no good reason, let him pay five *merkur* [plural of *mörk*; see Appendix 1 under: Units of Value] to the king, and to the person whom he has bound full amends according to the judgment of twelve men legally appointed by the magistrate. A man may bind a thief without penalty, and likewise any person whom he knows to have committed a criminal act, provided there are witnesses to verify that the person could not otherwise have been brought before the magistrate. If there are no such witnesses, let him confirm the fact with the oath of one person."
[From: *Jónsbók*, 1970 edn., p. 58.]
8. The assembly of 14 December 1655; see p. 76.
9. Appendix 3.
10. It is curious that this important event—the refusal of *síra* Jón to allow Jón the younger to marry his stepdaughter—is mentioned nowhere else in Chapters I to X except in this short paragraph.
11. According to Sigfús Blöndal (the first editor of the *Píslarsaga*), the word *transskriftarbréf*, translated as "explanatory document," means here a document giving explanations of magical staves. See *Píslarsaga*, 1914 edn., *Athugasemdir*, p. 192 (just before the *Registur*).
12. The "Christmas register" (Icel. *jólaskrá*) may mean a weather forecast that covers the twelve days starting on Christmas Eve. (See *Íslensk orðabók*, 3rd edn., under: *jólaskrá*.)
13. See Appendix 1 under: Magical Spells and Staves, [4].
14. See Appendix 1 under: Magical Spells and Staves, [5] (Farting runes).
15. This was Markús Brandsson of Seljabrekka, whom *síra* Jón later regarded as also being a practitioner of the evil arts. See p. 143.
16. Icel. *glímugaldur*, a form of magic that gives victory in the traditional Icelandic sport of wrestling.
17. These names of magical staves are by no means self-explanatory, but they do indicate a strong connection between the practices of Icelandic magic and the pre-Christian runic alphabet (see Introduction, §6). The word *hagall*, for instance, occurring in *Hagallinn blá*, is the name of the runic letter "h," which was similar in form to the modern capital H, and was much employed in 17th-century Icelandic magic. The word *hagall* is cognate to the Icelandic *hagl* (hail) or *haglél* (hailstorm), and is said to point to the god Þór, who was lord not only of thunder and lightning but of all manner of foul weather such as violent winds and hailstorms that could deprive men temporarily of their vision. An example of the use of the *hagall* is Spell no. 29 of the *Íslensk galdrabók*, which explains how to keep unwanted guests out of one's farm by sorcery. The magical stave to be employed for this purpose consists of ten runic *hagall* letters, intertwined and pointing in all directions. (See Matthías Viðar Sæmundsson, *Galdrar á Íslandi*, pp. 361–364; also Matthías Viðar Sæmundsson, "Rúnamessa, Hagall, Rúnalýsing 7:16," *Morgunblaðið*, Lesbók, 29 November 2003.)
18. See Appendix 1 under: Magical Spells and Staves, [6].
19. For this event see p. 65.
20. The metamorphosis of *síra* Jón's sufferings referred to here is probably the bout of sufferings described on p. 66.

21. Einar Már Jónsson considers this verse to be an echo of the fifth verse of the *Sigurdrífumál*, a poem from the ancient *Poetic Edda* (Sæmundar-Edda). In this *Sigurdrífumál*, the valkyrie Sigurdrífa teaches good counsel and runic lore to Sigurður, who has awakened her from an enchanted sleep during which she was surrounded by a wall of fire. (For the Eddic original see *Eddukvæði*, 1968, p. 343.)
22. See Note 11.
23. This was not Þuríður but Þorgerður, the younger sister of Þuríður.
24. See Chap. I, Note 15.
25. The "book of the laws of our country" referred to here is the *Jónsbók*. The passage quoted here comes from the 2nd Paragraph of the *Mannhelgi*. See *Jónsbók*, 1970, p. 38.
26. See Appendix 2.
27. The "ancient laws of our land" refers to the *Grágás*, the code of laws valid in Iceland during the period of the Commonwealth. The passage referred to here regarding the penalty for practicing black magic is found in *Grágás: Lagasafn íslenska þjóðveldisins*, 1992, p. 19. (Actually it is in the 18th, not the 10th, section of the *Kristinréttur*.)

    This passage from the *Grágás* lays down "full outlawry", not death, as the penalty for practicing black magic. But "full outlawry" meant that no assistance of any sort could be rendered to the outlaw, and that anyone in a position to kill him was obliged to do so. In the harsh environment of Iceland this was equivalent to a death sentence.
28. Kirkjuból in Langidalur is a quite different place from the Kirkjuból in Skutulsfjörður where the Jón Jónssons father and son lived.
29. 1656.

VII. The Second Verdict, Regarding the Disposition of the Property of the Executed Father and Son[1]

On 11 April 1656, at the same assembly of three *hreppar* in Eyri, Skutulsfjörður, at which the verdict was passed on the Jón Jónssons father and son, sorcerers who have now been executed, the same magistrates, Þorleifur Kortsson and Magnús Magnússon, appointed the following men to form a court: Gísli Jónsson, Snæbjörn Torfason, Guðmundur Ásmundsson, Brynjólfur Bjarnason, Ásgrímur Björnsson, and Guðmundur Þorleifsson. The charge to the court was as follows: carefully to consider, weigh, and determine how the assets, left behind by those unfortunate prisoners and executed criminals the Jón Jónssons father and son, should be disposed of, and what persons should handle the settlement of the elder Jón Jónsson's wife's dowry, as well as other legitimate debts chargeable to them.

The first matter to come before the court was the request and demand of the priest, *síra* Jón Magnússon, for a legal decision regarding the following:

1. He requests compensation for his injuries and the attempt made upon his life.
2. For damage done and for his inability to work.
3. For the costs incurred by him.
4. That his wife should have right to compensation.

Moreover the dean, *síra* Jón Jónsson, points out that the late Jón Jónsson the younger may not have tithed correctly for the preceding year (*anno*) 1655. According to the information given by good men he admitted to owing a tithe[2] on four hundredworths[3] of property; but now, in the estimation of intelligent men, it turns out that his assets were sixteen hundredworths, from which we see that the remainder of his correct tithe is based on assets amounting to six hundredworths and eighty ells—since one third of the inanimate part and two thirds of his livestock are to be added to the four hundredworths which he had already correctly reported. Therefore, since the younger Jón committed this trespass in order to injure the priest before he was convicted as a criminal and lost his rights, we, the members of the court just named, in accordance with the law and the *Kristinréttur*[4] and in view of the statutes contained in *Mannhelgi*[5] and the Amendment regarding money belonging to criminals, have decided that the first items to be deducted from the abovementioned six hundredworths and eighty ells should be all the tithes and the fines for withholding correct tithes. These amount to 440 ells, and are to be given to the bishop, the priest, the church, and the poor in one lump sum, which they are then to divide among themselves.

In the third place the *sýslumenn* have laid claim to certain taxes and penalties (Icel. *gjaftollur*), and fines for nonpayment of these, to be deducted from the assets of Jón the younger. Our verdict in regard to these is given on the same legal basis as the above deduction of tithes. The tax, together with fines for nonpayment, amounts to fifty-six ells. For the penalties to be deducted (and the fines for nonpayment of them) they are content to receive a certain gun which he owned, along with twelve *aurar* and two ells. This is in addition to the abovementioned fines and ten hundredworths of assessed items which have been earmarked to be awarded in toto to the priest, *síra* Jón Magnússon, along with any other amount that may remain after the legal expenses of the trial have been paid. [This decision is taken] on the authority and force of those legal regulations and precedents which are relevant here and the texts of which support our opinion and verdict.

Now as regards the assets left behind by Jón the elder. Our judgment is that the *sýslumenn* should hand over her dowry to his wife, according to the amount that she can be proved to have brought into the marriage, if that money, or its equivalent, exists. Otherwise let each *eyrir* (unit of money) be replaced by something of equivalent value—provided that the arrangement is convenient for her. (It is an act of great generosity and Christian compassion to regard her in the most merciful possible light.) Likewise all his other legal debts are to be earmarked and paid to his other creditors out of his assets. The total amount of all the assets and monies that Jón the elder had in his possession was: 19½ hundredworths of inanimate assets, and eleven hundredworths and ten ells of livestock—altogether thirty hundredworths and twelve *aurar*. From this we first deduct the property and dowry of his wife, namely seventeen hundredworths; then a land rent for five hundredworths of land, amounting to forty ells, due to Torfi Jónsson; then Stefán Brandsson claims a debt of thirty-five ells in three tithes, amounting to ten quarters and a half[6] (which should be earmarked and paid first of all). The remainder, after his debts are paid, is twelve hundredworths and twenty-five ells, to which must be added the value of the livestock [Icel. *kúgildi*] that goes with the rental farms,[7] less that which goes with the church (which for lack of knowledge we cannot estimate).

And now as regards what the priest, *síra* Jón, petitions and demands as his right under the four headings set forth at the beginning of this verdict of ours. Our opinion and conclusion are the following—as we stated earlier in our discussion of the property of the younger Jón: The priest ought to receive no less than twenty hundredworths in compensation for his injuries and for the assault against his life. In addition to all the effort, loss, expense, and trouble that he has been put to because of this trial, his respected wife and his household have been subjected to most violent attacks. Above all, he himself is now completely bedridden and God alone knows how long he will survive or what his end will be.

Our national lawbook,[8] in *Mannhelgi*, Chapter 11, speaks about those who plot to kill or injure others, and says: It is a plot if a person speaks words or performs acts with the intention that, if the words are acted upon as he intends, some other person may be deprived of life or subjected to some disgrace. He must give full compensation to the plaintiff, according to the decision of the law, and also to the king.

Item as regards assault by slander, see *Mannhelgi*, Chapter 24: Full compensation has been decreed by the governor (Icel. *höfuðsmaður*), according to [the said Chapter] 24, just as if an innocent party had been killed, even though he was not killed.

Item Mannhelgi, Chapter 5: If he cannot restore[9] the man, let him pay full weregild for the man, according to the latter's status.

Mannhelgi, Chapter 21: If two or more men wound another man, each of them separately shall be guilty and liable to pay full compensation on his own behalf, and also to the king, etc.

Item Mannhelgi, Chapter 2, where [various kinds of injury] are enumerated, such as shameful murder, malicious injury, or greater or lesser irremediable injury. For those injuries—such as the cutting off of a foot or hand or similar injuries—which are of comparatively lesser degree, compensation of twenty hundredworths is awarded.

But how much greater and more serious than these acts does the hellish assassin's work, the devil's own murderous plot, seem and appear to us to be, affected as we are in heart and soul by earnest compassion, disgust, and zeal for censure, in this present case in which it is the devil himself who is instigated and set on to torture a man day and night—a man who preaches God's word, in fact the very pastor of the miscreants themselves! And we have seen written verdicts of bygone times before us, to the effect that the compensations for priests and other honorable men have been adjudged by the country's leading men to be forty hundredworths or sixty hundredworths, according to their dignity and birth. Moreover, besides the abovementioned tortures which he suffers on his own person in bed in weakness and pain, he has been deprived (to the extent that this sorcery has been able to accomplish it) of his livelihood and priestly salary and also of the ability to carry out his priestly duties. May God remedy this misfortune! Therefore, as payment to the priest of the aforesaid sum of twenty hundredworths, we charge ten hundredworths to the Kirkjuból farm, since we consider that the movable assets of the farm will bring twenty hundredworths if they are sold, or if the heirs have the money to redeem them within ten years, according to the provisions of our law. We propose to submit to the consideration of a higher authority the question of how we should proceed in this situation. It may be that the authorities—the *lögmenn* with the counsel of the fief-holder of the estate—will consider that *síra* Jón and his respected wife have a right to further compensation from the aforementioned movable property worth twelve hundredworths and twenty-five ells, which would otherwise be divided between the king and the heirs (who are near the upper age limit of minors, and in addition sickly). We rule further that the decision be left to them, to be made according to the relevant rules of the section of the laws dealing with travel to the Althing (Icel. *þingfararbálkur*). Let the *sýslumenn* take this oft-mentioned movable property into their custody—but without being liable for it—until a decision is handed down at the next session of the Althing as to whether the leading men of the country will award compensation to *síra* Jón under the four headings specified earlier, over and above the aforementioned ten hundredworths of real estate. We are not able, nor would we venture, to make any further ruling, since this would have wider implications. It is a new thing in our day, that one has to hand down judgment on compensations for harm, damage, spells, and injury due to Satan himself and his minions. But everything else shall be paid out to each individual as indicated in writing by the *sýslumenn* and the six named dignitaries (Icel. *dánumenn*), in all respects impartially and conscientiously.

The aforementioned *sýslumenn* have approved this verdict of ours, affixing their signatures below to our [document]. This verdict was written up in the same place and on the same day [as the court session], and was recopied at Kirkjuból in Langidalur[10] on 12 May of the same year [1656].

Þorleifur Kortsson, *manu propria* (i.e., signed with his own hand)
Magnús Magnússon (signed with his own hand)
Brynjólfur Bjarnason (signed with his own hand)
Snæbjörn Torfason (signed with his own hand)

Notes

1. This Chapter VII covers the following material from the three printed Icelandic editions of the *Píslarsaga*:
    1914 edn., p. 55 (line 1) to p. 58 (bottom);
    1967 edn., p. 109 (line 15 from bottom) to p. 113 (bottom);
    2001 edn., p. 225 (line 1) to p. 228 (bottom).

2. See Introduction, §3.

The Icelandic tithe law differed from the tithe laws in many other Christian countries in being largely based on 1% of the total worth rather than 10% of the income (yearly increase of worth) of the individual. For more detailed information about the Icelandic tithe and tax laws in general, see Jóhannes Hraunfjör Karlsson, *Frá tíund til virðisauka: Saga skatta og kvaða frá upphafi til vorra daga.*

3. For an explanation of the units of commercial value encountered in this chapter see Appendix 1 under: Units of Value.
4. See Appendix 1 under: *Grágás.*
5. See Appendix 1 under: *Jónsbók.*
6. I.e., 105, or 3 times 35, ells.
7. The value of the livestock that "went with" a farm when the latter was leased was called the *kúgildi* or *leigukúgildi* of the farm. This livestock was the property of the owner of the farm, and the tenant rented it (his rental payment for the animals being included in the rent he paid for the farm). The tenant was obligated to maintain these animals, and hand them over to the next tenant. If they were decimated by disease or harsh weather, he had to compensate the owner.
8. This is the *Jónsbók.*
9. Chap. 5 of the *Mannhelgi* (see *Jónsbók*, 1970 edn., p. 42) deals with compensation to be paid for a free man who has been sold abroad into slavery. In this context "restoration" means bringing the man out of slavery back to Iceland.
10. See Chap. VI, Note 28.

PART II

The Second Part of the Story of the Sufferings of Síra Jón Magnússon

VIII. Reflections on the Punishment of Wizards. The Assaults on Síra Jón Do Not Cease, in Spite of the Burning of the Jón Jónssons[1]

Such was the character of the first phase or part of my torments, up to the final assembly here in Eyri which lasted four days and led to the burning [of the Jón Jónssons]. In those proceedings the Lord God worked marvelously on the judges, so that they were of one accord in their investigation of the accused. It had seemed to me most unlikely that the verdict should turn out as it did on the basis of my earnest and weighty demands, both by word of mouth and by letter, to Magnús Magnússon, the nearer of the two *sýslumenn*. The latter, I think, undertook the case unwillingly, more because of my galling and compelling demands than out of compassion or his own free will. But above all, the Lord demonstrated His almighty power on those hapless men. Previously they had been so insistent in their own defense that they swore a most solemn oath denying that they had practiced any magic on me. But then, without being tortured, or put to any distress except for the irons that fettered them, they became so compliant that they freely confessed to having committed unspeakable crimes in the manner already related. Admittedly leading men came to me where I lay in bed in my *baðstofa* and reported to me what tactics had been used on the younger Jón—tactics that no one can blame—whereby they thought they would catch him out by cunning. But both the Jón Jónssons were sharp and shrewd enough to avoid being trapped by the wiles of these men who assembled for the purpose. The tactics that the latter employed would have availed them little had not the Lord been at work. This, it seemed to me, should be clear as daylight to everyone.

Similarly when the two Jón Jónssons were arrested in accordance with the demand that I made of the *sýslumaður* Magnús Magnússon. I sent this demand to him in an open letter—a procedure that he later reprimanded me for—and I had my servant read the letter to him in the presence of witnesses in his home in Eyri at Seyðisfjörður,[2] a fact clearly confirmed by their signatures. The *sýslumaður* Magnús reacted to this letter by taking action: he put the father and son in irons, following the counsel of the worthiest men present at the time. The cause of my making this demand was not only the intensity of the sufferings to which I was subject because of diabolical assaults, then as at other times throughout that period, but also the fact that news reached me that Jón the elder had evidently advised and urged his son, Jón the younger, to save his life by flight. We received word here from Kirkjuból that at that time the younger Jón had begun to collect his belongings and for some nights had been sleeping with his clothes on. This made me realize, knowing how unscrupulous these two men were, how unprotected my farm here would be if the younger Jón at the outset of his flight chose to make his way hither. This is the way of murderers, who care nothing about what miseries they let fall on the unprotected heads [of their victims]. So it was painful for me to expose myself to the barefaced witchcraft of these wretched men by letting them remain at large any longer than the law permitted. I well knew what befell me on past occasions when these men had passed by or called in at my farm. So it was that I made my demand of the *sýslumaður* Magnús in harsh language, since I saw that nothing else would be effective. I am ready to answer for what I said and did, and defend it against whoever wants to challenge it.

When the father and son were about to be arrested and put in irons, some thought it would be no easy task since it was generally rumored that they had guns and defenses prepared and were on the watch for men approaching from a distance. Besides, both of them were capable and resolute men, so that people feared that they would be difficult to apprehend. In spite of this, when it came to the test they were no more difficult to seize and arrest than a domesticated ox in a stall. People wondered at this, for it seemed a work specially arranged and carried out by God. Another thing too was unforgettable to me—the judgment passed by God almighty on those hapless men. The elder is said to have declared that he had no desire to live longer even if he were given the chance to save his life. The other was quite different: he had been very much afraid of death, but in spite of that he confessed his many acts of witchcraft.

At that time I often wished for the opportunity to speak to them, for I was well aware that they had need of this, even though more than one cleric had spoken to them and urged them to mend their ways. But I did not dare to have them brought before me because of their evil magic. Also I was much surprised at the wrong judgment of my dean regarding their penitence and conversion of heart, and also of other intelligent men in the crowd, who told me their belief that the two men were by now truly repentant and back on the right path. Hearing this I [at first] became only too glad to have myself brought out to meet them at the front door of [my] house. When I saw them at the door I stretched out both my hands to them, for I had been told that they would probably want to ask my forgiveness. The older Jón came up to me first. He seemed to me to have some rudiments of contrition, so that I would have been hopeful of a better outcome for him if the poor wretch had been worked on, and [his rough edges] smoothed away, for a longer time. He asked me humbly for forgiveness, and when he took his leave he prayed that God would be with him. After that the younger Jón approached me at my farm door and I also stretched out my arms to him. But he never asked me for forgiveness. When he saw me stretch out my arms to him, all he said was: "May God stretch out His arms to receive my soul as you are doing." After that he knelt down outside the threshold and set his arms on it as people do when praying, while I was inside the threshold supported on my knees by two persons. I began to feel a revulsion at the younger Jón's presence and the prostration with which he imitated the manner of those who pray, but I could not move away because of my weakness. However I suppressed my revulsion, and said some words to him which I thought might benefit him and encourage him to repent. As for him, he lay with his arms outstretched, until at last he reached out with his hands and struck me with his hand on my left side so that I shrank back in pain. This event brought to a halt my admonitions to this wretched man. I was nonplussed by such behavior. It occurred to me that, while he was lying on the threshold, the younger Jón might have been mumbling under his breath and reciting some magical spell of which the stroke of his hand was perhaps expressive—a stroke that pained me under my side for a long time thereafter. The last words of Jón the younger as he left me were: "May God grant us all a good night!"[3] I could not see the least sign of repentance in the man. I was surprised that I had been so deceived and given over into the hands of a wretched man like that without anyone to restrain him. For the other people stood afar off when he was allowed to approach me, and I was unable to back away myself. Also, I heard later from those who guarded this prisoner in the kitchen that he had apparently asked the men to permit him to come into my presence before his father. Some people were perplexed as to what this might mean. But it did not happen that way; it fell to his lot to come before me after his father.

From this one can see the stupidity of those who believe what magicians say. The latter are even more faithless than foxes and snakes, since they are confederate with the devil himself. The signs and appearance of damnation were clearly to be seen in Jón the younger. I was astonished to see how this man had changed since I saw him before Christmas. At that time I thought him to be an unusually handsome man in face and form. His hair was curly and of golden color, and he had an attractive complexion and fair skin. If he had lived and attended the Althing[4] in the summer of 1658, he would not, I think, have stood much chance of being convicted of the charge of witchcraft if looks had carried any weight in procuring an acquittal—just as his sister Þuríður, because she was admired there for beauty and intelligence, was considered unlikely to be a witch (though no one here in the west has been much impressed by her good looks). But when I saw him again in church after Easter week (when I was carried there and was lying on the pew and there caught sight of him), I was afraid to look at him, and I could not refrain from speaking about it. His face had become black, swollen, and repulsive, and his hair, which I had expected to be yellowish-red and close to the color of gold, had become dun or ash-colored. It struck me that this was what the man was going to look like when I would see him in future among the damned, before the judgment seat of the righteous One. Such was his appearance when I saw him in the doorway of my farmhouse on the occasion just mentioned. But though I had seen Jón the younger in this condition before my very eyes in church, I was so easily duped that I was persuaded to believe the dean and other intelligent men when they claimed that both men were truly repentant. But in fact I saw only *utpote contritionis quædam initia* (as it were some rudiments of contrition) in the elder Jón, and not a sign of contrition in the younger one who seemed completely hardened in his malice. And yet the latter had a painful fear of death, which was manifested most clearly (as I have heard) when the fire refused twice to take hold of him,[5] if not more often. Then he is said to have called on the devil by every name when the fire [finally] began to scorch him.

This makes me increasingly aware of two things bearing on the two arms[6] of the Christian community, that ought to help scour them clean in such cases as the present one. First, it sickens me when unrepentant, hardened criminals, especially those involved in this sort of wickedness—even individuals who are very limbs of hell[7]—are pressed into receiving the most holy Supper of the Lord, without the proper repentance that is evinced by circumcision of the heart and visible fruits. Therefore I think there is a need for more than one learned priest to be available in such situations, to provide judgments and solutions when the necessity arises of acting in closest accord with God's word, in conformity with the Church Ordinance.[8] The second point is also something, it seems to me, which is not carried out as it should be. When the Lord God works marvelously for our poor country so that sea-monsters like [the Jón Jónssons] are caught in nets, and evil deeds like [theirs] float up from the bottom of the ocean (which happens, I think, less often than it should), the only interest that is shown is in bringing the case somehow to a conclusion. No matter if the whole cargo is thrown into the fire along with the boat and the ballast![9] (Magnús the *sýslumaður* had to bring charges against the estate of the men who were burned, on the grounds that two of their taxes were unaccounted for.[10] Why was there no [prior] supervision, Magnús? I wonder whether trousers full of fear might have been the cause![11]) As far as I know, neither of the two, father or son, was at any time tortured to give any information. In this regard I attach no blame to that good man Þorleifur Kortsson. Indeed, I remember well that he once questioned me whether there were any tongs on my farm and coals sufficient to heat them. He told me why he wanted them, and was quite determined in his purpose. Both tongs and coals were in fact available here. But I did not encourage this, so as to avoid being censured for undue hatred of the two men. Still, I believe that this initiative of his was both wise and useful. Just what brought on or who thwarted this intention and plan of Þorleifur Kortsson I do not know. I heard no further mention of it as far as I can remember. But, far from their being tortured to gain information, the rumor was that the younger Jón, who was sent for custody to Gísli Jónson, ate at table with Gísli himself and lacked none of the amenities that the latter's mother could provide—or so at least it seemed to some, who had not seen him looking so fat and sleek since he returned from the west. A similar tale was told about his father, the elder Jón, who was in custody with Magnús. It will do me no credit to pass judgment on this behavior. But I believe that the best procedure with a proven offshoot of witchcraft is to cleanse and cauterize it as far as lies within the power and intelligence of man. One purpose of this is to reveal evil ways which taken by themselves cannot be recognized but can be discerned for what they are by comparison with similar cases. This is a better course than to slumber in the same stupidity, indifference, and the sleep of death, like some of the magistrates and officials that are set over us, taking no measures and conducting no interrogations—a course that leads to the downfall of oneself and one's country. Another purpose, easy to guess, has to do with the guilty themselves: what good does it do to sorcerers to protect them and keep them from humanly kindled fires? It is a pitiful thing to write about, but I think I am more qualified to answer the question than anyone else. For I have experienced a different fire, that sears more excruciatingly than any other. And yet what will they experience who on top of all this suffer the wrath of God, which surpasses every weight [of misery]? [Even] I have not been touched by this. So I shudder with fear for those who are supporters and defenders of wizards. All they are doing is to pile more fuel on the fires of hell for the very people whom they are defending. Also, they are unaware that they themselves are likely to be plunged into the very same fire. For "he who is not with Christ is reckoned to be against Him, and he that gathereth not with Him," etc.[12] Therefore I know of none who do a greater favor to sorcerers than those who track them down and arrest them promptly—if possible before they manage to fill up the measure of the crimes that will consign them to the fires of hell. For if these poor fellows cannot escape eternal damnation by being pitied in this world or [even] with the aid of the prayers of God-fearing men (in so far as it is permissible before God to pray for such), I cannot see any hope of salvation for them if they die with their sin unpunished. For those who are wise enough there is little need for me to expatiate on this by quoting the express word of God.

When these hapless men were parted from me in this manner and taken away to be burned in the flames, I suffered an attack—though not one of the most intense—so that I could not give any reply to the magistrates who returned to me from the burning. Some thought that this was a retaliation, stemming from the jab that the younger Jón gave me at our meeting. He had made efforts to come into my presence, indicating thereby that he wished to ask me to speak words of blessing over him. But some felt that this was hardly likely from his ilk, so the matter was not settled. So the burning of these wretched men became an accomplished fact. But it was carried out more hastily than it should have been, and my sufferings did not abate at the first burning. After the burning was over a vision of the younger Jón was also seen—not as he had been, but as people saw him begrimed by the fire. *N.B. hic visionis modum ut et alibi.*[13] I heard that the message had been conveyed [to others] in dreams that, if my torments were to abate, the residue of the fire should be examined more carefully. Also, the same dreams pointed out that part of the younger Jón's face had survived unburned—a circumstance not without relevance. Moreover it turned out, so people thought, that parts of the brains of either father or son had been found. So the men of the district got together and rummaged through these remnants and burned them to ashes—in fact did so two or three times or more. Only then did the visions of devils and hauntings cease throughout the district. No such visions were reported at any farms other than mine.

Nevertheless *my* sufferings persisted just as before, even after the burning of these remnants of the original fire, with peaks and recessions just as before. Quite exceptional was the terrible attack that I suffered on the Monday following Ascension Day, the day when Þuríður was traveling past here on her way to Hnífsdalur. This was the trip on which she had stroked a cow belonging to Jón Jónsson and Margrét Arnórsdóttir according to the latter's account, on the evidence of a pious girl, Ingibjörg Ívarsdóttir, who (she said) had been with her in the cowshed. That attack on Monday lasted from the beginning of the day until about the middle of the afternoon. It was so terrible that I thought that in all my former distresses I had never endured such a violent assault. I could not speak a word to anyone without, I felt, putting myself in the gravest danger. In my great peril and bewilderment my only recourse was to lament and cry aloud to the Lord and beseech Him with the utmost fervor. Sometimes I felt as if I were detached from the mattress I was lying on and would be thrown out of the bed and onto the floor. That day seemed to last longer than two or three [ordinary] days, for I could not for a moment break off the intense ardor with which I was calling on God in prayer, though my heart felt harder than steel or stone. The colder and more shriveled my heart was, the more energy I had to expend in order to sustain the fervent repetition of the prayer. On that day as twilight drew on, I turned my face to the wall or the crossbeam and set myself with all my might to constrain my heart to some act of piety. The substance of my prayer on that occasion was this: I begged my heavenly Father to grant me love for Jesus, my Redeemer, from whom I felt cut off. At the same time that I was constraining my heart to pray for this boon, I heard this phrase clearly spoken to me: "I shall be victorious tomorrow!" This phrase came to me through the hearing of my ears; it was not spoken in my heart. I was astonished at it, not knowing what it meant. I was fully awake and in great turmoil and uncertainty. Not knowing for certain from what quarter the angel had come who spoke these words, when my excitement had abated I enquired of those near me whether any of them had said anything about a victory, either aloud or to themselves; but no one knew anything about it. When my poor wife, Þorkatla Bjarnadóttir, asked me whether I had heard anything said about it, I answered that I would tell her on the morrow if God permitted. For I myself was in doubt whether it was a bad angel or a good one that had spoken to me. The thought entered my head that perhaps my vicious enemy, who had persecuted and plagued me, was boasting of his success in advance and promising himself the victory. To this my mind responded that, however furiously the devil threatened me, I would counter him similarly by prayer and appeal to my God, the Savior of all mankind—whether the Lord granted me to live or to die. So I bided my time, waiting for whatever the Lord should be pleased to bring to pass.

The next night, which was Tuesday, such an ardent sense of devotion was infused into my heart, with such joy and rapture, that I cannot write about it or describe it. I lay, as it were, in a flood of rapturous tears, feeling more than compensated for all my injuries, willing and eager to endure every load of misery that the Lord might see fit to impose on me—if only I might hold on to this one thing, namely, the grace of the Lord in His only-begotten Son Jesus. So the night passed and likewise the following day which was mild for me in comparison with the day before. From the evidence of this experience I perceived and concluded that it was a holy angel of God that had given me this message for my comfort and restoration, not an evil spirit.

On that Monday when I was stricken with this intense, racking seizure, my wife and household had been gloomy and distressed at this calamity. For we were expecting and awaiting help and restoration, since the Lord had given us such a splendid victory over those wretched men whose devilish arts and witchcraft had now been publicly exposed and proved, and who in addition had been executed by burning. But just the opposite had happened: a new seizure and attack came over me, more violent, it seemed, than any I had suffered in all the times of torment up till then, even while the two sorcerers were living and raging most intensely against me. In view of this the good people of my household, as I came to know, were conferring in their simplicity and ignorance about seeking a remedy for my troubles. So, when I began to feel better and could answer her, my disconsolate wife, Þorkatla Bjarnadóttir, asked me whether I did not think it advisable to send for a certain man who lived in the north, and who was said to have methods for counteracting this sort of malady and seizure, to come and heal me. I gave the matter some thought, reflecting that in extreme distress and dire necessity it is hard to oppose and completely dismiss the advice of friends and relatives. I thought to myself: could it be that it is the Lord's pleasure to spur me to seek out good advice? I called to mind what St. James says in his fifth chapter: "Let the sinner and the sick man call for the elders of the church," etc. Also: "The fervent and frequent or continuous prayer of a righteous man avails much."[14] So I began to look around for one whom I might select for the purpose. Averse to my family's naively ignorant ideas regarding a trip to the north, and unwilling to make requests of this man whom we knew only by name, I redirected the desire and urgency of my family and friends along a different path, following the counsel of St. James. I had heard reports of a certain well-known devout and learned priest, *síra* Páll Björnsson of Selárdalur, who was said to be outstanding and to have few peers in virtuous living, moral admonition, and powerful teaching of the word of God. On the afternoon of that same Monday, without consulting anyone else, I had a few lines written to him in which I let him know my request in God's name that he should favor me with his assistance in praying to the Lord our God. Without delay this worthy man of God made me a partaker of his prayer, as the comforting and touching letter that he wrote me clearly showed. Moreover this good man went to the considerable trouble of travelling here to see me and give consolation to my soul. Surely the Lord will reward his compassion by showing compassion to him at the right time, according to His kindly promises.

So time passed as I have already told, in assaults by devils which I was able to face and cope with only by persistent prayer in the manner described above, until the time foretold for me. For on the evening before holy Pentecost (in that year 1656), after three days of continuous and intense battle, I was relieved of the worst monstrosities of the devil and had complete relief from them. I was then lying in a state of weakness, experiencing the symptoms of a mild feverish heat. This heat was always in the part of the body that was turned toward the bed, whether it was the back or either side. This lasted almost a week and a half while I was getting stronger, until finally my feet were able to bear me up. At this point I was granted a rapid recovery—unexpectedly rapid in fact, so that many were surprised at how quickly the gift of life and health was restored to me. At the mass of [the nativity of] John the Baptist it was granted to me to conduct the service in church, and this went on until the later diabolical attacks struck me on the day of the mass of [the beheading of]

John the Baptist in the fall of the same year.[15] This followed the occasion when I was in the near presence of Erlendur Ormsson and Þuríður Jónsdóttir, after giving the latter some wholesome advice and admonition.

Nevertheless there was one occasion during the course of that summer, between the two dates mentioned above, when I experienced a grievous diabolical assault after speaking a few words of admonition to a certain man who was then in our district and was thought to be involved with runic staves. These words I spoke to the man in the Eyri church, in the hearing of the congregation. Afterwards I experienced a demonic assault, so that I had to get up from my bed, but it did not last very long at its peak. Another time, when the same man took me by the hand, I reacted to it with a disorder of the hand, but this was cured when Sigmundur of Seljaland, whom I visited for the purpose, drew blood from that hand. I do not hold Þuríður Jónsdóttir accountable for these two episodes, nor for every act of witchcraft that has taken place in this district. For if we look into it carefully, we will see the truth of what the elder Jón is reported to have said—"that something will outlast [him] in Skutulsfjörður even though he depart."

Now, since the Lord of glory had rescued me out of those flames of hell and raised me up out of that devils' bath, I had determined to have no fear of the devil's agents, and not to be intimidated from doing the priestly duties committed to me or from admonishing those whom I knew to be in need of it. But even so, in thus admonishing, I cannot expect anything else from those diabolical men whom some specific individuals, who are so minded, think it fashionable to shield. But I am well aware of what that support will bring to pass for them within a short time.

My household knows of these happenings, and in fact news of them has spread through the district, if not beyond. I was granted a certain amount of strength that summer so that I sometimes undertook strenuous work, helping to make hay and working in the smithy. I do not remember suffering any attacks other than those I have already mentioned until I went with Erlendur Ormsson to Kirkjuból. My only business there was to see Sturli Bjarnason who lived there, and I did in fact meet him. My business with him was to ask him to let me see the letters and inventories for the Kirkjuból estate which he had in his possession. The reason that this had been delayed until that time was that I have never made it my habit to pursue much worldly business with my congregation on holy days. I am not fit for it at those times; such things escape my memory, as my congregation is well aware. In fact, if I have business with any parishioner I have generally had to ask somebody of my household to transact it on my behalf on the days when people meet at church. Otherwise it would be put aside and not attended to. That is the true reason for my trip to Kirkjuból on that occasion, as I expect that Sturli Bjarnason will still acknowledge. Thus it happened by chance that on that occasion I was present at a conversation between Erlendur and Þuríður. Every story must have some background.[16]

Notes

1. This Chapter VIII covers the following material from the three printed Icelandic editions of the *Píslarsaga*:
   1914 edn., p. 59 (line 1) to p. 71 (line 15 from bottom);
   1967 edn., p. 114 (line 1) to p. 127 (line 11 from bottom);
   2001 edn., p. 94 (line 3) to p. 103 (bottom).
2. Eyri in Seyðisfjörður, the residence of Magnús Magnússon, should not be confused with Eyri in Skutulsfjörður, the residence of *síra* Jón Magnússon. Seyðisfjörður is a small fjord that indents the Djúp a short distance east of Skutulsfjörður; see the map.
3. These last words of the younger Jón Jónsson to the priest sound a little strange under the circumstances. Could it be that he intends them to suggest the sentiments of a certain evening hymn quoted by Margrét Eggertsdóttir on p. 192 of *Kristni á Íslandi*, vol. 3? This hymn (like some other Christian literature) has an erotic flavor. The words *Guð gefi oss öllum góða nótt* (may God grant us all a good night!) occur as the refrain of each of its four verses.
4. Icel. Öxarárþing. See pp. 6, 7.
5. Literally, "the fire twice spat him out."
6. By the "two arms of the Christian community" *síra* Jón probably means the ecclesiastical authority (represented by the administration of the Lord's Supper) and the civil or secular authority (that concerns itself, among other things, with the trial of alleged practitioners of witchcraft).
7. *Síra* Jón's word for "hell" here means literally "damnation."
8. This refers to the Church Ordinance originally decreed in 1537 by the Danish King Christian III, and amended about a century later by King Christian IV (see Introduction, Note 17).
9. The phrase "the whole cargo .... ballast" presumably refers to information about the circumstances surrounding their practice of sorcery, which was allowed to perish along with the burning of the malefactors.
10. See Chap. VII.
11. I take the Icel. word *hveiti* here to be derived from *hveitur* (fear) rather than from the much commoner *hveiti* (flour). The phrase "trousers full of fear" is reminiscent of the Icel. phrase "to have one's heart in one's trousers," i.e., to be terrified. The above sentence is then a sarcastic insinuation that Magnús was reluctant to investigate the Jón Jónssons too closely out of fear of their magical powers. I owe this interpretation to Bishop Sigurbjörn Einarsson.
12. *Matthew* 12:30.
13. This Latin phrase means: "Here [I ought to describe] how the vision appeared to me, as in other places." Evidently *síra* Jón intended this phrase as a memorandum to himself that he ought to give a further description of this vision, but he evidently forgot or omitted to follow it up.
14. The *Epistle of James* 5:14–16.

15. The mass celebrating the nativity of John the Baptist was held on June 24th, while the mass commemorating his death (by beheading) was held in the fall on August 29th. Thus the period of relative calm enjoyed by *síra* Jón lasted for about two months.
16. At this point in his French translation of the *Píslarsaga*, Einar Már Jónsson suggests that *síra* Jón is being less than truthful in his account of the real reason for his pivotal journey to Kirkjuból on 29 August 1656. In presenting it as purely a business trip to meet with Sturli Bjarnason, he does not explain why he went in company with Erlendur Ormsson. For Einar Már's conjectural reconstruction of the real background of the journey see Note 89 of the Introduction.

IX. He Attributes his Continued Sufferings to the Witchcraft of Þuríður[1]

Here begins the presumptive evidence for Þuríður's practice of witchcraft—that is, if we do not count the violent attack that I had suffered on Monday the day after the Sunday when she passed by my farm on her way to Hnífsdalur, as I mentioned before. On that trip Margrét Arnórsdóttir said she had seen the aforementioned Þuríður in the cow-stall with the cow belonging to Margrét, stroking the cow on its back with expressions of fondness—and this was the cow which some weeks later was killed by sorcery.[2] And Margrét had been exposed to considerable risk too, for after she had taken the cow in hand to help it along, she took a bad turn, with a surprising numbness which first affected one arm and then came out in unnatural convulsions in her chest. This was seen and recognized by several people on this farm and elsewhere.

Both these things happened on the same trip—the stroking of the cow, and the merciless attack that I suffered on that Monday. While those sorcerers who were burned, the father and brother of Þuríður, were still alive, whenever they came to the Danish Houses to meet the *sýslumaður* Magnús Magnússon or set foot on the property of my farm I usually had an indication of this because I then experienced worse attacks than usual. This sign on my own body is not to be taken lightly. On the other hand, during my former torments I most often noticed that I hardly ever suffered an attack so grievous that, if some stranger arrived or even someone from the same district but from outside our own household here, the attack was not alleviated thereby for a while, even if only for a short time. Men who are intelligent ought to take these and other circumstances seriously and give each its own weight, rather than sitting by idly, thoughtlessly, and lethargically, of no use to souls tortured with horrible sorcery, until such time as the birth pangs[3] of God's wrath reach their climax and overwhelm them. Then there is no further chance of amendment, and to each is measured out according to his life and deeds.

The account of the later outbreaks of sorcery, and of how Þuríður is implicated in them by signs both living and dead as recorded in the verdict of the twelve men,[4] is to some extent recounted and available there. The *historia* (story) is as follows:[5]

When I had arrived at Kirkjuból together with Erlendur Ormsson, he began talking with Þuríður, first in the churchyard there in the presence of her mother and some others. But I went off to Sturli's house since my errand concerned him. Then Erlendur and Þuríður moved toward the kitchen, by the yard below the farmhouse. I too was asked to go there. There were several others there, among them Örnólfur Jónsson and Þóra Einarsdóttir. This Örnólfur intended to marry Þuríður. Þuríður's siblings were also there. Guðrún, Þuríður's mother, came in now and then and listened to what Erlendur was saying. I and most of the others were surprised how plausibly Erlendur spoke to Þuríður, but she hardly replied to him at all except to say: "I don't think that is likely." Otherwise she was silent throughout.[6] From the kitchen they went into the church.[7] There too I heard Erlendur's exhortations to Þuríður, but to my surprise she was as silent as before. When Erlendur had left the church, I felt upset by what I had seen and heard, and I gave Þuríður some sound advice, to which she made hardly any reply. I also told her what I was then seeing around her. We were sitting on the same chest, on the men's side of the church.[8] I was nearer to the door of the church than she, and there was just a little space between us, enough for a half-grown child to occupy. Though it was a bright day and the sun was shining into the church, I saw a circle of darkness surrounding Þuríður, like the halo that one sees around the moon. The darkness reached as far as my right side, which was turned toward Þuríður. When I saw that circle of darkness making contact with me, I quickly rose from the chest and withdrew from it as far as the door. I told Þuríður what I saw, and stretched out my foot as far as the ring of darkness, but she made no reply. There were no witnesses present except for Him who is the most clear-sighted of all, and He saw and heard all that passed between us. During our conversation there in the church something happened that surprised me: Þuríður turned to face the chest she was sitting on, and fell on her knees as people do when saying their prayers. She remained kneeling at the chest for a short time, while I paced around the church floor. I did not like the way Þuríður prayed. She seemed to me dry and hardhearted, since I did not see any tears fall from her eyes. But I felt that Erlendur must have made every effort [to arouse repentance in her] before he went away. I addressed her again when she rose from the chest at which she had been kneeling, and told her my presentiment—that this prayer of hers would probably not be heard or accepted by God. My heart pointed this out to me, in terms more repulsive than I care to put on paper, but the Lord saw to it that the outcome was not any worse than it was. I was admonished to show good will to the children[9]—which indeed it had been my intention to do—and so, when I bade goodbye to the people, I admonished the two of them who were standing outside next to their mother to fear God and to be diligent and eager in showing submissiveness and obedience toward their mother. Indeed, I was afraid on their behalf, that something unfortunate would befall them if they did not fear and hold fast to God. The people bade me farewell outside, but Þuríður remained alone inside the farmhouse. Erlendur had a change [of behavior at this point] which he might have explained [but didn't]: in the yard he drew back and retreated surreptitiously to a spot from which he could see nothing to confirm what the others testified to[10]—or so it seemed to me. But I did not pursue the matter further, since I left the place before he did.

I rode homeward from Kirkjuból as evening drew on. But when I was nearly at the mouth of the fjord, on the landward side of Hafrafell, I had a sense that a ghostly visitation was increasingly haunting my journey. I paid no attention to it until the evil spirit came upon me when I was already near my home, at a place called Torfnes. When I reached home and sat on the bed in the *skáli*, I felt as if my face were being attacked by the biting of gnats. Thereafter I began again to suffer agonizing torments. They were especially violent for three nights, most of all on the third. Not until that time did I realize how savage were the racking tortures that the devils could cook up. In my sleep I felt as if I were being drawn out limb from limb and then, in between, slammed and snapped together again into fetters. Never do I remember having experienced this kind of torture—never in all the former attacks of witchcraft, as far as my memory reaches—except on this one occasion. I was stripped of all my strength and almost completely drained, so that I doubted whether or not I would even be able to drag myself out of bed. But I thought that, if I did not make the effort to move myself, I would be forced to lie in the same bedridden condition as before. So, for good or ill, I exerted myself to crawl out of bed.

On the following Saturday I was lying down by the church walkway with the intention of looking into my catechism book, but it was of no use. So I put the book under my head, and lay as if crushed and weighed down by an overwhelming burden. But my greatest dread was to go into the farmhouse, for there my pains were cruelest.

On Sunday I dragged myself in great weakness down to the church. I did not trust myself to go up to the altar or into the pulpit, not even to sit upright in a pew. So a seat was prepared for me at the entrance to the choir on a little chest, so that I could support my back against the post of the choir while I read the gospel and said a few short words about its meaning and substance for the benefit of the congregation. After the parishioners had gone, I dragged myself back to my farm. But I had an aversion to being inside the farmhouse, and went outside again as far as the mound by the farmhouse. I lay down on the mound while my household were taking their meal inside, turning to face the farm, and wondering whether or not the Lord was going to show greater leniency to the wretched abode that had been my refuge during all the former devilish horrors, or whether He was going to plunge me again into the same torments that had engulfed me before. Such were the reflections that occupied my mind as I lay prostrate on my shoulder there on the mound, alone, gazing at the farm and wondering anxiously whether I was going to be assaulted again. At the very time when I was reflecting thus, I received an answer, coming not through my ears but spoken in my mind and heart, as happened formerly on the church walkway and in my bed. The answer was: "Why don't you go and talk with her? You don't know whether you will get a better opportunity later if you don't go now!" These words relieved me of almost all my depression, and I received strength and courage. I stood up and went inside the farmhouse—though no further than between the doors of the *baðstofa* and the *skáli*—and called out to my household and asked which of them would venture to ride with me to Kirkjuból. The people were surprised at my request, but my relative Pétur Einarsson answered that he was prepared to go. I asked him to get ready as quickly as he could. He did so, and we rode up the fjord to Kirkjuból. When we arrived there, it so happened that the mother and daughter, Guðrún Bjarnadóttir and Þuríður, were walking together and conversing on the walkway between the churchyard and the farm. Markús Brandsson, then living at Seljabrekka, was walking in between the mother and daughter and talking with them both. The two women were walking on either side of him as Pétur and I rode up to the farmhouse. Afterwards I spoke with Þuríður, but not in the gentlest manner and with no words of flattery, for my state of mind this time was different.[11] Anyone else who had my cause for speaking, even if he were no more than my equal, would have addressed her just as harshly as I did. I then set out for home. That pious couple, Sturli Bjarnason and his wife Kristín Sigmundardóttir, walked with me down to the river and showed their good will toward me. Sturli asked me if I had any objection to his arranging an escort for Þuríður over the mountain, to which I answered no. He then told me that she had asked for an escort westward over the heath on Saturday. Margrét Þorvaldsdóttir, who was then a servant at Kirkjuból, has told me that she had not known anything about this journey of Þuríður until they packed the horses that she [Þuríður] and her escort were to ride. I now turned back homeward.

When I and my companion Pétur Einarsson reached Seljaland, Sigmundur Guðmundsson, who farmed there, came to meet us. He knew about our journey, and must have been surprised at my journeying on that day when I had been in such a wretched state during the church service. When we saw him, we headed over the home field to meet him. His wife and her children, and likewise her mother, also flocked out of the farmhouse and down over the home field to meet Pétur and me. But just a few moments before we met, this message was spoken in my heart: "You are not worthy to be riding on horseback when you meet this woman who is coming toward you on foot." I immediately consented to this unexpected message. Indeed, I knew that Randíður Ólafsdóttir,[12] the mother of Hildur Halldórsdóttir, was a most God-fearing woman. She had withstood grievous, prolonged temptations and assaults of the devil, beginning when she witnessed the pains and agonies of her husband, the late Halldór Ólafsson, who had been subjected to the torments of diabolical witchcraft, recognizable as such by sure signs and characteristics. This couple lived in Súðavík, Álftafjörður, and had a reputation for benevolence and works of mercy beyond many of their peers. This Randíður herself had been subjected to grievous, protracted, and dangerous temptations for a long time thereafter, but the Lord had given her the victory over all these miseries. This aged widow was now walking down the field with her daughter Hildur to meet me, and I knew at once that the message spoken to me referred to her. So without hesitation I dismounted and fell on my knees before her in full view of all. The couple, Sigmundur and Hildur, wanted to make me stand up again, but I refused to do so until I had received a blessing from the woman's hand, for in my eyes she was a person of great consequence. Those who stood nearby did not understand this. For what was she but an infirm old woman, poor and destitute, supported by the resources of her children? So it seemed to them astonishing that I should fall at the feet of a pauper like her. But I understood the matter quite differently—that in this person the Lord wanted to show me how precious in God's eyes are His saints, even though they are despised and considered worthless by ignorant people since they have no gold or silver or worldly finery to flaunt.

After I had received a blessing from this woman I rode back home to my poor dwelling. The next day I was admonished in the same manner that I should show thanks and some service in return for the good deed done to me by the woman. So I also sent my boy to her when I was told to do so. Other amazing things of this sort also happened to me about this time, even though I was suffering grievous buffets and temptations from the assaults and torments of the devil. But this [one incident] I am relating here so that intelligent people may assimilate it, avoid the rash foolishness of human reason in regard to God's works, and come to realize that even now God's power is mighty in those who, though weak, hold fast to Him with pure and simple hearts. I also cite this episode for the benefit of those who are wise in their own esteem, who think they know and understand everything, and who fit everyone's shoes to their own size and will, reserving nothing for God but the leavings of their own counsels, strength, and wit. Such is the tune the world pipes!

From these violent fresh diabolical pains I had little hope of extricating myself by human remedies. Still, I took counsel with myself and decided that I ought not to despise the remedies that God himself had provided. It was quite dubious whether I would live or die, and I knew that the following winter would not be a better time for legal action, judging by my previous experience. For these reasons, even though I shuddered at the thought of the legal proceedings that I had initiated during the former witchcraft trial, [I remembered the proverb] "necessity makes no bargains"; and I sent a message north to Þorleifur Kortsson in Hrútafjörður, asking him for legal redress and requesting him to institute legal proceedings. I made the same request to Magnús Magnússon—though only after [the request to Þorleifur had been sent], as the letters indicate.

At the time of this outrage against me, the devil's presence was visible in the appearance and demeanor of Þuríður, just as it had been in the appearance and bodily form of the two Jón Jónssons, her father and brother, before they were burned. Even people who were not clairvoyant saw the same. I admit that I never saw the devil's images in the two Jón Jónssons who were burned, though others (e.g., Katrín Ísleiksdóttir, Kristín Ólafsdóttir), some of whom were not clairvoyant, saw them. But to me, the image most closely resembling Þuríður was that of the wench whom I once saw here when I had stepped out of the farmhouse at Eyri in the fall of 1656. She was standing a short distance from the gable of the *baðstofa*. She had on a wide black coat and a broad-brimmed hat, and the skirts of her coat fluttered in both directions. At that time I was not very strong. Still, I was going to drag myself out over the yard to meet this troll-woman. I knew, as soon as I laid eyes on her, that she was the fiend! My purpose in wanting to approach this devil was to speak God's word to it. But the woman's form disappeared from my sight so quickly that I could not clearly distinguish it.

Magnús the *sýslumaður* said here at Eyri that he had seen a vision like that at Seljabrekkunaust. The young man Páll Egilsson of Hafrafell was badly affected by illusions of this sort both in the former plague of devils evoked by the two Jón Jónssons, and now again since this new demonic turmoil has befallen us, first in the guise of Þuríður but later of others also. Judging by the signs, these others may at some stage turn out to be of her ilk, though perhaps not until Judgment Day. Material regarding this matter will be found written up elsewhere.

Þuríður herself moved away from her mother and fled for refuge first to Halldóra Jónsdóttir of Holt and then westward to Brynjólfur Bjarnason in Hjarðardalur, where she had also lived off and on. But the devil in her likeness then started riding a brown mare (the same color, as I have been told, as the one on which she rode out of our district) by the crossroads from the west. In this connection four honest, adult women of my household told me that in the fall, close to the later Mary's Mass,[13] when they were all milking ewes in a sheep-pen, they all saw someone riding a brown mare along the shore toward the ocean as far as the farmhouse. Some of the women said it was a female figure wearing festive headgear that they saw, with a tassel hanging behind, but others said they did not see a female figure clearly enough to have recognized it as such. The ewes, they reported, instantly rushed helter-skelter out of the pen on all sides, but [the women] stood there quiet and downcast. A great many such visions have been seen in this district, and very many people have reported how openly the devil has been on the move. After the burnings he was seen first in the likeness of Þuríður, after that in the form of Snæbjörn Pálsson, and then, when these visions ceased, in the shape of Markús Brandsson. All these persons have taken fright and left the district in haste, being generally recognized as tarred with the same brush—though no one is willing or bold enough to say anything about it because of the danger to be expected from sorcery and witchcraft, and also because of the endorsement and support of some men who see fit to stand by [the sorcerers] in this affair.

It happened that, before Þuríður set out for the west, she asked for an escort in Engidalur from Magnús Jónsson and some other people. This was on the Saturday following the Friday commemorating the beheading of John the Baptist.[14] On that day, after the departure of Þuríður, I experienced in the evening the attack of witchcraft that I have already described. So quickly did Þuríður resort to flight (for "seldom does the hand that strikes a blow derive joy from it"[15])! Magnús refused [the request for an escort], as he has testified. After this refusal he suffered an assault of the devil, as his testimony relates. This came out even more clearly in the account which Signý Ólafsdóttir, the wife of Björn Jónsson who lives in Engidalur, gave in the church in the hearing of myself and the congregation. The clearest account, which tallied with that of Signý, was given by another pious young woman named Þóra Einarsdóttir, who at that time lived at the same farm.

In the winter of 1656, before Christmas, Þuríður travelled eastward from Holt in Önundarfjörður and came here to Eyri to visit me. I would not have known what her business with me was if she had not pretended to ask my forgiveness (following Njáll's counsels[16]), so that she might get [from me] a sacramental certificate.[17] I had no inclination to invite her into the farmhouse, in view of the old saying: "Tiresome are those who are constantly in need." Some of our household must have thought that she had already frequented our farm often enough in spirit, even though she cost us little expense or sustenance. Thus there were no witnesses to our conversation. In the light of this journey of hers, it is clear that there is either little truth in the accusation made in her letter of self-defense (which is included in the verdict of the twelve-person court[18]), or else a great deal of underhandedness and hypocrisy in the claim that she had prepared herself for the reception of the sacrament, as stated in that document.

On that journey something occurred which Jón Þorsteinsson of Tunga related to me. His testimony is as follows:

"I the undersigned, for the sake of truth and also at the request of my priest *síra* Jón Magnússon, bear witness to an event that occurred before

Christmas in the winter of 1656, when I gave a ride to Þuríður Jónsdóttir, seated behind me on the same horse, from here at Tunga to Kirkjuból. I felt pain in and under my side—the side that she was holding on to. The pain decreased the following night. This sensation seemed to come upon me in a surprising manner. To confirm this happening, I sign my name here below with my own hand, at Tunga, 6. *Septembris anno* 1658."

Here Jón Þorsteinsson signed his name with his own hand.

Similar shocks and buffets, I have been told, have been felt by various women in the proximity of Þuríður. Some, like Herdís Arnórsdóttir and Ólöf Guðmundardóttir, have felt them in church. Of some of these I have heard this told at second hand, of others by talking to them myself. Some, like Ingibjörg Pálsdóttir and Margrét Þorvaldsdóttir, [felt it] while sharing a bed with her, and others, like Halla Arnórsdóttir, in other places. I have not wanted to take the trouble to make out testimonies for these, since those who have to pass judgment on them will be inclined to throw them out. Still, I think that such shocks, which one person experiences in the proximity of another, are not a good sign. Indeed, this is the way poisonous snakes and adders are told apart from other creatures even by men whose eyes have been put out, for they can be felt even if they are not seen.

[The following are] pointers as to what happened at Kirkjuból on [the day of] the fall mass of John the Baptist, [when I was] in the company of Erlendur Ormsson:

"I, Sigurður Jónsson, testify that when *síra* Jón Magnússon was at Kirkjuból along with Erlendur Ormsson, on a Friday in 1656, I walked past the lower farm door at a time when Þuríður was the only person indoors. I then saw what looked like flying sparks of fire coming out of the farm door. I want this testimony of mine, written at Tunga on 6 September 1658, to be made public."

"With our signatures below, written at the same place and on the same day, we confirm that we heard Sigurður Jónsson give testimony by the above statement,

Gunnlaugur Skeggjason (signed by his own hand) and Jón Þorsteinsson."

"I, Margrét Þorvaldsdóttir, testify that I was present at Kirkjuból, Skutulsfjörður, on the day of the beheading of John the Baptist, 1656, when *síra* Jón and Erlendur Ormsson were also present. I saw the following apparition in the sky above the Kirkjuból farm: A red light was visible to me in the sky, round, and resembling the northern lights except that it was somewhat redder, and it struck me that out of this light came darkness. I was disconcerted, and covered my eyes with my hand. After a short while I looked again, and saw what looked like a ball of fire floating over the farmhouse. At that time Þuríður was alone inside the farmhouse. This happened at the time when the priest was with the people of the household there, between the churchyard and the farmhouse. But after he had ridden away, I saw something like a black dog going after him. I watched it as long as it was within sight, anxious to know what would come of this and expecting that it would have its effect on the priest. I want this testimony of mine to be made public, whatever may be the outcome."

"This testimony was given at Eyri in Skutulsfjörður on 6. *Septembris anno* 1658, and handed over to the priest, *síra* Jón Magnússon, in the hearing of those of us whose names are signed here in the place, day, and year just mentioned.

Pétur Einarsson (by his own hand) and Jón Jónsson (by his own hand).

N.B. She states that she was near the southeast corner of the churchyard when she saw the apparition in the sky over the farm, and in the upper farmyard when she saw the likeness of a dog."

Before Christmas in the winter of the same year, during the same journey on which Þuríður came to see me, Snæbjörn Pálsson of Kirkjuból had accompanied her over Þverdalsheiði to Önundarfjörður. I have heard it said that an evil female spirit and satanic tricks preceded them and were manifested at Kirkjuból in Korpudalur—or so it is generally rumored. But nowadays little attention is paid to such things. Nevertheless I am aware that those who have a persistent reputation for wizardry are very often accompanied by this sign— that something is wafted along with them or ahead of them, something that makes itself felt most often in dreams. Examples of this are not hard to come by in the West Fjords.

After Snæbjörn had done Þuríður the favor of escorting her, it was said that the devil had shown himself in the guise and appearance of Snæbjörn Pálsson during the period when devilry was at its peak in our district that winter. Snæbjörn was also in church here at Epiphany, at which time I felt as if there were a ball of fire hanging over my head. A man of my household named Guðmundur Ísleiksson saw these visions, as did other clairvoyants. He was struck down and carried speechless out of the church. Another girl too, likewise clairvoyant, was ushered out of the church by two persons in an almost helpless condition, Margrét Þ.[19]

This same Snæbjörn is far from having had a good reputation in these matters. Those who live in Álftafjörður will know whether there is any truth in the assertion that Snæbjörn Pálsson was excluded from church for sorcery, or that that honest priest *síra* Magnús Einarsson, after an investigation, found in his house and burned some material bearing on [magic], in his virtuous and pious zeal for the duties of his office. Likewise some of the Eyrarkirkja congregation will remember the promises that Snæbjörn made in order to receive absolution and the sacrament there. People know too what Gísli Jónsson found on Snæbjörn's breast[20] after his arrival here, especially at the first session held at Eyri in the trial of the father and son who were burned, and how he described what had been there. These signs confirm the apparitions, even though little account or notice was taken of them. Snæbjörn also fled this district later in the winter. He stayed with his brother at Langadalsströnd, while his wife and livestock stayed here until he fetched them. What was the objection raised against him in Álftafjörður? Why could he not settle on the royal property of Hattardalur which he was said to have rented? Was he not trying to avoid all court sessions, both here and elsewhere, at which the issue of magic was raised? But he has now moved north to Strandir. Many such cases are very well known, and some people in our country defend them zealously.

After Christmas that same winter, on 10 January 1657, I had an open letter[21] read to my dean, *síra* Jón Jónsson of Holt, in which I demanded that he take the measures appropriate to his office—measures explained very clearly in the letter. I did so in view of the clear fact that no response to me or my fitness or my demands was forthcoming from the secular authorities, the *sýslumenn*, even though the diabolical assaults and tangible signs, visible to all, were increasing in number and severity throughout the district. I remember that the dean wrote to me in reply that he had sent out summons and demands to the *sýslumenn*,[22] as a result of which they had responded to his summons and had arrived in Holt with Þuríður and unpacked their horses by the wall of the *stofa*. But for no good reason the summons to the assembly[23] was publicized before the meeting at Holt got down to business, and sent, along with a letter, to those [in the district] who were to attend the assembly. So all the earnestness faded away at the Holt meeting. It was reported that Halldóra Jónsdóttir, the wife of the dean *síra* Jón Jónsson, who was the aunt of the *sýslumaður* Magnús Magnússon and the sister and legitimate [heir] of Gísli Jónsson, Þorleifur Kortsson's deputy over his part of the *sýsla*, took sides with Þuríður. This became evident, and will be shown in what follows. Still, the case was dropped at Holt, so that I was not awarded any verdict, and there was no further investigation of this witchcraft case all the rest of that year. But they [Magnús Magnússon and Gísli Jónsson] did send out a hypocritical letter from Holt, very revealing in its grave style, and giving the reports and conclusions of those men.[24] Meanwhile I and my household were in torment, receiving no verdict and no further action in the case. This letter is given elsewhere, in order not to confuse the story by inserting it at this point.

On 7 April 1657, Gísli Jónsson arrived here at Eyri in Skutulsfjörður and conducted a public assembly concerning the transactions of the *hreppur*. I understood that the assembly was going to deal with accounts, taxes, and fines in the *sýsla* rather than with investigations into witchcraft—in spite of the fact that, on my farm and some other farms, storms of devilry had so escalated during the Easter season just past that, in addition to my own distress, one man of my household had been diabolically smitten to the point that for some days he lay between life and death, barely able to speak. The *sýslumenn* themselves testify to this in the *acta* (proceedings) of that assembly, having seen it with their own eyes. Also the majority of the people of our district presented a letter demanding an investigation into the cases of witchcraft that had started up anew here in Skutulsfjörður after the removal of the [two Jón Jónssons] by burning.[25] The letter gives perfectly clear evidence of all this, and was inserted into the proceedings of the assembly. But all was to no avail, though the *legenda* (records) made at this assembly do clear up the obstacles and confusion surrounding the matter if they are carefully attended to.

When I saw before my very eyes that I had been checkmated by a wretched pawn and that the chess game of witchcraft investigation was about to end again this time as it had before, I did not permit the assembly to convene on this farm [of mine], since I believed that I would derive no relief from the court procedures of these honest men—a surmise clearly attested by their acts (several of which are recorded in another place, outside this *historia*). By this ploy I wanted to find out whether the mandates of His Royal Majesty were going to be neglected and disregarded over and over again by his Icelandic ministers.[26] Indeed, I thought that in the present state of my affairs it would not be very hard to prove that some Icelandic officials were guilty of so doing—if I cared to embark on this.

And so the period of my distresses passed by. I suffered great weakness as well as many severe attacks, with intervals of respite and abatement in between. But I was never so devastated that I was unable to drag myself out of bed, however bad the attacks were. The most severe attack lasted from over Christmas into the month of *þorri*, when the number of devilish apparitions seen in our district finally dwindled. For in these later attacks by witchcraft as well as in the former ones, the demonic turmoil always increased and decreased along with apparitions, as those who were clairvoyant assured us.

Now I felt fully convinced that none of our local authorities were willing to undertake any investigation into why I and others were once again showing the same or similar symptoms [to what had been manifested before]—symptoms relating to living individuals in the same way [as the former ones did] to the men who had died. It struck me as hopeless to keep on begging for the means of relief from a quarter which I had already petitioned ad nauseam—appealing to my dean and also both *sýslumenn* and incurring perhaps the mockery of some, in addition to my sufferings and all the expense involved. So I decided to drag myself from here—from Eyri in Skutulsfjörður—to the Öxarárþing, following the fjords. Though I was in a state of such weakness that I felt hardly able to ride on horseback even the distance between neighboring farms, I set out, not knowing whether or not I would make it there and back, but taking the risk anyway, since I thought I could easily return by boat as long as I was still following the fjords. How the business of my ride to the Althing fared, as well as all the reverses and difficulties that I endured there—all this is well known to the *lögmenn* and the *lögréttumenn*. I had foreseen, as clearly as in the palm of my hand, that the representatives at the Althing would by no means do proper justice to my business, considering the little time they had and their great lack of interest. So, when I rode back home, I carried with me a short ambiguous note of assent addressed to our *sýslumenn* regarding the scrutiny of witchcraft cases.[27] The ambiguity of the document of agreement escaped my notice when it was read out at the Althing on that occasion. Moreover I did not obtain a copy of it until more than six months had passed. Even then I never heard what had been entered into the proceedings of the Althing regarding this issue, in spite of the fact that, as far as I know, such information is available at all the other assemblies and synods in our country. I would have made a verbal response before setting out homeward, had I realized that this resolution, with its open-ended phrases such as "after due process of law," served no other purpose than to be available as a "spare horseshoe," which a person is free either to attach to a horse's foot if he wants, or to throw it back into the fire and make something else out of it. Every "due process of law" that I have come across in my own torments, and in those of other fiend-afflicted individuals that I know or have known, has long since been submerged like great whales. This is especially the case with some magistrates and men in authority—as I also found when I had returned to my poor home from this trip to the Althing, and also during the period thereafter.

At that time Þuríður had come here to Kirkjuból in Skutulsfjörður, and was staying with her mother. The diabolical torments that I suffered now once more redoubled, so that neither in the *skáli* nor inside the farmhouse did any rest or sleep relieve me at night. Sometimes I tried to find sleep and relaxation in a little tent, sometimes under a sail, sometimes in the open air, and sometimes in a hay-barn. I remember one night at that time, when I had lain down in my little tent and my poor wife was beside me. She wanted to share what I suffered from being driven out of doors, as she had in all my former torments. One of our servant-girls was also with us. When I lay down in hope of sleep I felt, as usual, as if things were crawling over me, like mice creeping and jumping. However, in spite of these goings-on—a condition that I clearly recognized—I fell into a doze, sound but terribly painful, the like of which I don't think I could ever describe. It seemed to me that, had I not quickly awakened from that sleep, at least my reason and senses, if not my life itself, would have been torn from me and blotted out. But I *did* wake up in the following way: It seemed to me that I had been whipped or lashed all across my chest, but that the pain I felt did not do me any harm. I was aware, when I woke up, that it was the angel of the Lord who had struck me thus so that I should not go to pieces and be destroyed. I sat up just as I had lain down, in my underwear. But the sleep that had overtaken me was so poisonous and had given me such a shock that I could not shake it off until I went outside and stood by the church, for on these nights it was my practice to do so from time to time.

On another night of this sort, when we were lying outside in the vegetable garden under a sail, I again had to get up because of similar horrors. When I came back and stood by the hut in which my wife was lying and the girl with her, my dear Þorkatla questioned me why I was standing outside and letting myself get wet. She said she heard what seemed like rain or a heavy shower beating on the canvas roof above her. But at that time I felt not a single drop of dew falling. Such monstrous supernatural prodigies of the devil befell our household about midsummer, as soon as I returned from the Althing and up to the time of Þuríður's departure. But in the daytime I had greater tranquillity.

Magnús Magnússon the *sýslumaður*, on his return from the Althing, failed to hold the customary *leiðarþing*.[28] But I freely admit that, to the best of my knowledge, he had a valid excuse for this omission, because the Danish merchants with whom I could see that he and others had necessary business to transact were on the point of sailing away. Therefore I did not put more urgent pressure on him to carry out the investigation than I knew it would be feasible for him and his household to accede to without great inconvenience. But when I felt confident that the *sýslumaður*'s affairs were no longer in a state of emergency and that he had recovered his composure, I made my men leave off haymaking on the home field, and had myself taken by boat to meet the *sýslumaður* Magnús. This was at the time when I and my household were being severely molested by attacks of devilry. I presented my complaints before him, but he was not confident of being able to collect people to attend an assembly at the peak of the haymaking season. So the aforementioned *sýslumaður* decided on the plan of trying to get Þuríður to leave the district, whereby he could test whether the diabolical persecutions would abate or not when she was far from my home, as they had intensified when she was nearby. So he wrote her a letter, which he showed me before he sealed it. In the letter, as I remember, he invited Þuríður to move to his house and have free food and drink and freedom with respect to labor and amenities.

So I journeyed back toward home from my meeting with the *sýslumaður*, taking with me his letter to Þuríður, and sent one of my men, named Jón Jónsson, to deliver it to her. Word of her reaction to the letter came back to me, to the effect that she did not wish them to deal with her in the same way as with her father and brother. Whether or not Þuríður actually said this, the fact remains that she did not want to move anywhere. I reported this in a letter to the *sýslumaður*, whereupon he took the trouble to go to Kirkjuból [himself], and forbade Þuríður any [further] residence or sojourn in this district.

On that same journey Magnús the *sýslumaður* had a clairvoyant experience[29] at Seljabrekkunaust or Kaldaðareyri, according to what he mentioned when he stayed the night here at Eyri on that journey. On that night when he stayed here he was able to see for himself my condition. For I had been spending the nights at that period on the floor of the *baðstofa* here at Eyri lying on felt (since I could not tolerate any other bedding because of my increasing restlessness), but on that night I had to flee out of the *baðstofa* into the hay-barn. But on the second night and thereafter, when Þuríður had moved away, these devilish attacks gradually subsided.

This is the charge which Þuríður levels against me—that I was the cause of her being torn forcibly from her mother. But the facts are just as I have stated. It should be noted here that the intentions of the *sýslumaður* (Magnús Magnússon) in deciding on this ban were all to the good, in so far as my torments could be brought to an end by this expedient and I could be given rest from pursuing and scrutinizing this horrible affair further. Indeed, I had been thinking of dragging myself off to the southerly districts,[30] as long as I could stay upright, provided it were possible for me to meet once more with the higher authorities before the end of the summer. But I gave up this plan because of the relief, mentioned above, that I felt after the departure of Þuríður.

At this point the incident occurred which Sigmundur Björnsson, stepson of Sturli Bjarnason of Kirkjuból, testifies to in a statement that he wrote on a loose sheet of paper *quod intercidit*.[31]

So the summer passed, and winter began. On 20 November Magnús Magnússon the *sýslumaður* journeyed out to Bolungarvík. Because I saw that no official was ever going to make any investigation of any witchcraft cases, I once more demanded of Magnús Magnússon an investigation, sending a letter that was read to him, which sets forth the matter very clearly. This letter egged Magnús on, and he reported it to Þorleifur Kortsson. This became the *processus* and source of litigation in the first assembly,[32] which was set on foot by the sort of pressure combined with inducements[33] that is indicated by this whole narrative, with the documents, letters, and proofs here presented, along with the general awareness of the public in our district.

So I shall cut short the thread of this narrative, now that its theme and conclusion have been established.

*****

We, men and women of the household of *síra* Jón Magnússon, who have signed our names below or had them signed for us, bear witness in good conscience to the truth of this story of our priest's sufferings and of the two distinct periods of torment that befell him, according as this has been related in the preceding document of thirty-three leaves. There are no untruths in this whole document that we know of, nor to our knowledge can any be detected. This applies also to the two periods of his sufferings as described there, in so far as each of us could perceive and recognize them. This we did not only from their visible signs and his complaints, but also from the attacks that his wife and all of us have also suffered—though very little of the latter has been related in this account. Everyone on this farm (with the exception of one five-year-old girl) has been subject to these wicked and devilish attacks, struggles, and injuries, some more violently than others, some more often than others. Likewise some guests who have lodged here overnight have complained of similar experiences. As regards events mentioned in this document that occurred in other places, and which we may or may not have had the opportunity to observe ourselves, we forgo the right to testify to these, except to say that, from the reports that we have heard, we are not aware of any person contradicting a single item that bears on this narrative. As token and confirmation of this we hereby sign our names, or permit them to be signed, at Eyri, Skutulsfjörður, on 25 May 1659:

Pétur Einarsson (by his own hand)	Guðmundur Ísleiksson
Jón Jónsson (by his own hand)	Guðrún Guðmundsdóttir
Hallbjörg Ólafsdóttir	Halla Arnórsdóttir
Kristín Ólafsdóttir	Guðlaug Gunnlaugsdóttir

Notes

1. This Chapter IX covers the following material from the three printed Icelandic editions of the *Píslarsaga*:
   1914 edn., p. 71 (line 14 from bottom) to p. 90 (bottom);
   1967 edn., p. 127 (line 10 from bottom) to p. 148 (bottom);
   2001 edn., p. 104 (line 1) to p. 119 (bottom).
2. Literally, "killed by trolls" (Icel. *trölldrepin*).
3. The Icel. word used for "birth pangs" here is *kollhríðir*, literally "head-pains." This is said to be a woman's most agonizing moment of childbirth, when the baby's head emerges.
4. It is not entirely clear what court session is indicated by the "verdict of the twelve men." According to Einar Már Jónsson it is probably a court convened at Eyri in the spring of 1658 to review the accusations of *síra* Jón against Þuríður, the outcome of which was to refer the whole case to the 1658 session of the Althing at Þingvellir. The proceedings of this Eyri court session are no longer extant, but in all likelihood they contain the arguments presented by *síra* Jón in his apologetic tract *Rök og andmæli* (Arguments and Objections; see *Píslarsaga*, 2001 edn., pp. 165–180). The 1658 session of the Althing also reached no conclusion (see Appendix 5 under: *Anno* 1658). It was left to the local court at Mosvellir finally to acquit Þuríður in the autumn of 1658.
5. The events of *síra* Jón's visit to Kirkjuból along with Erlendur Ormsson, on 29 August 1656, are also related, in abbreviated form, in *síra* Jón's apologetic tract *Rök og andmæli* (see *Píslarsaga*, 2001 edn., pp. 168–170).
6. In his description of this scene as given in *Rök og andmæli* (see Note 5), *síra* Jón comments that "all those present could see that Þuríður seemed overcome by his [Erlendur's] words."
7. This is of course not the parish church at Eyri but the chapel or "half-church" attached to Kirkjuból (see Introduction, §7).

8. That is, on the right-hand side as one faced the altar from the door of the church.
9. The elder Jón Jónsson and his wife Guðrún Bjarnadóttir had at least three children other than the younger Jón Jónsson, though only two of them are named in the *Story of Sufferings*, namely Þuríður and Þorgerður.
10. The phenomena to which "the others testified" may well have been the supernatural events recorded on pp. 144, 145.
11. In her accusation against *síra* Jón (see Appendix 6) Þuríður speaks of this visit of *síra* Jón to Kirkjuból, and states that in the course of it he spat in her face, but that there were no witnesses to this act.
12. This Randíður Ólafsdóttir, the mother-in-law of the farmer at Seljaland, who was "of great consequence" in the eyes of *síra* Jón, was the widow of the deceased brother of Jón Ólafsson *Indíafari* (see Appendix 1). The latter mentions Randíður in his *Reisubók* as a "virtuous, most excellent woman" (*erleg dándiskvenna*). See *Reisubók Jóns Ólafssonar Indíafara*, p. 8; also *Píslarsaga*, 2001 edn., p. 29, Note 58.
13. Sept. 8th.
14. The beheading of John the Baptist was traditionally commemorated on August 29th.
15. This is a version of an old Icelandic proverb: "A blow causes but short-lived joy to the hand that strikes it." See for example *Njáll's Saga*, Chaps. 42, 99, 134.
16. Njáll (the main character of *Njáll's Saga*) was famous for his skill in devising legal stratagems for securing the acquittal of accused persons. The mention of Njáll here is evidently a disguised reference to the dean at Holt, *síra* Jón Jónsson, who doubtless supported Þuríður with legal advice but whom *síra* Jón Magnússon feels it undiplomatic to criticize openly.
17. For "sacramental certificate" see Appendix 1 under: Church Attendance, the Sacrament, Sacramental Certificates.
18. For the document referred to here see Note 4 of this Chapter.
19. The manuscript leaves her name in the abbreviated form "Margrét Þ." Probably this is the Margrét Þorvaldsdóttir who gave the testimony above.
20. Gísli Jónsson's search of Snæbjörn's belongings is described in greater detail on p. 76.
21. This letter, written on 9 January 1657, is the first document translated in Appendix 4.
22. The dean's letter of "summons and demands" to Magnús Magnússon and Gísli Jónsson is the second document translated in Appendix 4.
23. The "assembly" referred to here may have been the 1657 session of the Althing.
24. This "hypocritical" letter is the third document translated in Appendix 4. It gives two reasons for postponing to a more favorable time the proposed meeting at Holt to discuss *síra* Jón's accusations against Þuríður: first, the violent winter storms then prevailing in the West Fjords, and secondly, the fact that both Þuríður and Magnús Magnússon were ill at the time.
25. This letter, dated 27 March 1657, and signed by twelve individuals (including, strange to say, Jón Ólafsson the friend of the Jón Jónssons father and son) is to be found in the apologetic tract entitled *Prósessus* (see *Píslarsaga*, 2001 edn., pp. 145–146).
26. Evidently the Danish king had issued an edict forbidding the use of priests' rectories for assemblies that were likely to prove tumultuous. In his apologetic tract *Prósessus síra* Jón discusses this edict at some length, but here, in the *Story of Sufferings*, he mentions only his real reason for invoking it. (I owe this Note to Einar Már Jónsson.)
27. This "ambiguous note of assent," dated 30 June 1657, is still extant and is given in Appendix 5 of this book, under: *Anno* 1657.

28. See Appendix 1 under: *Leiðarþing*.
29. See p. 142.
30. He means that he was considering another journey to the Althing.
31. Latin for "that has been lost."
    This is the incident recounted on p. 166.
32. The "first assembly" mentioned here may refer to the court session at Eyri conjectured in Note 4 of this Chapter.
    Though the *Píslarsaga* was written in the winter of 1658-1659, *síra* Jón never mentions in it his crowning defeat—namely, the verdict of the local court at Mosvellir, which in the fall of 1658 acquitted Þuríður of the charge of sorcery brought against her by *síra* Jón.
33. The Icelandic word *mungát*, translated "inducements" in this passage, means "ale, beer," and may be intended to imply that the verdict of the Mosvellir assembly (and perhaps also of the "first assembly" conjectured in Note 4) was "assisted" by bribes of strong drink. See Ólafur Davíðsson, *Galdur og galdramál á Íslandi*, p. 218.

X. Considerations Regarding Those Later Devilish Torments, of which I Believe Þuríður Jónsdóttir to have been the Primary Instigator[1]

I lay the following account of these latest occurrences of sorcery before clear-thinking and healthy-minded persons so that they may attend carefully to what is presented here in a nutshell regarding the infestations and signs of that witchcraft and sorcery that has befallen me once again. It came upon me after I had talked with Þuríður Jónsdóttir and admonished her in the chapel at Kirkjuból. On this matter I, Jón Magnússon, a poor minister of God's word, long plagued by spells and sorceries, leave behind me this written record, inasmuch as one who occupies the noble office [of priest] has a sworn duty to do so.

I notice that some Icelandic jurists and lawyers hold, to say the least, a firm opinion regarding those who, having suffered from magic and sorcery, have once managed to win their case, identifying the wizard or witch and exposing his (or her) deeds. (However, I think that the laws of our country make it impossible for anyone to do this, judging from what I have seen of the way such cases are handled, understood, and interpreted at the present time, unless God almighty—whose every word is potent—comes to his aid with special miraculous help.) Their opinion is that such a person, whom God has once assisted, has no hope of being vindicated in an Icelandic court of law on any future occasion. It does not matter whether the one performing the [subsequent] sorcery is doing it to avenge the exposure and death of the former [sorcerer], or out of ambition and vanity in the art to see if he can do it better than the former one. [He is exempt from conviction] for the sole reason that the former sorcery was exposed and the guilty parties convicted and executed. The one who is denounced later is safe as long as any loopholes at all can be found—even if it is only the question of whether *all* the devilry [both past and present] is to be attributed to the former devil's [tools] who are now dead and no longer available to defend themselves. So, out of one half-baked precedent attaching itself somehow to a case like this, a full-blown, hard-and-fast rule is established and concluded, according to the wishes of those who believe that from now on I must never bring complaints of magic and witchcraft, no matter what sorcery may befall me or what evidence and proofs I can adduce—and all because the first practice of wizardry against me was attested and confirmed.

To my understanding, those people adopt a narrow, circumscribed line of reasoning who hold that all the acts of witchcraft that have been practiced in Skutulsfjörður on me and on others since the time when those wretched men were burned who were found responsible for the former sorceries—that all these are attributable to none other than those same wizards now burned and dead, as if they were still living and perpetually active in the devil's [work], one outbreak of demonic frenzy[2] succeeding another and so on indefinitely into the future. So these two burned sorcerers are made into scapegoats and means of defense for all other sorcerers, as if, with the removal of these two, there were no other people of that sort left. But the very narrative itself and the events as they occurred easily refute the partiality and stupidity of those [who hold this opinion], and tangibly negate it as idiotic stupidity not worthy of notice by intelligent men. Be that as it may, I must endeavor first to oppose these persons by setting forth what, as I think and feel, effectively refutes their opinion, so that their continual murmurings may be silenced. Another task is to reply suitably to those who accuse me of being too hard on Þuríður, whom I think I have established, on valid and documented grounds, as being no less than an adoptive heir of the sorceries of her father and brother. It is my intention to write about both of these opinions in what follows.

But first I want to mention an opinion regarding magic and sorcery, held even by some who are considered intelligent, that devilish attacks, worked through magical means, are likely to be irreversible, incurable, and permanent. I cannot reply to this, not being a doctor qualified to judge of these matters. I can only tell what I have experienced in support of both sides—namely, that both have happened: assaults of this sort have been cured and have also not been cured. The truth of the matter is that both have been found to take place.

I willingly go along with any good man who maintains that these wretched men who were burned did try out on me all their sorcerer's expertise, every trick of the sorcerer's art that they knew. They must have devised their magical practices not only so that I would never recover, but first and foremost so that I might suffer everlasting hurt and injury to both body and soul. It was in accordance with the law of the land—or so it is claimed by those who maintain this opinion—that I was subjected to all their magical tricks and practices. For the court gave them a period of thirteen or fourteen weeks in which to [find people willing to testify to their innocence] under oath. During this time they had leisure to practice their tricks on me and my household, as is evident from my account of the escalation of the torments that I suffered, and also from their confession. However, their intentions, plans, and endeavors completely failed them, came to nothing, and recoiled on their own heads. Little did these poor men dream that the wheel of fortune would roll out from under them, as they found happening when the Lord so exposed their works that everything came to nought—what they had planned and resolved regarding both me and themselves. Indeed, these poor men—and others who share their outlook on wizardry—had no idea that an agency which they had not bargained for would take charge of their destiny,[3] that the Lord God would intervene between them and the demons in their employ, eager to demonstrate on me, His most wretched creature, the riches of His mercy and His infinite power and omnipotence, in defiance of the devil and all the powers of darkness. And all this was clearly confirmed in two ways: the Lord apprised me of the duration of my recovery, and this was verified when I was granted a ten-week period of relief after the removal of the two Jón Jónssons. I was also apprised of the coming period of distress on the day before it began. Both of these came to pass. Moreover the Lord relieved me of my torments and granted me a marvelous restoration of health in full view of everyone, while the others were cast into the flames. Both of these facts overthrow and nullify the stupid ideas and opinions of people who put excessive trust in the devil, as if the Lord's power did not suffice to destroy or restrain his power. It is hardly surprising if the devil and the courts of hell are jubilant when blasphemies and poisonous opinions of this sort are published and blazoned abroad in various places, communities, and districts. Still, we should be thankful that this shameful outlook and belief has not already gripped more people than it has in this poor country—people who fear the devil and his fiends more than they fear the true and living God who is blessed for ever and ever.[4]

But let me answer those who maintain that the later prodigies of witchcraft that befell me came from those very sorcerers who had been burned. To this I venture to reply: One of two possibilities must be true. If the attacks of sorcery and the resulting agonies that befell me at John's Mass in the autumn were the result of the wizardry of the father and son who had been burned in Easter Week the previous spring, how is it that I was granted the gift of health and recovery beyond all expectation, so that, as I mentioned before, I could even do some work? If the magical schemes and preparations of the two who were burned had still been effective, they would not have been cut short. But since they *were* cut short, it follows that nothing of them was preserved. For a thing does not exist if its existence ceases. They planned greater and worse evils for me; they intended to murder me by their sorceries. But, as everybody can see, they did not succeed. So, just as the Lord God was capable of maintaining my life through these enormities that befell me as a result of their sorceries, so He had the power to grant me health and recovery in spite of all the devices of magical art and the power and potency of all the fiends—a fact which was made manifest to all. Thus this stupid opinion refutes itself in the light of truth and contrary experience.

This is supported by other evidence too, not least by the fact that the fiends changed their appearance. Since the time that the remaining ashes and all traces of the men who had been burned were repeatedly and meticulously cremated, the visions of devils ceased, and the afflictions that came and went along with those visions also ceased. God granted that the disturbances came to an end, both here at Eyri and elsewhere in the district, during the aforementioned period of time that my good health lasted. But after the conversation with Þuríður at Kirkjuból and other signs that appeared there at the same time and were testified to by persons of honor,[5] the demonic attacks flared up and likewise the visions of devils in the form and shape of living people, just as had previously occurred with the burned father and son. My experience leads me to regard these as certain *experimentum* (proof)—granted that at the root [of these attacks] lie the effects and injuries caused by the devil, so that second-sighted people can see the forms of the individuals involved. Otherwise we must presume *fascinum*[6] or illusions, if this is possible, which deceive only the eyes without affecting the feelings. This is my opinion, which I think I could support with documented arguments if I were to set it forth at greater length—especially if [we allow that] it has been clearly and truthfully demonstrated in the case of other sorcerers, as I have heard it reported regarding those who were burned in Strandasýsla.[7] I do not know what more weighty facts others could possibly adduce to invalidate these arguments based on experience and other grounds which I could adduce (though I have not yet done so)—particularly when they go hand in hand with several other true and provable signs of magic which have been verified and have long been apparent (and more than apparent!) in Þuríður and, I believe, several of her cronies. Who will tell me, in opposition to this, how it happens that when the visions of devils cease, then the ill effects of the torments caused by these fiends also cease? Is not the master known by his works? Does not a stream point to its source, even though it has flowed from afar?

So I think I have sufficiently demonstrated that the later deluge of wizardry is not just a residue left over from the men who were burned, but has its source elsewhere. And this will be the better confirmed as more and more documented evidence is found pointing in the contrary direction.

Perhaps an objection will be raised by someone who has read, or has heard read, the story I have written about these sorceries and [especially] the fiendish horrors that have befallen me more lately: "You have written and recorded complaints about two other events that befell you this same summer which you do *not* attribute to Þuríður.[8] Then why is she a more likely [culprit] in the later attacks than those whom you hold responsible for the earlier two?" The response to this is easy, since the occasion itself and the narrative give a very clear explanation. But now let us answer the question: assuming there were others, apart from Þuríður, whom I had documented grounds and occasions for suspecting of sorcery after the burning of the two sorcerers—which of my countrymen will dare to put me under the obligation of doing battle with [all] those devils? As far as I can tell, there is no one man qualified to undertake to uproot this evil from our country in a right and proper manner. I would be an object of pity to sensible men if I alone, a small insignificant person, should distress myself by striving to put my hand into the jaws of wolves like these—especially since those who ought to be protecting me join in beating me down. So I have decided, the law being applied and interpreted as it is in our country, to spare myself any such major undertaking, provided I can [at least] rid myself of those and similar deadly buffetings that have driven me to prosecute Þuríður. Indeed, as far as I can see, no legal cases in this country are more effectively defended than witchcraft cases. So I think that the devil can now celebrate his marriage here in Iceland whenever he wishes, for he has got himself the dowry, namely the legal support of persons who nevertheless are called Christians, along with other perquisites. Those are most likely to be rewarded who have done most to deserve it. So I have decided never again to have recourse to legal redress at the hands of those Icelandic High Court judges of whom I have had experience, or their fancy legalese regarding magic and witchcraft—no matter what opportunity I or any other of our Lord's martyrs may have for seeking legal redress. It belongs to the Lord God to determine the outcome. This is what I have to say about the first point.

What follows is valid proof that Þuríður is not only *likely* to have committed sorcery, but *is* in fact a demonstrable sorceress. It is based on telltale evidence reviewed from the past and perceptible in the present.

1°. The evidences from the past, from the ashes of her father and brother, are the following: First, she is the daughter of her father, the elder Jón, who after more than twenty years of notoriety as a magician, dating from or before the time of his acquaintance with the late Þorleifur Þórðarson, was burned to death. It was under his care that his daughter Þuríður was brought up. Also she is the legitimate sister of the younger Jón, who spent by some reports twelve years, by others fifteen, in the study of the art of sorcery—as he himself acknowledged at the session at which he was condemned to be burned. During the same period his sister Þuríður was acquiring book-learning, and it seems unlikely that she knew nothing of his stock of lore, especially if we consider the fact that he confessed and admitted to testing his magical skill on the dogs and also to having made runes for farting for the girl (as is recorded in the verdict[9]). I have talked with a mature man who lives on that farm, who told me that two women had suffered from the pranks of Jón the younger, namely, Hallný and Unnur. The same man repeated to me the following droll verse that was current on the farm at that time:

> Unnur makes her backside
> Blow in its usual way.
> In a Christian chapel
> She shouts out louder than anyone.

Who can imagine that Þuríður would have been unaware of these home-grown pranks of her brother, the younger Jón, and of other such exercises in the magician's art? And it is unlikely that the younger Jón would have played these pranks by himself without some partner.

II°. If anything can be concluded from the evidence, it is the *hardness of heart* of this Þuríður, which must be manifest to everyone. For what person, having reached the age of responsibility, could be so steeled as not to melt at the death by burning of a father and brother in a proceeding such as this one? But this is just what is truly reported about both mother and daughter at the assembly, and most of all about Þuríður, and subsequently spoken of with astonishment, as the twelve-man court has testified. At the present time very few will admit to having heard of this, especially those who were nearest to the scene, who examined, appraised, and divided the belongings of the condemned men. But their behavior[10] at that time and place confirms it. For on the very same day when the father and son were burned, when firewood, charcoal, brushwood, tar, fish oil, and all loose pieces of wood large and small (all this being mostly the property of the elder Jón Jónsson) were moved by the people of the district from the Kirkjuból farm to the place where the two men were to be burned, in full view of the mother and daughter and of the other people of that household—on that very day, while or even before the disposition of the property of the father and son was recorded, Þuríður asked the authorities to give her the silk cap trimmed with fur that had belonged to her father, and wore it on the Saturday following the burning of the father and son, as I have been told. The *sýslumenn* themselves know about this, even though they have kept quiet about it as they have about other matters bearing on the case. I think the reason for this concealment is that I myself was not up and about and so could not adduce witnesses to the facts. So I shall refrain from writing more about it here.[11] According to the admission of leading men, Guðrún, the mother of Þuríður, asked to have a velvet cap with silk ribbons which had belonged to her son, Jón Jónsson the younger. This velvet cap with copious silk ribbons Guðrún presented to Erlendur Ormsson [as thanks] for his admonitions to repentance directed at Þuríður. This indication in itself, it seems to me, would be worthy of note to any right-minded, impartial person who looks over the whole matter and cares to appraise it justly. Where will you find an adamantine heart, a hardened and unfeeling human creature, if not here? We have seen what sort of men her father and brother were. But I believe that if they had seen or heard of *her* being burned to death, *they* would at least have looked downcast. One very rarely comes across examples of this sort, even if they are disregarded in court cases of magic and sorcery, as happened here.

III°. The third indication that should be considered is what I call the "sorcery corner," the school of sorcery on that farm, which can be inferred from the proficiency shown by Jón the younger. The other pupils on that farm are not to be named, according to our Icelandic jurists, "unless ten persons come with him before an assembly [to confirm the allegation]," etc.[12] For the time being I will let their judgment prevail and keep quiet about these fellow pupils and sick limbs [of society], since they are *Plutoni dicati*[13] and so will be cosseted by people of this sort. Still, I thought that this legal clause would not be given free scope except perhaps in time of war,[14] when such clauses would be enforced by [a decree of] the authorities. If this evidence based on sameness of domicile is indeed nonsensical, then I think it makes little difference where a person settles with his possessions, or whether he spends his years among wicked people or devout. And yet prudent men have considered it a matter of no little importance that one should move in good society rather than bad—a principle that is certainly to be gleaned from the word of God.

IV°. As indications of [Þuríður's] guilt there are insinuations gleaned from the father and son,[15] which I have brought out and caused to be inserted in the verdict of the district court. Among other evidences of Þuríður's practice of magic there are the following confirmations:

1°. I think it most unlikely that these utterances were lies or fancies, or were openly attributed to the father and son without any occasion or basis in fact. I think it more likely that the identity of those who heard these utterances from their mouths has been suppressed, as I believe I have noticed in other similar and yet verifiable situations. For I know that partisanship carries great weight, as I will soon show in Þuríður's case.

2°. Another matter, on account of which I submitted these insinuations to the district court without any backing, was that I wanted to test whether or not the authorities would be willing to perform the duties of their office and take up what they themselves had [formerly] ignored. They had not shown themselves willing to make any investigation during the nearly one and a half years since I had demanded that they take measures, or even to make an outward show of doing so. At that time I did not know that I—not to speak of the truth itself—would have to suffer for this neglect. Had there been an investigation as soon as I was subjected to these new tortures, when I asked and summoned the *sýslumenn* to make an inquiry and investigation of the matter while the recent case of the Jón Jónssons, father and son, was fresh in everybody's memory, it would have been easier to report these words which are now open to question since I alone in the face of many opponents will not be able to pursue them effectively. Above all, the time elapsed since then, along with other contributing causes of the neglect, has erased the evidence.

3°. My purpose was as follows: I realized, from the protective walls put around Þuríður, that the case would encounter no little delay in coming before the higher authorities and being chewed over by them. So it was a quite deliberate tactic on my part, that these vague hints, which many persons testify to having heard spoken or repeated from the lips of the Jón Jónssons father and son, should be in danger of suppression when I came before the High Court. For in this way it could be put to the test whether sorcery was going to be defended or impugned within the precincts of the National Assembly and the Öxará Lawcourt,[16] and so it would be determined whether concealment and cover-up would have a sweeter taste when applied to sorcery than to other wicked acts. In this way I might be of benefit and service to some people, in return for the harm that has been done to me. For the obliteration of sorcery, if it is to be properly carried out, will depend in large measure on observance of this point.

V°. Þuríður's astonishment that I had not lost my life, or at least my wits, should be attended to and not disregarded—or so it seems to me, if it is an established fact. I shall have more to say about this elsewhere.[17]

VI°. As regards books on sorcery, my suspicions continue to be the same as those recorded in the verdict and elaborated on elsewhere.

VII°. Thoughts of revenge for the burning of her father and brother are more imperative for Þuríður than for any other surviving relative of theirs.

VIII°. As regards the cow belonging to Margrét Arnórsdóttir:[18] honest people acknowledge that it had been stroked and handled by Þuríður Jónsdóttir, and that after some weeks it was killed by sorcery; moreover, that Margrét herself—so she believes—suffered injury in her arm and chest from an evil spirit which afflicted her with unnatural illness for some days afterwards. She said that it came over her when she was intending to do something to help the cow—a fact that some still remember. People of the West Fjords still have the vague recollection of more than a few similar effects produced on sheep and cows in the days of the the late Þorleifur Þórðarson.[19] So this sign ought to be noted.

IX°. I cannot but nurse suspicion because of the terrible attack that I suffered in connection with Þuríður's journey when she passed nearby. I suffered this attack on a Monday, the day after the Sunday when Þuríður was passing near here. This was the same journey on which she stroked the cow and so forth. I and various others remember the occasions when the two Jón Jónssons passed nearby, and how the diabolical assaults increased as they came near here and abated on the arrival of other people.

These observations and conclusions I call [genuine] evidence.[20] To my mind they associate Þuríður, with greater probability than other persons unconnected and unrelated to these signs and evidence, with this later sorcery that attacked me since the former diabolical wizardry was laid to rest along with its tokens, visions of witches and demons, and other devilry. With my weak understanding I have tried to have these evidences evaluated elsewhere in the light of our country's laws. But last summer, in 1658, I was not able to raise the issue at the Öxará Assembly [i.e., the Althing], or to describe it to the judges who preside in that place. For I notice that other business is more congenial to them than extirpating sorcery from our country (assuming that I am dealing with generally clearheaded persons). For this reason I believe that this evil will proceed apace and make unimpeded headway unless the Lord Himself intervenes with hand outstretched to help us.

The other evidences, which seem to me more convincing, more accessible to eyewitnesses, and directly observable, are the following:

I°. When I had spoken words of wholesome advice, admonition, and warning to Þuríður, I was attacked with such violent sorcery and demonic torments that they became known and evident to my household and to the whole parish and district. It happened just as it had when I spoke words of exhortation and God's word to the Jón Jónssons, the father and brother of Þuríður. The same manifestations of sorcery were inflicted upon me at my meeting with her as at my former meetings with them. Also, in my opinion Þuríður's posture of prayer when she fell on her knees by the chest so strangely—in which position I think it most likely that she was mumbling some magical spell—points in the same direction, being similar to what the younger Jón Jónsson her brother displayed when he prostrated himself on the threshold of the farm door, bowing his head on his arm as if he had been saying his prayers.[21] This is how Þuríður's behavior struck me. I also suspect that the same meaning attaches to the darkness surrounding Þuríður which I saw in the chapel and which I told her of, pointing to it with my foot.[22] Also I think that the very same meaning must be attributed to the vision of sparks of fire which Sigurður Jónsson declares in his testimony that he saw issuing from the farm door, when Þuríður was by herself indoors after our parting in the church—or so it appears to me. Likewise to Margrét Þorvaldsdóttir's vision of the portent that she affirms that she saw above the farm at that same time; and also of the form of a dog that she says she saw following me, in conformity with my own fancy about the unclean thing that I felt to be with me on my journey.[23]

II°. Another significant item, I would say, was the silence of Þuríður at the very plausible words of Erlendur,[24] and on top of that the gift made to Erlendur by Guðrún Bjarnadóttir, the mother of Þuríður, and affirmed by witnesses (Sigurður Jónsson, Örnólfur Jónsson, and Magnús Jónsson). This gift was the velvet cap with silk ribbons[25] which had belonged to her son, the younger Jón Jónsson, and which she had asked the *sýslumenn* to allow her to keep and cherish. If in addition a feast took place, many will have taken note of lesser indications.

III°. Then there is Þuríður's extremely hasty flight from her mother's [house] at the approach of winter. Nobody whom I have spoken to at that farm expected it, and I have not heard any reason given for it. It was her prompt reaction to the tricks of sorcery that she practiced on me on Friday, which was John's Mass.[26] At daybreak and during Saturday, the day after, she solicited and obtained an escort, applying first to Magnús Jónsson and Hallur Tindsson of Engidalur—according to their report—and afterwards to Sturli Bjarnason of Kirkjuból. To the latter, as I have heard, she gave a choice grindstone in payment for his services as an escort.

IV°. Palpably and demonstrably attributable to this Þuríður are the tricks and signs of magic that affected these men, Magnús Jónsson and Hallur Tindsson. Both of them were then living at Engidalur and had refused to serve as escorts for Þuríður. They were attacked by the devil and tormented with strange nocturnal terrors and phobias, according to their testimony. Where can there be a closer parallel between Þuríður and the two men, her father and brother, who were burned? When individuals refused to support [her father and brother] with oaths confirming [their innocence], the devil straightway pounced upon them with similar terrors, phobias, and nocturnal attacks. This, I think, is genuine, irrefutable evidence that sorcerers are at work, when the devil so perceptibly goes to their aid, plays their game, and resents and avenges any injury done to them as if he were their most loyal friend.

V°. Then there is the poisonous touch or contact or brush described in the testimony of Jón Þorsteinsson.[27] He states that, when he was riding with Þuríður from Tunga to Kirkjuból (this is twice the average distance between neighboring farms), he felt pain on his flesh under the spot where Þuríður was holding on to him. I have heard more of this sort of thing from honorable persons, some of whom live in Önundarfjörður. This phenomenon, though it is dismissed by those who protect sorcery, is easily recognizable in venomous animals and is natural to sorcerers. These indeed have, all of them, become venomous creatures, merged with the devil himself. They are like apostles and mighty potentates in the devil's kingdom, able to slay and wound by their mere touch and contact, just as Christ's apostles were able to heal and give life by theirs.

N.B. Margrét Arnórsdóttir reports that Þuríður went to Hnífsdalur on Ascension Day. The cow died half a month before midsummer.

N.B. One of the two Jón Jónssons, when he was being held prisoner in the kitchen at Eyri, reached out with his foot toward a goat that was indoors, and I was told that five days later the goat lay dead.

VI°. [Then there is] the fiend's change of garb. After Satan had put aside the clothing and appearance of the Jón Jónssons who had been burned, the father and brother of Þuríður, he changed his clothing and did not recoil from putting on a skirt, a long woman's cloak, and an apron, so that he looked just like Þuríður Jónsdóttir. Sometimes he wore a large wide-brimmed hat, or a hood down to the eyebrows, sometimes with a fringe and a tassel hanging from the back of the neck. As she changed her apparel so did Satan, copying her. The same happened with the two men who were burned and are dead, as well as with others who are still living and who by all indications, I think, would turn out to be of the same ilk as Þuríður if the matter were faithfully and devoutly investigated. But the evil one gave that dignity to Þuríður which he did not grant to her two family members, the father and son who were burned, that he rode like a knight in her likeness, on a brown stallion or horse, just as she had ridden from Kirkjuból to Holt in Önundarfjörður. I have not heard it mentioned that the father and son had done any riding after they had poured themselves out into the devil's chamber pots with their sorcery aimed at my destruction. If this piece of evidence could be established for the three sorcerers who were unmasked in Strandasýsla[28] as well as for the two relatives of Þuríður who were burned here in Skutulsfjörður, it could not be dismissed as irrelevant, however limited [in applicability] it might prove to be. It is no wonder that evil beings are the darlings of the powerful, since this is the case [at least] in the West Fjords![29]

In considering this evidence, one must exclude *fascinum* (bewitchments) in which it is only the eyes that are deceived, without any of the feelings or sufferings or other symptoms that should accompany it. But with this exclusion I believe, from my own experience, that it is a sure and most incontrovertible *experimentum* (direct evidence) of this kind of sorcery.[30] True, it does not cover all those situations from which valid evidence can be deduced according to [other] examples well known from ancient times in our country. For example, when evil beings are raised by heathen sorcery, it is said that the same body is raised with the same appearance. *Item*, when the witch raised Samuel, [saying:] "I see gods rising from the earth."[31] From this I gather that when a person employs his own body—his hair, nails, blood, and so forth—in the practice of wizardry, so that Satan lacks nothing that he demands, then the latter is parading [as it were] in the bridal finery which a baptized Christian person has handed over to him. In that [finery] Satan can celebrate his triumph, to the person's greater degradation, in the face of the living God and His holy angels and as it were to their chagrin. For the angels of God rejoice at the repentance of a sinner,[32] *et vice versa* [they are grieved when he falls into sin].

VII°. The *sýslumaður* Magnús, as an experiment, forbade Þuríður to reside here, to see whether my sufferings would abate when she departed as they had intensified when she was nearby. When the *sýslumaður* had issued that ban, Þuríður asked Sturli Bjarnason to escort her over the mountain. But he refused because of the urgency of getting in his hay crop, since he had no one capable of acting as her guide except himself and his stepson Sigmundur Björnsson. Subsequently that same Sigmundur Björnsson suffered an accident and injury to his hand, which stopped him from working and caused him more delay and inconvenience than if he had crossed the mountain with Þuríður. His testimony affirms this in the clearest terms. When one considers this event, and compares it with what one learns of other similar acts of other sorcerers, it strikes me that here is one of those genuine pieces of sorcery demonstrating the open fellowship of Þuríður with the devil.

VIII°. The same applies to the magic practiced in Önundarfjörður on Bjarni Snorrason. When Þuríður was in Holt, he read out in her presence the open letter that I had written to my dean,[33] in which I called on him to do the duty of his office in the case of the suspicions regarding Þuríður. Whom should I blame for that wizardry other than Þuríður, to whom the affair pointed, as the contents of the letter show?

IX°. In the ninth place, witchcraft and sorcery on the part of Þuríður was manifested in the visible events themselves, since the demonic commotion in our district escalated on her arrivals here and died down on her departures, as anyone can see who looks at the narrative with an eye to comparison. The trip to Kirkjuból also attests this, and likewise the events of the assembly, as witnessed in writing both by the authorities and those present at the assembly.[34] It was also [proved] when the *sýslumaður* Magnús delivered the prohibition to her, testing whether these events were of her doing or not, by forbidding her to live or to sojourn in this district. The test proved the truth of the matter without further ado.[35]

I have now set forth satisfactory arguments showing that the sorcery that was practiced on me when I went to Kirkjuból, and assailed me the same evening that I returned from there, was *not* an aftereffect of the sorcery of the same men who had been burned—the men convicted of the former witchcraft that had assaulted me and my household and also other farms in the district. I have presented nine items of evidence which point to Þuríður and fit her to a tee. In view of these I say that this Þuríður is more liable and likely to be involved than other persons to whom this evidence does not apply—the more likely indeed as this evidence is stronger, weightier, and more compelling. It is my hope that this will be allowed and admitted in my favor by fair-minded people following the authority of the court.

In addition I have presented nine other visible signs, more weighty than the other evidence. In the light of these signs and acts of sorcery performed and practiced on me and others I believe, first, that Þuríður, daughter of that proven warlock Jón Jónsson, is unmasked and proven guilty by virtue of the cogency of the proofs adduced and inserted there. But what I have gathered is not even one half of the miscellaneous evidences for witchcraft that I believe would come to light if one were to get to the bottom of the matter. But these evidences have been suppressed by those who defend Þuríður—who are of no little consequence in the West Fjords—as well as being ignored by others who might be aware of them, taking advantage of our country's legal procedures, and who are at the bottom of the frightful risks attending lawsuits against vicious men.[36] I can see that all this is making headway here in Iceland uncurbed. Indeed, the hooks and fishing gear that might be dragging it from the depths have not made their way to the harbor in the West Fjords where I have lived for the past several years. For [such gear, to be effective,] would have to be very cunningly fashioned.[37]

Nevertheless I think that I have said enough. Any person who bears all the distinctive marks that this Þuríður bears cannot escape the appellation of sorcerer, whatever other title he may bear. At least this is my considered opinion.

Perhaps some obstinate adversaries may insist as follows: "With all your testimony you have not yet proved that Þuríður is a witch." To this I would reply: In this *objection* you raise two points at the same time. The first of them involves the account and truth of the narrative. For this I am responsible, as long as it is in accordance with the *terminus* (bounds) and limitations, power, and authority of all the relevant laws in so far as they concern me and me alone. The second point concerns other people, those who are involved in such cases, both in the investigation and in the procedural matters, such as their presentation in syllogisms, in accordance with the strictest format of the laws.[38] Assuming that both of these aspects are equally well constituted on my part and on theirs, I can draw no other rational conclusion than that Þuríður is a proven sorceress. I think that, to consign her to the flames, only one step of the platform remains to be mounted.

All clear-sighted men can see that I have made some efforts in these sorcery cases—though with relatively little hope or expectation on my part. But as for what others may have done, I have no awareness or perception of it. As concerns the court session that in my view should properly have been expected to act in this sorcery case, I can see nothing whatever except people stumbling, as it were, through dense clouds of smoke, like a creature which, dazed by ocean breakers, bobs now toward and now away from the shore, not knowing what direction it should take. Though it sounds like bragging, I by no means lack confidence to demonstrate and prove my case, even before men of greater stature than those here at the Öxará *lögrétta*.[39] I am ready to rise up somehow from the humiliation[40] to which people see me reduced by the conduct of the Þuríður affair, and stand erect once again. I would indeed be ready, were it not for the *nexus naturae* (natural bonds) and obligation that I feel for my country and also certain individuals here within it, notably Árni [Oddsson] the *lögmaður*— not so much because of *his* benevolence toward me as that of his most noble parents,[41] whose acts of kindness toward me I am bound to remember always. But I have been waiting a while, not so much out of diffidence or timidity because of my poverty and obscurity (*siquidem furor arma ministrat*[42]), but out of circumspection, in order to spare myself from having new pains added to old. To cast down and debase this country of ours brings no honor or fame. Indeed, to do so is quite within the power of the most insignificant of men,[43] since the country has already succumbed.[44] I would much more gladly employ my weak powers to support and bolster it, crushed as it is under the burden of such sins and abominations as prevail at present—especially those that relate to demons[45] and sorcery. Such a task, I think, would be more arduous than all the labors of Hercules, and greater than any degree of fame [could reward]. But this is beyond the power of the people of our country to accomplish, so long as the wounds of our poor country are kept open by the weapons of iron that are obvious to every right-minded person.

Hereby I commit all honest men to God.

Notes

1. This Chapter X covers the following material from the three printed Icelandic editions of the *Píslarsaga*:
    1914 edn., p. 91 (line 1) to p. 108 (bottom);
    1967 edn., p. 149 (line 1) to p. 168 (bottom);
    2001 edn., p. 121 (line 1) to p. 135 (bottom).
2. The Icelandic word for "demonic frenzy" here is *phýtonsskapur*. See Chap. I, Note 15, and Chap. IV, Note 15.
3. Where this translation reads "agency which they had not bargained for," the Icelandic text has two idioms: *skáld var í skipinu*, and *skröggur í skjali*, both of which convey the idea of something quite unexpected coming out of the background and directing the course of events.
4. This strong faith, that the power of God far surpasses the power of the devil, is shared by *síra* Jón with his enlightened contemporary Bishop Brynjólfur Sveinsson of Skálholt. See the latter's conviction expressed on p. 19.
5. See pp. 144, 145.
6. Latin for "bewitchment." Compare the English "fascination."
7. In 1654, a year before the outbreak of sorcery in *síra* Jón's parish of Eyrarkirkja, three men were burned to death as convicted sorcerers in the remote community of Trékyllisvík in Strandasýsla, a district of the West Fjords. They were accused of having used sorcery to cause such hysterical outbursts among the women of the community during church services that the latter had to be discontinued.
8. See p. 133.
9. The reference here is to p. 110. See also Appendix 1 under: Magical Spells and Staves, [5].
10. I.e., the behavior of Þuríður and her mother.
11. A more emphatic description of the "hardhearted" behavior of Þuríður is given by *síra* Jón in his apologetic tract *Rök og andmæli* (see *Píslarsaga*, 2001 edn., p. 166). There we read (under heading II):

    "Next, I and other right-minded persons must regard the impudence and adamantine brazenness shown by the aforementioned Þuríður (or courage, as some may be pleased to call it) as an ugly piece of evidence [against her] which shocked everybody and caused great astonishment. For when she heard and realized that her father and brother were burned on the same day in one fire, Þuríður laughed. And she is said to have dangled her feet over a box and shown high spirits, amusing herself and joking. This feminine ostentation (according to what I have heard) produced the utmost astonishment among the many people, both near and far, who heard about it. It seems that there were kindhearted people unrelated [to the Jón Jónssons] who wept and grieved over the tragic event. To find a comparable case I think one must search in stories from antiquity. Even the evil spirit himself is said to have had more loyalty toward his friends. It is like [the story of] the witch Medea—though *she* did have some motive for her disloyalty [toward her children]. Fortunately, such an example of unfeelingness is rarely to be found in a normal human being."

This comparison of Þuríður with the notorious witch Medea of Greek mythology reveals the full intensity of *síra* Jón's antipathy to the unfortunate young woman.

12. The reference here is to the section *Um fullréttisorð ok úkvæðisorð* (On Damaging and Offensive Language) of the chapter on *Mannhelgi* in the *Jónsbók* (p. 64 of the 1970 edition of the *Jónsbók*). The opening clause of this section runs as follows:

"No one, whether a *sýslumaður* or other person, shall tell anyone else that he has been disgraced [by offensive language] unless ten persons come with him before an assembly and verify his allegation as the law requires. That is, two must swear, and eight must verify his allegation. The two [who swear] must take the book in their hands and swear as follows: 'We place our hand on the holy book and swear that we have heard these words spoken, but we do not know whether they are true or not.'"

The requirement that ten people should concur in naming other pupils of the "school of magic" is also mentioned in *Rök og andmæli* (see 2001 edn. of *Píslarsaga*, p. 173, line 16).

13. Latin for "given over to the devil."
14. A further explanation of "except in time of war" is given in *Hugleiðingar mínar* (see 2001 edn. of *Píslarsaga*, p. 187, middle paragraph). According to this explanation, the "war" here is the war against sorcerers, who are the agents of the kingdom of Satan.
15. These "insinuations" are not explicitly quoted here. But, as Einar Már Jónsson points out in Note 13, p. 167 of his French translation of the *Píslarsaga*, they are evidently the same as those mentioned in *síra* Jón's third apologetic tract *Rök og andmæli* (see *Píslarsaga*, 2001 edn. pp. 166–167): (a) the elder and younger Jón Jónssons said that *síra* Jón's sufferings would not abate even if they were burned; (b) they hinted that something would be left behind in Skutulsfjörður even if they departed; (c) the elder Jón Jónsson had said that after him his daughter Þuríður would also be burned.
16. I.e., the Althing and the *lögrétta*.
17. See *Rök og andmæli*, *Píslarsaga*, 2001 edn., p. 167.
18. See p. 137.
19. See Appendix 1 under: Þorleifur Þórðarson.

According to Dr. Sigurbjörn Einarsson, "vague recollection" is a deliberate understatement, implying that in fact the West Fjords people had very vivid memories of the feats of sorcery practiced by Þorleifur Þórðarson.

20. For *síra* Jón's view of the cognitive status of this "genuine evidence," see Note 125 of the Introduction.
21. See p. 127.
22. See p. 138.

23. For the visions of Sigurður Jónsson and Margrét Þorvaldsdóttir see pp. 144, 145.
24. See p. 138.
25. See p. 160.
26. August 29th, the day on which the beheading of John the Baptist was commemorated.
27. See pp. 143, 144.
28. See Note 7 of this Chapter.
29. I.e., since an evil being like Þuríður is pampered by powerful people in the West Fjords, why should she not also be pampered by a powerful being like the devil?
30. The mixed Latin-Icelandic original of the phrase "of this kind of sorcery" is: *þess galdralags in specie.*
    The evidence referred to here is of course the appearance of the devil in the likeness and garb of the sorcerer.
31. *I Samuel* 28:13.
32. *Luke* 15:7.
33. *Síra* Jón Jónsson, the priest at Holt in Önundarfjörður, was at the time of Þuríður's flight to Holt the dean whose jurisdiction included *síra* Jón Magnússon's parish at Eyri. See Appendix 1 under: Jón Jónsson, priest and dean at Holt.
34. Is this the assembly (Icel. *þing*) conjectured in Note 4 of Chapter IX?
35. "Without further ado." Lit., "as if one were speaking to someone."
36. *Síra* Jón is probably referring here to those who, insisting on the letter of the law, allow vicious sorcerers a period of freedom in which to try to collect compurgators who will swear to their innocence, and who use that period to practice black magic on their victims.
37. "Would have to be very cunningly fashioned." Lit. "would have to be dwarfs' work." "Dwarfs' work" was an ancient epithet for works of rare art and cunning.
38. Presumably in the 17th century, as well as in the Saga Age and at the present time, correct wording was essential and cases could be thrown out of court for errors in procedure or presentation.
39. I.e., at the lawcourt at Þingvellir, where *síra* Jón is presumably writing these words.
40. "Humiliation." Lit. "squatting position" (Icel. *hnipur*).
41. Árni Oddsson (1592–1665) was a son of Oddur Einarsson, bishop of Skálholt from 1589 to 1630 who fostered *síra* Jón Magnússon after the death of his mother and got him admitted to the Skálholt school. Árni Oddsson's brother was Gísli Oddsson, his father's successor as bishop of Skálholt. Árni himself was appointed *lögmaður* for the southern and eastern quarters in 1632. Most of his life he showed himself to be ambitious and quarrelsome, and it was all that his fellow officials could do to pacify him and settle his quarrels. But in his old age he calmed down and became humble, devout, and public-spirited. (See Páll Eggert Ólason, *Saga Íslendinga, vol. 5, Sautjánda öld*, pp. 109–112.)
42. A Latin proverb meaning: "For frenzy lends weapons."
43. "The most insignificant of men." Lit. "buntings" (Icel. *tittlingum*).
44. Einar Már Jónsson, in the Introduction to his French translation of the *Píslarsaga*, suggests that this final paragraph of the *Story of Sufferings* contains a hint of *síra* Jón's original intention to appeal the acquittal of Þuríður to the king of Denmark, over the head of the Icelandic Althing, and also hints at his reason for deciding finally against doing this. See Note 97 of the Introduction.
45. The Icelandic word for "demons" here is *phýtonsskapur*. See Note 15 of Chap. I.

Appendix 1

Explanations of Historical Terms, Place-Names, Persons, Etc., Relevant to The Story of Sufferings

Æðigaldur *(Madness Magic)*

A magical spell (or type of spells) used by 17th-century Icelandic black magicians, by which the victim against whom the spell is directed is made to lose his wits (Icel. *missa vitið*) for the time being, becoming mentally incapable of performing the ordinary duties of life. An example of the alleged effect of *æðigaldur* is found on pp. 72, 73, where *síra* Jón becomes temporarily incapable of conducting the church service.

Baðstofa *(Communal Room)*

In early (12th-century) Icelandic farmhouses the *baðstofa*, as its name indicates, was the bath-room, where the household could enjoy a sauna-type bath. It would naturally be the warmest room in the house. As the forests began to disappear and firewood ran short, the *baðstofa* soon began to be used for sleeping and indoor work, and in the 17th century it was usually the largest, warmest, and most important room in the house. Here would be the beds where most of the farm household would sleep (other than the master and mistress, who usually had a smaller private room), and where most of the indoor work (such as carding, spinning, and knitting) would be carried on.

Calendar

All dates are given in the *Story of Sufferings* according to the (old style) Julian calendar, which in Denmark and its dependencies (including Iceland) was not officially replaced by the (new style) Gregorian calendar until 1700. To convert 17th-century dates from the old to the new style one must add 10 to the old style date. Thus an event dated in this book as occurring on 20 October 1655 would have occurred on 30 October 1655 by the new style (modern) calendar, i.e., ten days further into winter than would appear if one did not take account of the reform of the calendar.

In official documents the Julian calendar was used in Iceland in Jón Magnússon's day. But in the old rural Icelandic society a different calendar of months was also in use, in which two main seasons were recognized, summer and winter. The former began on the first Thursday after April 18th, and consisted of six summer months. The latter began on the first Saturday after October 21st, and consisted of six winter months. The only month of the old rural calendar that is mentioned by name in the *Story of Sufferings* is the winter month of *þorri*, which ran from the latter part of January to the latter part of February.

Church Attendance, the Sacrament, Sacramental Certificates

The 17th century (at least the first half of it) was a period in which the outward signs of piety and religious devotion were very marked. Bishop Guðbrandur Þorláksson (bishop of Hólar from 1571 to 1627) and his contemporary Bishop Oddur Einarsson (bishop of Skálholt from 1589 to 1630) made strenuous efforts to kindle the spirit of Lutheran devotion throughout the land. Special emphasis was laid on church attendance (fines being imposed on households which for no good reason failed to attend church services on holy days). Again and again episcopal decrees were issued urging priests in their sermons to teach their flocks about prayer and the sacraments, and on the need for awareness of sin and for repentance.

The original Lutheran teaching had been that congregations should partake of the Lord's Supper at every celebration of the mass—or at least as often as possible. But soon, for practical reasons, this requirement was reduced to the reception of the sacrament at least four times a year (in spring, summer, autumn, and winter). Even so, the common people of Iceland showed an extreme reverence for the Lord's Supper. One important feature of the celebration of the sacrament at that period was that no one was allowed to partake of the sacrament unless he or she had first made a personal confession of sin and had been absolved by the priest. (See Helgi Þorláksson, *Sautjánda öldin*, pp. 56–59; *Kristni á Íslandi*, vol. 3, pp. 91, 171–174.)

In connection with the reception of the sacrament, one should mention here one custom prevalent in Jón Magnússon's time: If a person left his home parish to stay for a while in another parish, he would not be permitted to receive the sacrament in the latter parish unless he could present a "sacramental certificate" (Icel. *sakramentisvottorð*) from the priest of his home parish, stating that he was in good standing and fit to receive the sacrament (see for example *Kristni á Íslandi III*, p. 103). Indeed, receiving the sacrament was considered a mark of one's good moral standing in the community.

This custom plays the following role in our story: Þuríður Jónsdóttir, suspected by *síra* Jón Magnússon of practicing sorcery against him, had fled from her home at Kirkjuból in September 1656 and taken refuge with the family of the dean, *síra* Jón Jónsson, at Holt. Wishing to receive the sacrament at Holt but having no sacramental certificate, she visits Eyri that winter, before Christmas, with the hope of inducing *síra* Jón Magnússon to give her one, but evidently she failed of her purpose. (See p. 143.) However, in the following May (1657), a synod of five priests met at Holt and, evidently setting little store by *síra* Jón Magnússon's accusations, gave her special authorization to receive the sacrament (see Appendix 4, 4th Document).

Deacon (Icel. djákni), Choir Deacon (Icel. kórdjákni)

Generally speaking, each parish had only one priest serving in it, and he would need much help from lay people in the running and supervision of different aspects of parish life, especially in the conduct of church services. In 17th-century Iceland any layman to whom fixed duties had been assigned in the running of the parish was called a deacon. (At that time the post of deacon was not one to which ordination was required, as it is now.) The responsibilities of deacons were various. Some (who at a later period were called *meðhjálparar*) had duties that were both liturgical and disciplinary. In preparation for the church service they had to light the altar candles and any other candles that were needed for illumination, and also to make sure that sacramental wine was available if the Lord's Supper was to be celebrated. They helped the priest to vest and unvest, and read opening and closing prayers. They served as ushers, showing visitors to their proper places, kept dogs out of the church, and saw to it that people did not step out of the church during the sermon to take a nip of *brennivín* (the favorite strong alcoholic drink consumed by Icelanders). Other deacons had duties which were confined to the chancel or choir (Icel. *kór*) of the church and the time of services. They recited some of the prayers, or, if they had good voices, they led in the singing of hymns. These deacons (like those of the first kind) would sit in the chancel by the altar, as distinct from the rest of the congregation who sat in the nave (Icel. *framkirkja*), and they were referred to as choir deacons. (For this and further information on the organization of church life in the 17th century, see *Kristni á Íslandi*, vol. 3, pp. 242–246.)

It is interesting to note that in *síra* Jón Magnússon's parish of Eyri both the Jón Jónssons, father and son, were choir deacons (see p. 65), who sat in the chancel during services. They probably had good voices and helped lead the singing.

Dean (Icel. prófastur), Deanery (Icel. prófastsdæmi)

In the 17th century Iceland was divided for ecclesiastical purposes into 17 geographical districts called *deaneries*. Church affairs in each deanery were supervised by a *dean*, who was appointed from among the parish priests in that deanery. The duties of a dean included visiting and inspecting each parish in his deanery every so often, and reporting to his bishop on his findings. It was also his duty to summon synods of the priests of his deanery when necessary, and to preside over them as deputy of the bishop.

At the time of the events of this book the dean, in whose jurisdiction *síra* Jón Magnússon's parish lay, was *síra* Jón Jónsson, priest of the parish of Holt. In May 1657 he convened a synod of five priests to discuss the question of whether Þuríður Jónsdóttir should be allowed to receive the sacrament even though she had no sacramental certificate from her home parish. (See this Appendix under: Church Attendance ....)

Erlendur Ormsson

The role of Erlendur Ormsson in the sorcery trials recounted in this book is somewhat mystifying. He probably played a more important role than *síra* Jón is willing to admit. Other sources declare that he was a vagrant from Snæfellssýsla, a priest's son but without formal education, a great talker, and known to have practiced magic himself. He pretended to be endowed with prophetic gifts. (See Matthías V. Sæmundsson, "Galdur og geðveiki," *Píslarsaga*, 2001 edn., p. 364.) He evidently made a good impression on *síra* Jón, who admired his apparent intellect, insight, godliness, and hatred of all sorcery. (See *Píslarsaga*, 2001 edn., pp. 171.) Nor was *síra* Jón the only person to be impressed by him. In April 1656 he called on Bishop Brynjólfur Sveinsson at Skálholt, evidently to procure from him a certification of the genuineness of his (Erlendur's) spiritual gifts and understanding of the scriptures. The bishop gave him an excellent commendation for Christian piety and aversion to sorcery, but refrained from certifying him as a "prophet" (see *Úr bréfabókum Brynjólfs biskups Sveinssonar*, pp. 64, 65).

This was the man whom *síra* Jón seems to have taken as his principal witness in his case against Þuríður Jónsdóttir (see Note 89 of the Introduction).

But by that time the authorities apparently were suspicious of Erlendur's testimony, and at the 1658 session of the Althing he was ordered either to substantiate his testimony or to face punishment for making irresponsible accusations (see Appendix 5). This suspicion is probably the reason why *síra* Jón plays down Erlendur's role in the witchcraft trials.

Ruth C. Ellison's article "A Prophet Without Honour: The Brief Career of Erlendur Ormsson" (see Bibliography) gives a clear account of what is known about Erlendur Ormsson.

Evening Wake

The evening wake (Icel. *vaka* or *kvöldvaka*) was the period of the day between the setting of the sun and bedtime. It would of course have been an especially lengthy and important part of the day during the winter season. During the evening wake the family would gather in the *baðstofa* and do all sorts of indoor work, such as the manufacture of clothing from wool or skins. Some literate member of the family might read aloud from an entertaining book (such as an old saga), and the House Reading (q.v.) would also form a part of the evening's program.

Gísli Jónsson (died 1679)

Gísli Jónsson, like his nephew the *sýslumaður* Magnús Magnússon, was a member of the Svalbarð family, the most influential family in the West Fjords. At the time of the events of this book he was deputy (*lögsagnari*) for Þorleifur Kortsson (who was his wife's sister's husband) in the northern part of Ísafjarðarsýsla, and later himself became *sýslumaður*. He was said to be very rich (by the Icelandic standards of that time).

Grágás

This was the book of laws in force in Iceland during the Commonwealth Period (i.e., before Iceland lost its independence in 1263). Though it was superseded by the *Jónsbók* after Norway took control of Iceland, it was still being quoted as authoritative even in Jón Magnússon's time. For our present purposes the most important part of *Grágás* is the *Kristinréttur* or *Kristinna laga þáttur*, a collection of laws governing the Church and the practice of Christianity.

Hallgrímur Pétursson (1614–1674)

The great Icelandic poet-priest, a contemporary of *síra* Jón Magnússon (though there is no evidence that they ever met or corresponded with each other). His *Passion Hymns* are said to have had more influence on Icelandic Christianity than any other book except the Bible.

Hólar

The seat of the northern diocese, located in the mountain-ringed valley of Hjaltadalur in the Skagafjörður district of northern Iceland. The diocese, along with a school designed primarily for the training of prospective priests, was founded in 1106. The diocese and school lasted until 1801, when the two separate dioceses of Hólar and Skálholt were abolished and replaced by a single diocese embracing all of Iceland, with its seat at the new capital city of Reykjavík.

Holt in Önundarfjörður, seat of the dean síra Jón Jónsson

Holt is a parish church and priest's farm lying on the fjord Önundarfjörður in the West Fjords, about ten miles west of *síra* Jón Magnússon's church at Eyri. It has fertile farming land, and in the 17th century was considered one of the most affluent and desirable parishes in Iceland. To reach it from Eyri (in Skutulsfjörður) one had to cross a steep and formidable mountain pass named Breiðadalsheiði.

One of *síra* Jón Jónsson's predecessors at Holt was *síra* Sveinn Símonarson, who was priest and dean there from 1583 to 1632. He was the father of Bishop Brynjólfur Sveinsson.

House Reading (Icel. húslestur)

This was a feature of Christian observance on which the early Icelandic Lutheran bishops, such as Bishop Guðbrandur Þorláksson, laid great emphasis. They realized that, to instil Christian teachings and practice into their people, the requirement of church attendance on holy days was not enough. For one thing, the long distances from the remoter farms to church, through harsh weather and over rough mountainous trails, made it difficult or even impossible for many (especially the sick and infirm) to attend church regularly. It was therefore laid down that each household should assemble regularly (usually in its *baðstofa*) for home prayers and hymn-singing and the reading of some edifying devotional work. The long winter evenings, when there was little pressing farm work to be done, provided the most convenient occasions for the House Reading, but it was also commonly observed on Sundays the year round for those who for one reason or another could not get to church. The House Reading of course required that at least one member of each household (usually the master of the household) should be more or less literate (see this Appendix under: Literacy).

Church decrees on the conduct of the House Reading were not rigorously enforced during the 17th century. Not until the 1740s were stringent laws laid down by the Danish government enforcing the rules regarding the House Reading in Icelandic households, and making them an almost universal part of Icelandic life.

Hreppur *(plural* hreppar*), hreppstjóri (plural* hreppstjórar*)*

The *hreppur* (commune) was an administrative subdivision of a *sýsla*; and a *hreppstjóri* was an official who managed affairs in his *hreppur*. Usually there would be three to five *hreppstjórar* in each *hreppur*, elected by its inhabitants. The original role of the *hreppur* was to provide a "safety net" for those unable to care for themselves—the aged, the sick, orphan children, and so forth. Each such needy individual would be assigned by the *hreppstjórar* to a viable household, and the household would receive an allowance from the *hreppur* for his or her maintenance. Later, the duties of the *hreppstjórar* were broadened and came to include assisting the *sýslumaður* in the enforcement of law.

Jón Jónsson (died 1680), priest and dean at Holt, and his wife Halldóra Jónsdóttir

Síra Jón Jónsson was priest and dean at Holt in Önundarfjörður during the events recorded in this book. He and his wife both came of distinguished families. His father, *síra* Jón Sveinsson (died 1661), who was priest and dean at Holt before him, was half brother to Bishop Brynjólfur Sveinsson; and his mother, Þorbjörg Guðmundsdóttir, was aunt to the poet Hallgrímur Pétursson. His wife Halldóra Jónsdóttir was the sister of Gísli Jónsson and aunt of the *sýslumaður* Magnús Magnússon.

Síra Jón Jónsson's ecclesiastical jurisdiction, as dean, included Jón Magnússon's parish of Eyri.

Jón Ólafsson of Arnardalur

This Jón Ólafsson (to be distinguished of course from Jón Ólafsson *Indíafari*) was a friend of the Jón Jónssons father and son of Kirkjuból. Within a few days of the burning of the Jón Jónssons this Jón Ólafsson was arraigned on suspicion of having conspired with the Jón Jónssons to practice witchcraft against *síra* Jón. He was condemned to be flogged, rather than burned to death, since the only evidence against him was that he had in his possession a manual of sorcery (see *Píslarsaga*, 2001 edn., pp. 229–230).

Jón Ólafsson Indíafari

Jón Ólafsson (1593–1679), nicknamed *Indíafari* (Voyager to India), was brought up in the West Fjords, travelled as a young man to England and Denmark, and from 1616 to 1626 served in the Danish navy. In that service he travelled widely, and spent some time in India. In 1626 he returned to Iceland, and lived for most of the rest of his long life as a farmer by Álftafjörður (the next fjord east of Skutulsfjörður) in the West Fjords. In 1661 he wrote reminiscences of his travels under the title *Reisubók Jóns Ólafssonar Indíafara* (Travel Journal of Jón Ólafsson, Voyager to India). This book earned him fame. It is remarkable for its vivid depictions of life in foreign countries of that era, and has been translated into Danish, English, and German.

Jónsbók

This is the Icelandic Lawbook which was adopted by the Althing in 1283, after Iceland had come under the suzerainty of Norway. It contains much material from the older Commonwealth Lawbook *Grágás*. Much of the *Jónsbók* was still in force in the 17th century.

For the purposes of the *Story of Sufferings* the most important part of the *Jónsbók* is the section on *Mannhelgi* (Personal Rights), the rights of persons injured or arrested.

Kirkjuból in Skutulsfjörður

Apart fom the priest's farm at Eyri, Kirkjuból was the most important of the farms in the Eyri parish for our story. It was home to three households, headed respectively (in *síra* Jón's day) by the elder Jón Jónsson, Snæbjörn Pálsson, and Sturli Bjarnason. The dominant role in our story is played by the family of the first of these: this consisted of the elder Jón Jónsson himself, his wife Guðrún Bjarnadóttir, and their children, of whom three are mentioned in the *Story of Sufferings*, namely, the younger Jón Jónsson and two daughters Þuríður Jónsdóttir and Þorgerður Jónsdóttir. At the time when the events described in this book took place (1655–1658), the younger Jón Jónsson and his sister

Þuríður were young adults (Þuríður in 1656 being probably about eighteen; see Note 96 of the Introduction). Both of them are described as very handsome (see pp. 127, 128). The study and practice of sorcery played a large part in the lives of the two Jón Jónssons and (if we are to believe *síra* Jón's accusations) of Þuríður also (see p. 159). Along with their exposure to sorcery all three probably became literate.

Kristinréttur

See this Appendix under: *Grágás*.

Leiðarþing *(Informative Assembly)*

This was a meeting, held in each local district after the conclusion of the annual session of the Althing at Þingvellir, at which a leading district delegate to the Althing would inform the people of his district of the proceedings of that session (including his own participation in it).

Literacy

The question of the extent of literacy in 17th-century Iceland is an important one for our purposes. Not only was it essential for the spread of Christianity through the institution of House Reading (q.v.) that at least one person in each household should be able to read printed books, but the practice of witchcraft also required an ability to read manuals of sorcery (Icel. *galdrabók*) as well as to copy spells (Icel. *særingar*). This note will give a brief synopsis of what is known or conjectured of the state of literacy in Iceland in the 17th century. For further discussion of literacy in Iceland through the centuries, the reader is referred to Loftur Guttormsson's article "Læsi," *Íslensk þjóðmenning 6, Munnmenntir og bókmenning*, pp. 118–144.

The active printing establishment at Hólar in north Iceland, first set up around 1530 by Jón Arason, the last Roman Catholic bishop of Hólar, was almost continually occupied for more than a century in turning out a stream of devotional works for the building up of Lutheran Christian faith and practice in Iceland, under the supervision of Bishop Guðbrandur Þorláksson of Hólar and his successors. (See Steingrímur Jónsson, "Prentaðar bækur," *Íslensk Þjóðmenning 6, Munnmenntir og bókmenning*, pp. 91–115). This printing enterprise would have been of little use if some degree of literacy had not been widespread in Iceland in Bishop Guðbrandur's lifetime. Since many of these books would have been used in the House Reading, one may conclude that a large proportion of farm households had at least one literate member. A similar conclusion can be drawn from the Church's regulations concerning the religious education of children. It was first laid down around 1575, and confirmed by royal decree in 1635, that no child should be permitted by the local priest to receive the sacrament of the Lord's Supper until he or she had demonstrated a knowledge of the contents of Martin Luther's *Lesser Catechism* (which was first printed and published in Icelandic translation in 1562). At this early stage this did not mean that every child was expected to be literate enough to read the *Lesser Catechism* for himself (or herself); memorization of a simplified version of the text, after hearing it read by others (presumably their priest or a family member), was considered to be enough, and up till 1700 a substantial fraction of the population had satisfied the requirements in this manner. This suggests that a substantial number of farm households must have had at least one member who was at least minimally literate and so could support the oral tradition, and assist the local priest in carrying out his teaching responsibilities.

As for writing ability in post-Reformation times, it lagged far behind reading ability, for the good reason that the Church considered writing less important than reading for the Christian education of the common people, which after all, in its view, was the main purpose of literacy. Moreover, for girls, and for boys of mediocre aptitude for study, the effort of learning to write was generally considered a distraction from more useful kinds of work.

There is one interesting piece of evidence from the year 1649 regarding the writing ability of so-called tax-farmers (Icel. *skattbændur*). These were farmers whose economic status entitled them to sit on commissions, courts, and other responsible bodies. In 1649 the Icelandic tax-farmers who were present at the session of the Althing that year were required to sign an oath of allegiance to King Frederick III, who had newly ascended the throne of Denmark. The documents that they signed are still preserved. Each signature is accompanied by the notation either "by his own hand" (Icel. *með eigin hendi*) or "has his signature written by another" (Icel. *lætur skrifa*). The proportion of each notation shows that only about 20–25% of the tax-farmers in that year had enough writing ability to sign their own names. (See the aforementioned article of Loftur Guttormsson, pp. 131, 132.)

Magical Spells and Staves from the Íslensk galdrabók *(Icelandic Book of Magic)*

The *Story of Sufferings* describes many specific occasions on which *síra* Jón believed himself and others to be the victims of attacks of sorcery by the Jón Jónssons and Þuríður. In [1]–[6] below I point out certain spells from the *Íslensk galdrabók* (see Introduction, §6) which appear designed for producing

Appendix 1 || 181

effects similar to those described by *síra* Jón. But it should be remembered that in the 17th century there must have been many manuals of sorcery current in Iceland, and we have no way of knowing which of them was actually used by any particular sorcerer. Also, except for Solomon's Seal and Fjölnir, the text of the *Story of Sufferings* does not name the magical techniques used on each occasion.

The English translation of the spells is taken (with slight modifications) from Stephen Flowers, *The Galdrabók, an Icelandic Grimoire*. The numeration of the spells is that of Matthías V. Sæmundsson, *Galdrar á Íslandi*. The forms of the staves associated with spells in the *Íslensk galdrabók* will be found in any of the three printed editions of the latter.

[1] A soporific spell for causing one's enemy to fall into a long and unnatural sleep:

"If you want to put someone to sleep, then carve these staves [of which diagrams are given] in alder wood and lay it under his head, and he will surely sleep until you take it away."

This is Spell no. 32 from the *Íslensk galdrabók*, and an occasion for its possible use is found on p. 64.

[2] A spell for overawing an enemy by gazing at him:

"If you want your foe to be afraid of you whenever he sees you, then carve these staves [illustrated in the *Galdrabók*] on an oak branch and wear it in the middle of your breast—and see to it that you see him before he sees you."

This is Spell no. 8 of the *Íslensk galdrabók*, and an occasion for its possible use is to be found in the episode on p. 76, where the elder Jón Jónsson is in a hurry to look Björn in the eyes. One who *sees* gains magical power over one who does not see.

[3] The Ægishjálmur.

The magical power of the gaze of the eyes, exemplified in the preceding [2], is also dwelt upon in Spells 25, 26, 41 of the *Íslensk galdrabók*, where it is presented in connection with the magical stave known as the Ægishjálmur ("helmet, or mask, or covering, which arouses fear or awe in the beholder"). (See Matthías V. Sæmundsson, *Galdrar á Íslandi*, p. 290, 353–354.) This is the best known of all the Icelandic magical staves of the 17th century; it is in the form of a cross with four (or eight) arms, the end of each arm being split into three branches. Five variants on the form of this stave are pictured on p. 146 of Matthías V. Sæmundsson, *Galdrar á Íslandi*.

The Ægishjálmur is not mentioned by name anywhere in the *Story of Sufferings*, but it does appear in four of the Spells (nos. 7, 25, 26, 41) of the *Íslensk galdrabók*. In Norse mythology it appears in verses 16, 17 of the pre-Christian Eddic poem *Fáfnismál* (*Eddukvæði* 1968, p. 332), which describes how the hero Sigurður slays the serpent Fáfnir who had been guardian of the Nibelungs' hoard of gold. One of Fáfnir's "objects of power," which Sigurður takes as booty, is the Ægishjálmur, a "covering" which gave him the power to overawe and subdue his enemies (or at least did so until the advent of Sigurður), a power concentrated in or between the eyes and often associated with the power of serpents to paralyze their prey. (See Stephen Flowers, *The Galdrabók: An Icelandic Grimoire*, pp. 47, 48.)

[4] Solomon's Seal.

For the use of Solomon's Seal in the practice of magic, see Spell no. 10 of the *Íslensk galdrabók*, as described in Matthías Viðar Sæmundsson, *Galdrar á Íslandi*, p. 297. This spell is translated by Stephen Flowers as follows: "Whoever carries the following sigil [Solomon's Seal] on himself will never be harmed by any temptation of the Fiend, and his enemy will not be able to work any active hate against him. Nor will he fall victim to any poison in his food or drink. He will never fall victim to any treacherous dealings."

An occasion on which this spell was used will be found on p. 110.

[5] Farting runes.

Runes that cause farting (Icel. *fretrúnir*) are the subject of Spell no. 46 of the *Íslensk galdrabók*, translated roughly as follows by Stephen Flowers:

"Write these staves on white calfskin with your own blood; take the blood from your thigh and say: I write thee eight *áss*-runes, nine *nauð*-runes, thirteen *þurs*-runes – that will plague thy belly with bad shit and gas, and all of these will plague thy belly with great farting. May it loosen thee from thy place and burst thy guts; may thy farting never stop, neither day nor night. Thou wilt be as weak as the fiend Loki, who was bound by all the gods. In thy mightiest name Lord God, Spirit, Shaper, Óðinn, Þór, Savior, Freyr, Freyja, Oper, Satan, Beelzebub, helper, mighty God, protecting your companions and those of Oteo, Mor, Noht Vitales."

For a lengthy discussion of this spell see Matthías V. Sæmundsson, *Galdrar á Íslandi*, pp. 437–442. An occasion for its use is found on p. 110. A "droll" verse about a woman whose farting was supposedly induced by magic is found on p. 160.

[6] Fjölnir.

This is a magical stave whose form is given in Jón Árnason, *Íslenskar Þjóðsögur og ævintýri*, vol. 1, p. 432, and also in *Íslensk orðabók*, 3rd edn., p. 421. The name Fjölnir does not occur explicitly in the *Íslensk galdrabók*. However, Fjölnir is one of the names of the god Óðinn, and spells invoking Óðinn occur fairly frequently in the *Íslensk galdrabók*, especially in its latter part (see for example Spells 33, 43, 45, 46, in which the intent of the spells is clearly malevolent). We are assured in the *Story of Sufferings* (p. 110) that this was the stave which, scratched on the palm of Jón Jónsson the younger, caused burning pain on the hand of *síra* Jón after the two had shaken hands (see p. 65).

Magnús Magnússon sýslumaður (1630–1704)

Magnús Magnússon came of a distinguished family (the so-called Svalbarð family). He was a great-grandson of Magnús Jónsson (1525?–1591), a poet and *sýslumaður* who was so much admired for his scholarship and human traits that he has been referred to by the epithet "the Gentleman" (Icel. *prúði*) ever since. After a three-year sojourn in Denmark Magnús Magnússon returned to Iceland and in 1653 became the *sýslumaður* of the western part of the Ísafjarðarsýsla at the remarkably young age of 23. He was not only a magistrate but also a scholar who composed historical annals, and he had a genuine belief in the reality of black magic and the necessity of punishing it harshly. But when called upon by *síra* Jón Magnússon to take the lead in having the two sorcerers Jón Jónsson and (later) Þuríður prosecuted and punished he was at first reluctant to take up the case. But he was finally obliged (after the intervention of Þorleifur Kortsson) to join in overseeing the conviction and execution by burning in 1656 of the Jón Jónssons father and son. Þuríður on the other hand was ultimately acquitted (in 1658). In his *Story of Sufferings* (written after the acquittal of Þuríður) *síra* Jón bitterly berates the authorities, especially Magnús Magnússon, for what he sees as their lethargy and disregard of their plain duty to use every possible means for the eradication of sorcery.

Mannhelgi

This is the section on Personal Rights in the *Jónsbók*. It occupies pp. 35–69 in the 1970 edn. of *Jónsbók*, edited by Ólafur Halldórsson.

Páll Björnsson of Selárdalur (1621–1706)

Síra Páll Björnsson, a contemporary of *síra* Jón Magnússon, served as parish priest throughout his long working life in the remote parish of Selárdalur in the West Fjords. Not only did he have some personal contact with *síra* Jón, but in his dealings with sorcery he presents in some respects a parallel with the latter. For this reason it seems worthwhile to depict his life here at some length.

Síra Páll belonged to the "upper crust" of Icelandic society. His forbears, on both his father's and his mother's side, were among the most distinguished people in the country. On his father's side he was closely related to many of the foremost public officials of his time, including Brynjólfur Sveinsson, bishop of Skálholt from 1639 to 1674.

Like many promising young Icelandic men he was sent for his education to the University of Copenhagen, where he distinguished himself not only in classical and literary studies and theology but also in the sciences. In 1646, on his return to Iceland after completing his studies, he married Helga Halldórsdóttir, sister of the wife of Bishop Brynjólfur Sveinsson, and he and the bishop maintained a close friendship as long as they both lived. In the following year, 1647, he became priest of Selárdalur, and served in this parish until his death nearly 70 years later. There *síra* Páll became a rich man by the standards of the time. His wife had brought a considerable fortune to the marriage, and he himself improved the Selárdalur property by intelligent management of the farming and fishing that went with it. Around 1651–1653 he was made dean of his *sýsla* (district). In his later years he was invited to become bishop of Hólar, but declined because of advancing age.

But it was as a scholar, theologian, and preacher that *síra* Páll made the greatest impression on his contemporaries. Not only was his knowledge of the ancient Biblical languages of Hebrew, Greek, and Latin remarkable, but he also had some knowledge of Arabic, Chaldean, and Syrian (see p. 84 of Hannes Þorsteinsson, "Minning sjera Páls prófasts í Selárdal," hereafter referred to simply as H. Þ.). Among those who came to Selárdalur to study Greek and Hebrew with him was his younger relative Jón Þorkelsson Vídalín, who later became bishop of Skálholt and the author of a celebrated book of sermons called *Vídalín's Postil*. (Those who have compared this masterpiece of Jón Vídalín with *síra* Páll's essay on preaching, which survives in manuscript form, think it likely that the inspiration manifested in the former was at least partially aroused by the latter; see H. Þ., p. 80). He was considered to be a man of prayer, whose intercessions could be relied upon to bear fruit (see H. Þ., p. 61). In his later years he also devoted much time to composing translations and commentaries on parts of the Bible (See H. Þ., p. 82).

But classical languages and theology did not exhaust the mental energies of *síra* Páll. He also had a strong interest in science and technology, enthusiasm for which was then growing by leaps and bounds on the continent of Europe. From his remote rectory at the edge of the habitable world he carried on a scientific correspondence with the Royal Society of London, which had been founded in 1662 with the purpose of collecting and systematizing knowledge of natural phenomena. He sent to the Royal Society a report on the natural history of Iceland, which was sufficiently well received to be published both in English and in French translation (in 1674 and 1675). As regards technology, he made substantial improvements in the design of fishing boats.

Personally, he was renowned for his hospitality, cheerful disposition, magnanimity, manliness, and kindness (see H. Þ., p. 78).

After the above account of his character and intellectual accomplishments, it may come as a shock to a modern reader to learn that *síra* Páll Björnsson was also a burner of sorcerers: he was responsible for the death by burning of no fewer than six persons in his district who were accused of the crime of sorcery. The train of events leading up to these happenings was in brief as follows:

Síra Páll's first personal contact with sorcery seems to have taken place through his association with *síra* Jón Magnússon, who in 1656, after the burning of the Jón Jónssons father and son, wrote to *síra* Páll asking for his prayers and advice. Not only did the latter reply with a letter of consolation but took the trouble to travel north over fjord and mountain to visit *síra* Jón personally (see p. 132).

A few years later, in 1660, Helga, *síra* Páll's wife, became mysteriously ill. A contemporary describes her illness as a "mortal battle against the fiery darts of Satan" (see H. Þ., p. 63), from which it appears that the illness was a nervous complaint which, in the climate of opinion then prevalent, was attributed to demonic attacks. On this occasion she recovered. But in 1665 two priests died in the West Fjords under mysterious circumstances, and local self-styled wizards began boasting that they were no longer satisfied with tormenting the preachers of God's word but were resolved to kill them. This seems to have caused something of a panic in the district, and when in the winter of 1668–1669 Helga became even more seriously ill than before, events took a serious turn. Her illness was attributed to magic practiced on her by a parishioner named Jón Leifsson in revenge for Helga's refusal to allow him to marry one of her servant-girls. So violent were the alleged diabolical onslaughts on *síra* Jón's household that he and Helga and their children and servants were obliged to abandon their residence for a while and take refuge on a neighboring farm. Through the agency of the local *sýslumaður* Eggert (who was a brother of *síra* Páll) and the *lögmaður* Þorleifur Kortsson, both Jón Leifsson and his alleged instructor in sorcery, one Erlendur Eyjólfsson, were consigned to the flames in 1669. For their zeal in the cause of extirpating sorcery these magistrates received a vote of thanks at the 1669 session of the Althing.

But the panic over sorcery in Selárdalur continued. Within a few years two grown-up sons of *síra* Páll and Helga, named Björn and Halldór, became mysteriously sick, and their sickness was attributed to witchcraft practiced on them by a man named Lassi Diðriksson. This Lassi (who was also accused of inflicting diabolical illness on a servant of the *sýslumaður* Eggert) was burned to death at the Althing in 1675. Björn and Halldór never recovered from their illnesses, but died of them ten and fifteeen years respectively after the burning of Lassi.

Meanwhile Helga, *síra* Páll's wife, had not yet recovered, and soon three more individuals were burned to death for being supposedly responsible for her continued ailments: one was Magnús Björnsson, burned in 1675, and the other two were a mother and son, Þuríður Ólafsdóttir (the one and only woman burned to death for witchcraft in Iceland in the 17th century) and Jón Helgason, both burned to death in 1678.

These were the last of the burnings directly traceable to events at Selárdalur. Þorleifur Kortsson stepped down from his position of authority in 1679, and Eggert the *sýslumaður* (*síra* Páll's brother) died in 1681. So after 1681 *síra* Páll would no longer have enjoyed the same powerful backing by the civil authorities as he had before, even if he had wished to consign more alleged sorcerers to the flames. In fact, after 1680 his obsession with sorcery seems to have died down, and he devoted his later years largely to translations and commentaries on different parts of the Bible.

It is worth noting that *síra* Páll's wife Helga lived to a ripe old age, dying in 1704 at the age of 85, two years before the death of her husband.

Páll Björnsson's obsession with sorcery must not be judged by the standards of the present age. Like Jón Magnússon, and like very many men of solid intellect on the continent of Europe in the era of the witchcraft craze (such as Nicolas Remy and Jean Bodin, see Note 9 of the Introduction), he was caught up in the then dominant tradition of a literal interpretation of the Bible, which set great store by such texts as *Exodus* 22:18: "Thou shalt not suffer a witch to live." And, as in the case of Jón Magnússon, it was when he himself and his wife and family became the victims of alleged demonic sorcery that his intellectual convictions on the subject became obsessive and fanatical.

His crusade against witchcraft manifested itself not only in the burning of alleged sorcerers in his own district but also in his appeals to the authorities throughout the country, both civil and ecclesiastical, to close all possible loopholes by which suspected sorcerers might evade conviction and punishment. Bishop Brynjólfur Sveinsson, one of those to whom he directed this appeal, dismissed it on the grounds that "he did not have time to consider the matter properly."

Around 1674, when the witchcraft furor at Selárdalur was at its height, *síra* Páll wrote the treatise on the history of witchcraft entitled *Kennimark kölska* (Lat. *Character Bestiae* = The Mark of the Beast) which has been discussed in §5 of the Introduction. (This book was printed in 1976; see the Bibliography.)

As we have seen, from about 1680 onward he ceased his fulminations against sorcery and witchcraft and devoted himself to translations and commentaries on the Bible. Did he in his old age ever regret his earlier participation in the execution of sorcerers? Probably not. But in a letter (still extant) that he wrote to a young friend in 1703 at the age of 81, he complains that his life has been empty. "I have never lived," he laments (see H. Þ., p. 75). Evidently he felt that something important had been missing from his life. Was it worldly fame and advancement, of which he seemed to have been deprived by the isolation in which he lived? Or did he feel an interior poverty, for which even his intellectual achievements could not compensate, a sense that he had not made his peace with God? Perhaps there is truth in both of these interpretations.

Prayer of Jesus

In all spiritual traditions prayer is prescribed for those suffering any form of adversity. But in deep distress one may lose the ability to practice discursive prayer, or indeed to perform any mental acts of devotion. Here the so-called Prayer of Jesus, or Jesus Prayer, well known and practiced for many centuries in the Eastern Orthodox Church, becomes very relevant. It runs as follows: "Lord Jesus Christ, Son of God, have mercy on me a sinner!" This brief prayer is derived from the cry of the publican in Jesus' parable of the Pharisee and the Publican (*Luke* 18:13). The prayer can be used in even shorter forms, the shortest of all being the simple utterance of the name "Jesus." The Orthodox tradition holds that this prayer in the name of Jesus was instituted by the Lord Himself when, after the Last Supper, He told the disciples that prayer offered in His name would always be effective (*John* 14:13, 15:23; see also Brianchaninov, *On the Prayer of Jesus*, pp. 18, 19.) Moreover, the tradition maintains that, if a person has even a small degree of faith, his tongue can always be active in repeating the Jesus Prayer no matter how distressed his mind may be under the attacks of the powers of darkness; and that this repetition, mindless though it may seem at first, will if practiced faithfully bear fruit in the quieting and healing of the mind. (See *The Way of a Pilgrim and the Pilgrim Continues His Way*, pp. 183–192, especially p. 190.) "In the grim struggle with the enemies of our salvation," says Brianchaninov, "the supreme weapon is the Prayer of Jesus" (see Brianchaninov, *On the Prayer of Jesus*, p. 25).

The experiences of *síra* Jón Magnússon, as recorded in Chapters IV and V of the *Story of Sufferings*, exemplify this belief in the efficacy of the Jesus Prayer. In these Chapters he records experiences of spiritual darkness and desolation in the midst of which he finds his only solace in the repetition of the Jesus Prayer (though he surely had no prior knowledge of the Eastern spiritual tradition).

For more information on the Orthodox Prayer of Jesus, see the Bibliography under the headings: Kallistos Ware, Ignatius Brianchaninov, *The Way of a Pilgrim and the Pilgrim Continues His Way*, and *Writings from the Philokalia on Prayer of the Heart*. For parallels in Icelandic spirituality, see Guðrún Edda Gunnarsdóttir, *"Herra Jesú, miskunna mér......"*.

Sending

Icelandic folklore is full of stories of magicians who are able to raise evil spirits and then dispatch them to work mischief on their enemies. The

Icelandic word used for an evil spirit dispatched in this manner is *sending* (or *galdrasending*).

Settlement Age *(Icel.* **landnámsöld***)*

The period of the original settlement of Iceland, mostly by settlers from Norway and the British Isles. It is usually supposed to have begun around A.D. 870, when the first permanent settler in Iceland, Ingólfur Arnarson, appropriated a large tract of land around Reykjavík, and to have been more or less completed by A.D. 930 when the Althing was founded.

Side-alcove *(of a church) (Icel.* **stúka***)*

In Catholic times a *stúka* was a chapel within the church, containing a side-altar at which the saint of that particular church was venerated. After the Reformation these side-altars were mostly eliminated, and the alcoves in which they had stood were either left empty or used for other purposes such as storage.

Skálholt

Located in a fertile area of southwest Iceland, Skálholt was the seat of the southern diocese of Iceland. It had been the private estate of one of the earliest bishops of Iceland, Gissur Ísleifsson, but in 1082 he donated it to the Church as the episcopal seat of the southern diocese in perpetuity. Soon afterwards a school, primarily for the training of prospective priests, was founded there, which operated, with some lengthy interruptions, until the Reformation. Shortly after the Reformation, in 1552, the school was reorganized by royal decree, and continued to operate continuously until 1785, when an earthquake and economic disasters caused it to be transferred from Skálholt to the capital city of Reykjavík, along with the seat of the southern diocese itself.

Jón Magnússon's parish of Eyri (indeed, all the parishes of the West Fjords) belonged to the Skálholt diocese.

Skáli

In the oldest farms of the Commonwealth Period, the *skáli* was the principal room, where the household slept. As the centuries passed and the climate worsened and heating became more difficult, the farming household took to sleeping in the *baðstofa* (q.v.), and the *skáli* became an additional bedroom, mostly reserved for guests, on the larger farms.

Þorleifur Kortsson (ca. 1620–1698)

Of all the important public officials in Iceland during the latter half of the 17th century, it was Þorleifur Kortsson who acted most vigorously and successfully in bringing to trial and securing the conviction and burning of alleged sorcerers.

Þorleifur's great-grandfather was a merchant from Hamburg, Germany, who immigrated into Iceland. Þorleifur's father died when he was about fifteen years old, whereupon he was sent to Hamburg to be brought up by his relatives there. He remained there for many years. Eventually (no later than 1647) Þorleifur returned to Iceland, and in 1652 was married to the daughter of a noble and prestigious family in the West Fjords. Thanks largely to his wife he was now a wealthy man. In the year of his marriage he became *sýslumaður* of half of each of Ísafjarðarsýsla and Strandasýsla. In 1662 he received the highest promotion of his career, being appointed by the king to the post of *lögmaður* of the northern and western quarters.

The personal qualities of Þorleifur Kortsson have been variously described in the annals of the time. He is portrayed as acquisitive, but also as "wise, kindly, and mild." According to one historian (*séra* Jón Halldórsson, 1665–1736), Þorleifur was considered to be "reticent and unimpressive at public meetings, somewhat lacking in the qualities of a leading man, short in stature and one-sided in his views." (See Sigfús H. Andrésson, "Þorleifur lögmaður Kortsson," pp. 157, 158.)

Þorleifur's career as a public official is memorable in only one respect—his zeal in prosecuting and convicting supposed sorcerers. It is quite likely that this zeal had been kindled during his youthful years spent in Germany, where burnings of witches were almost a daily occurrence. The first victims of his crusade were three men in the remote area of Trékyllisvík, in Strandasýsla, who in 1654 were burned to death for allegedly using diabolical means to arouse violent manifestations of hysteria in some of the women of the parish during the church services, resulting in the disruption of the latter. Two years later, in 1656, in Ísafjarðarsýsla, he cooperated with *síra* Jón Magnússon in causing the principal event described in the present book, the consigning of the two Jón Jónssons to the flames. These events occurred while he was joint *sýslumaður* of the two districts (*sýslur*) in which they took place, before his appointment as *lögmaður* in 1662.

Þorleifur was much praised at the time for his role in these burnings. In the *Seiluannáll* (*Annálar 1400–1800*, vol. 1) for 1656 we read: "He [Þorleifur

Kortsson] was much praised of all men because of [his role in] this, and became well-known for his success in weeding out the evil art of sorcery."

Nor did his crusade against witchcraft abate after he became *lögmaður*: between 1669 and 1678 he was instrumental in getting six persons burned to death on the grounds that their sorcery was responsible for serious illnesses in the family of *síra* Páll Björnsson of Selárdalur (see this Appendix under: Páll Björnsson).

Þorleifur Þórðarson

Þorleifur Þórðarson (about 1570 to 1647) was a poet who lived at Garðstaðir in the West Fjords. He also had a reputation as an accomplished magician and was nicknamed Galdra-Leifi (Leifi the Wizard). Several folktales are told about his proficiency in the magical arts; see for example Jón Árnason, *Íslenskar þjóðsögur og ævintýri*, vol. 1, pp. 505–508.

Units of Value

It should be borne in mind that up to the 18th century relatively little money circulated in Iceland, so that most commercial transactions took place by barter of goods. It was therefore very necessary to standardize the relative values of different kinds of goods.

The basic unit of value was the *kúgildi*, the value of one cow. One cow was considered equal in value to six ewes, and also to a "large hundred" (120) of ells of homespun (see below). In view of the latter, the term "hundredworth" (Icel. *hundrað*) was often used as a synonym of *kúgildi*, especially in assessing the value of farms. A farm would be valued at one hundredworth if it were capable of supporting one cow or six ewes. A farm of the best class would be valued at 60 hundredworths or more; good average farms at about 20 hundredworths; and small inferior farms at 6 to 10 hundredworths.

As regards fish, 240 codfish, each weighing at least two or three pounds, were considered equal in value to one hundredworth.

One of the principal mediums of barter in 17th-century Iceland was homespun (Icel. *vaðmál*), a rough woolen cloth woven on Icelandic farms, the material out of which most Icelandic farmers' clothes were made. Amounts of homespun were measured in ells (Icel. *alin*), a unit of length, very roughly equal to two feet (originally equal to the length of the arm from the elbow to the fingertips). It was considered that 120 ells of homespun were equal in value to one cow, i.e., one hundredworth (i.e., that one ell of homespun was worth two codfish).

Appendix 1

Three other units of value mentioned in the *Story of Sufferings* are the *eyrir*, the quarter (Icel. *fjórðungur*), and the *mörk*.

The *eyrir* is, very roughly, the value of six ells of homespun (see *Íslensk orðabók*, 3rd edn., under: *Eyrir* 4), so that twenty *aurar* (plural of *eyrir*) would be roughly the equivalent of one cow.

A quarter (*fjórðungur*) is equivalent to ten ells (personal communication by Már Jónsson).

The *mörk* is, properly speaking, an ancient unit of weight, equal to about half a pound. When used as a unit of value (as for example in the passage quoted from the *Jónsbók* in Note 7 of Chap. VI), it is reasonable to suppose that it means the value of a *mörk* weight of homespun (see Magnús Már Lárusson, "Íslenskar mælieiningar," p. 234).

Appendix 2

Decree of King Christian IV[1]

COPENHAGEN, 12 OCTOBER 1617

We, Christian the Fourth by the grace of God, hereby declare to all men:
Common experience teaches us that certain secret arts—for example crossing oneself,[2] exorcisms, runes, magical staves, picking out certain days of the week,[3] revealing [stolen goods by sorcery][4]—are very prevalent, and are considered quite excusable. The reason they are not prohibited is that the people who practice such arts are revered as benefactors, able to restore health to human beings as well as to their livestock. Another reason is that certain words of holy scripture very commonly occur in practices of this sort. This leads people to disregard entirely the fact that arts of this kind are strictly forbidden by almighty God, as leading poor human beings away from God and from the natural means of aid and healing that He has ordained, and into the clandestine, unnatural machinations and agency of the devil. Moreover the aforementioned arts are the ABC of all sorcerers; they are the starting point and origin of their baneful and ill-fated purposes and undertakings. So, in hope that by God's help and assistance this kind of abomination and provocation of God may be removed and eliminated, we have graciously taken the occasion to devise a weighty means, procedure, and method to this end. With this in view we do ordain and determine, along with our dear Council of State, as follows:

If after this day it be found that any person is well instructed and learned in the above specified art, practices it, applies it, and makes use of it, then if they are of noble birth they shall be prosecuted and punished for this according to what we ourselves and our dear Council of State may decree and impose. But if they are not of noble birth they shall lose all their possessions and be exiled from our state, all our dominions, and all the districts over which we have jurisdiction. Also, any persons who are accomplices of such people, who make use of their advice or actions or permit use to be made of them for the benefit of themselves or their household—if they are of noble birth such persons must, on the first offense, receive public absolution and make a payment of 1000 *ríkisdalir* to the nearest hospital. Or if they are not of noble birth, they must likewise receive public absolution and as punishment must pay a fine to the extent that they are able. But those who for a second time are found to have committed such a crime, whoever they may be, will be subject to the same penalty and chastisement as the practitioners themselves who are learned in these arts and practices.

As regards genuine sorcerers, who have made themselves over to the devil to be joined in partnership with him or who are confederate with him— all such shall be dealt with according to due process of law. And those who put themselves into the hands of such people, desiring and coveting the realization of some benefit for their own people by means of these men's skill in sorcery— they shall be put to death without mercy.

Moreover, in order that this our gracious and earnest will and decree may be more effectual, to the glory of almighty God, we do hereby command and strictly enjoin all nobles and officials, all bishops, deans, priests, mayors, councillors, *sýslumenn*, and all who have been appointed and commissioned to offices of authority, as follows: they should one and all, each according to his rank and position, as soon as they become aware of cases covered by this our letter, denounce them publicly and have the culprits punished, provided that they do not wish to be prosecuted themselves for being accessory to people of this sort and consenting to their wickedness.

Published at our palace, Copenhagen, 12 October 1617,
Under our seal.

Notes

1. This letter, or decree, of King Christian IV was translated into Icelandic by *síra* Guðmundur Einarsson of Staðarstaður in 1627, and published at the 1630 session of the Althing. It is translated here into English from *Píslarsaga*, 2001 edn., pp. 51, 52.
2. The act of crossing oneself was thought to savor of magic by many Protestants. See for example the following words of Árni Magnússon (1663–1730):
    "As regards crossing oneself, we know that foolish superstitious people use it, or have used it, as a means of curing sickness." (Árni Magnússon, *Embedsskrivelser og andre offentlige aktstykker*, Copenhagen, 1916. See Orðabók Háskólans, under *signing*.)
3. Picking out certain days of the week, or of the month, as auspicious or inauspicious for undertakings of various sorts was evidently a widespread practice, but was thought to savor of astrology and therefore to be antichristian. Spell no. 21 of the *Íslensk galdrabók* (see Introduction, §6) lists two days out of each month which are said by the Egyptians to be especially unlucky.
4. I owe this interpretation of the Icel. *að koma aftur* to Helgi Þorláksson, *Saga Íslands VI*, p. 362.

Appendix 3

The Judgment of the District Court Regarding the Two Jón Jónssons of Kirkjuból[1]

14 December 1655

On 14 December 1655 a district assembly meeting was formally opened by the *sýslumaður* Magnús Magnússon at Eyri on Skutulsfjörður. He appointed the following men to form a court along with Gísli Jónsson: First the *lögréttumaður* Þorlákur Arason, [then] Guðmundur Ásmundsson, Guðmundur Þorsteinsson, Jón Þorvaldsson, Gunnlaugur Skeggjason, and Sigmundur Guðmundsson; from the western part Brynjólfur Bjarnarson, Bjarni Þorleifsson, Magnús Guðmundsson, Jón Þorsteinsson, Ásmundur Guðmundsson, and Einar Arnórsson. They were to consider and deliberate on the lawsuit which *síra* Jón Magnússon is instituting, and in regard to which he is now asking and demanding judgment, investigation, and legal redress (as he spells out and says later). It is true that some think the assembly has been summoned at an inappropriate time, for in the second chapter of the king's *Þegnskylda* (Civic Duty)[2] it is said that one should not summon an assembly unless necessity requires it and farmers themselves request it. But because it is so urgent that this case be discussed, it seems to us that this present time does not come under the ban stated in the book, but that there is a pressing need [for this assembly] if evil is to be eradicated and the Christian Church built up with the godly assistance of the priest, thereby serving the congregation to the praise of God, to the salvation of all God's children, and to the punishment and correction of the wicked if it should happen that they are exposed by this investigation of the authorities.

The first assembly that was summoned was prevented from taking place by reason of snow and stormy weather in this time of short, dark days, which made it difficult for the *sýslumaður* and other pious men to attend, even though a summons had gone out. But now it seems to us that the legitimate excuses of those who have been staying at home can no longer delay this assembly which has already been formally opened, or exempt them from serving as assembly witnesses. So we are not proposing to have the present [assembly] cancelled.

First of all, *sera* Jón Magnússon is presenting before our court the following evidence as confirmation of his suspicion: The devil (he says) has manifested himself in the appearance, size, and created form of the elder Jón Jónsson of Kirkjuból and of his son Jón the younger. Three of his household came forward in confirmation of his story—people who are related to the priest and connected with him by marriage.

Item, Egill Pálsson made known what he had heard from his ten-year-old child who, without being questioned, said (and had said [previously]) that he had seen the forms of these men—once the two of them together and at other times one after the other.

When Jón Jónsson and his son demanded that these same people should declare whether or not they had seen [the devil] in the forms of other men than them, Gvendur Ísleiksson acknowledged that he and some others, who had seen [such forms] on the night just passed and also at other times, had often seen them in the likeness of a dog or of mice and cats.

In addition *sera* Jón also says that, on each occasion when the aforementioned father and son came to church, it seemed to him and his household (as he and they affirmed) that these attacks of devils almost always increased and intensified, so that he and they say that they came to dread their coming to church. In regard to this he promised with a handshake to swear before the authorities an oath attesting to the truth of this testimony, as they should dictate to him. But since his wife and household wish to postpone presenting their testimony on the matter, we shall let this wait for further evidence supporting the priest's suspicions.

As regards the fourth matter that *sera* Jón presented for investigation, namely, to find out what Ólafur Sigmundsson and Ásta Narfadóttir, along with Björn of Engidalur, said about the insinuation and phrases that the younger Jón had used vigorously in his threats: they say they know nothing about it, so we are setting the matter aside.

At this point Jón Jónsson of *sera* Jón's household and a woman, Guðrún Guðmundardóttir, came forward saying that they wished to confirm on oath that, when the father and son came to church, the attacks increased and intensified beyond what was usual. With this purpose they placed their hands on the sacred book and declared to almighty God that as far as they knew this was true. When the oath had been spelled out ……. etc.[3]

As soon as this oath had been sworn, we came to a decision by full vote of the court, in accordance with the resolution passed by the Althing, dated

1631, regarding the finding of the late Jón Magnússon in the case of Benidikt Þorleifsson and Magnús Sigurðsson.[4] [According to this decision] the two Jón Jónssons, father and son, must swear an oath such as the following: Laying their hand on the sacred book, let them declare to almighty God that "you two have neither by magic nor sorcery, runes nor carvings, verses nor other means, caused loss or harm or injury to any man in soul or conscience, body or limbs, property or money, least of all to our pastor *sera* Jón Magnússon; nor have you availed yourselves of such acts by others, or conspired with others to cause harm to anyone; nor have you ever learned or practiced sorcery, runes, or carvings." Once this oath has been dictated to them may God show them his favor ...., etc.[5]

For this purpose, in accord with the text of the [Law]book, the *sýslumaður* along with Gísli Jónsson appointed the following men as oath-witnesses. All declare that these men are of age, upright, blameless of any misdemeanors, and also residing near [the accused]. Both parties are satisfied and pleased with this [choice]. They are to swear this oath by the next spring assembly with the oath-witnesses here named, provided they are able to do so with a clear conscience, either now or at the appointed time, either against or in favor of the innocence of [the accused]. [The oath-witnesses are as follows:] First Björn Jónsson, Sturli Bjarnarson, Ásmundur Guðmundsson, Egill Pálsson, Jón Ólafsson, Jón Þorsteinsson, Einar Arnórsson. In addition to these [seven], the remaining four may be obtained from anywhere within the *sýsla*. When the oath has been sworn by the accused and confirmed by the oath-witnesses according to the letter of the law, we declare that, if this procedure is completed within the aforementioned time period, by the next spring assembly, [the accused] shall be cleared of the sworn evidences and suspicions of *sera* Jón.

At the same time it was also laid down, with the advice of the judges, that [the accused] might now, if they were able and wished to do so, clear themselves immediately, with [the compliance of] the men named above. We the members of the court also thought that it was within their power to clear themselves immediately. And in fact they set about doing so—with massive oaths contrary to the law, mortgaging themselves and their souls to the devil with a handshake, but with all humility toward God and the priest, without any direction from the authorities that this is how they should swear.[6] Because of our ignorance we are submitting this matter to the directives of the highest and most exalted authority in this country, *Magister* Brynjólfur [Sveinsson]. Last year a twelve-man court verdict was submitted to the *lögmenn* and the *lögrétta*, but little reply to it was received. In the case just mentioned [the question was raised] also whether, in the light of one judgment of the Althing, the appointed oath-witnesses should not be bound to follow their consciences and affirm the most righteous [decision] of which they are capable before God and the law, and to declare themselves guilty if the oath should fail because of the oath-witnesses themselves—just as if they had wilfully refused to take either position. The resolution of the Althing which came out in the summer of 1655 puts us in a difficult position, since it refers to "some" rather than "all."[7]

Also we want to find out from the highest authority whether one may divide into two the oath as submitted, in such a way as [to accommodate] those who want to clear the [defendants] from this suspicion [of having injured the priest], but not from the charge of learning and practicing [sorcery] harmlessly. We submit all this to the judgment of the aforementioned highest authority.

Also, in the name of the holy Trinity the court unanimously declares that the *sýslumaður* Magnús Magnússon, and likewise the deputy of Þorleifur Kortsson, incur no blame for not putting the [defendants] into irons, since it is now a matter of collecting oath-witnesses, and ...... [Here ends the extant part of the Judgment.]

Notes

1. The Icelandic original of the document translated here is printed on pp. 201–204 of the 2001 edn. of the *Píslarsaga*. It is the extant portion of a longer document.
2. The *Þegnskylda* is the third section of the (Lawbook) *Jónsbók*. The second chapter of the *Þegnskylda* deals with the times of assemblies and the number of people who must attend them.
3. The sentence has been left incomplete in the manuscript.
4. On p. 118 of Ólafur Davíðsson, *Galdur og galdramál á Íslandi*, we find the following reference to the case mentioned here: "In 1631 the *lögmenn* and *lögréttumenn* reached a decision in regard to the sorcery case instituted by Benidikt Þorleifsson of Búðardalur. He had stated on oath that he suspected Magnús Sigurðsson of sorcery. Jón Magnússon, the *sýslumaður* of Dalasýsla, had tried the case in their home district. The assemblymen decided that Magnús should swear an oath in his home district denying his guilt, in the presence of Jón Magnússon the *sýslumaður*, within ten weeks of juridical days [i.e., days on which oaths can be officially sworn]. The *sýslumaður* was to prescribe the men who should swear the oath with him. Other than this we find no more information about the case either in the Althing Book for the year 1631 or for succeeding years. But [the annalists] Björn Jónsson of Skarðsá and Jón Espólín tell us that Magnús did swear the oath. His sorcery had consisted in causing illness in Benidikt."

    Björn Jónsson of Skarðsá (1574–1655) was a *lögréttumaður*, best known for his *Skarðsárannálar*, a book of annals of Icelandic history covering the period 1400–1644. Jón Espólín (1769–1836) was a *sýslumaður*, author of *Íslands árbækur í söguformi*, a year-by-year narrative of Icelandic history covering the long period 1262–1832.
5. At this point the copyist has omitted something from the Judgment.
6. See p. 77.
7. The reference here seems to be to the phrase, italicized below, in Item No. 1 of the Minutes of the Althing for the year 1655. This item concerns a dispute between

a certain Bjarni Jónsson and a woman (apparently subnormal mentally) called Þordís Símonsdóttir, and runs as follows:

"On 29 June 1655 a decision was reached by Thomas Nikolaison, the honored and respected deputy of our liege lord, along with the *lögmaður* Magnús Björnsson and his *lögréttumenn* (with the exception of Hannes Árnason), regarding the poor woman Þordís Símonsdóttir, whose case came before the *lögrétta* last summer, in the year 1654. It was then determined that the case should not be dismissed without an oath. So they enjoined a *tylftareiður* (oath of twelve) on Bjarni Jónsson, specifying that the full number of oath-witnesses should be assembled, because of the dullwittedness of the woman. By now Bjarni Jónsson has submitted an oath for himself (*eineiður*). So the men whose names appear above, together with half the *lögrétta*, have decided that he should pay a fine of four *mörks* [see Appendix 1 under: Units of Value] for failing to produce a valid oath, since he got *some of the oath-swearers but not all*, but that then he should trust in God to be cleared, since he has good testimonials. But the aforementioned stupid woman (ignorant though she is) should be punished for the ambiguity of her speech, in whatever way the *sýslumaður* in her *sýsla* considers suitable."

The conditions under which, in 17th-century legal proceedings, a plaintiff could be penalized for failing to produce the requisite number of oath-witnesses are not clear.

Appendix 4

Four Documents Regarding the Investigation of Þuríður Jónsdóttir[1]

Introduction

The two Jón Jónssons, father and brother of Þuríður Jónsdóttir, had been burned to death by court order on 10 April 1656. The sufferings of *síra* Jón Magnússon, which the latter had attributed to sorcery practiced on him by the two executed men while they were alive, now abated for a while, and during the summer of 1656 *síra* Jón seemed to regain his health. But, to his great disappointment, the autumn of that year brought a renewal of violent torments which, he felt sure, were again of diabolical origin. Who was practicing sorcery on him this time? From flimsy circumstantial evidence (narrated in Chapters IX and X) he fixed upon Þuríður Jónsdóttir, and began harassing her to the point where she felt she could no longer safely remain at Kirkjuból (her family home, located in *síra* Jón's parish). Early in September 1656 she fled from Kirkjuból over the mountains to Holt in Önundarfjörður, where the district dean, *síra* Jón Jónsson, and his family lived. The dean and his wife Halldóra were friendly to Þuríður, and seem to have set little store by the accusations of *síra* Jón Magnússon against her. Though Þuríður was now out of his physical reach, Jón Magnússon was determined to pursue her by every legal means, and if possible to consign her to the flames like her father and brother. To this end he wrote the first document below, a letter dated 9 January 1657 to the dean, *síra* Jón Jónsson, demanding that the latter take forthright action against Þuríður, and invoking as his authority the 1617 letter of the Danish King Christian IV.

The second document below is the dean's letter of response, dated 19 January 1657. It is addressed not to *síra* Jón Magnússon directly but to two senior magistrates of the district, Magnús Magnússon and Gísli Jónsson, whom he urges to begin an immediate and thorough examination of Þuríður, in the spirit of the 1617 letter of Christian IV. The dean's reply is cunningly phrased so that, on the one hand, he pays lip service to the king's 1617 letter requiring magistrates to take action against even merely rumored sorcery, and on the other hand leaves the question open whether he himself regards the evidence against Þuríður as convincing or not.

But the "immediate and thorough" examination of Þuríður did not take place. The third document below is another extant letter, dated 30 January 1657, from Magnús Magnússon and Gísli Jónsson to *síra* Jón Magnússon, in which the two magistrates excuse themselves from immediately assembling a court to look into the matter, on the grounds that travelling in the deep snows of midwinter is difficult, and in addition both Þuríður and Magnús Magnússon are unwell. As might be expected, *síra* Jón Magnússon branded this letter as "hypocritical."[2]

It was not until May 1657 that an effective examination of Þuríður's case was made—and this only of limited scope. Þuríður, having fled from Eyri, requested permission to receive the sacrament at Holt, and journeyed back over the mountains to Eyri to ask for a sacramental certificate[3] from *síra* Jón Magnússon. Not surprisingly her journey proved fruitless. In due course a special synod of five priests was convened at Holt, on 27 May 1657, to consider her case. In their decision, which forms the last of the four documents in this Appendix, her request is granted, on the grounds that "her behavior is Christian and the case against her is mere conjecture and insinuation."

The crowning defeat of *síra* Jón Magnússon's efforts to have Þuríður convicted of sorcery came in the fall of 1658, when a local court, meeting at Mosvellir (near Holt in Önundarfjörður) finally acquitted her of the charge of sorcery, on the basis of a *tylftareiður* sworn by twelve women (see Introduction, §8). Unfortunately the records of the trial and verdict at Mosvellir are no longer extant, though we do know that the Althing confirmed the acquittal of Þuríður at its 1659 session (see Appendix 5).

Letter of Síra Jón Magnússon to the Dean at Holt, Síra Jón Jónsson, dated 9 January 1657

May almighty God have mercy upon you, bless you, and preserve you now and for ever!

I, Jón Magnússon, a poor servant of God's word, by the grace of God a partner in the testimony of Jesus and of His sufferings along with His saints, was freed from the torments inflicted by sorcerers and brought back from death to life by the mercy of God. But now, my honorable, learned, and pious dean, *síra* Jón Jónsson, priest and dean of this district, I must inform your honor through

Appendix 4 || 203

this open letter of mine of the following fact: a crescendo of new attacks of sorcery has befallen me and swept over me, so that once again I have been in doubt whether my life will be preserved. This has been evident to my household and to those of my congregation who have attended church, especially on the two Sundays following Holy Cross Day[4] in the autumn of 1656. For this reason I have been obliged to send a message north to that devout man Þorleifur Kortsson, requesting and demanding in my letter, in view of his high office and the gracious letter of His Royal Majesty,[5] that he should conduct a new investigation of those whom the evidence points to and brands as being involved in this affair. I read [another] letter to the same effect before the other *sýslumaður*, Magnús Magnússon, at the Súðavík district assembly on 1 October 1656. But neither of these men has as yet taken any steps in the matter. Meanwhile the devilish activity has been on the increase, as I informed you in my other letter.

Therefore I request and demand that you take those measures to which you are obligated by your office, the gracious letter of His Royal Majesty, and the glory of God, so that those who may be proved guilty of causing these effects may be examined, exposed, and punished. I believe that a likely candidate for such an examination is Þuríður Jónsdóttir, daughter of the older and sister of the younger Jón Jónsson, who were [both] executed on the basis of the evidence that may be found there. As my aforesaid duty requires, I myself offer to take such measures as pertain to me, provided I am granted life and health, but I do request that *you* adopt measures, at the very first opportunity, in accord with the aforementioned reasons. But if you decline to perform the task entrusted to you in virtue of your twofold duty—the duty as prescribed by your office, and also the duty of loyalty to God and to His Royal Majesty—then I say that you must bear full responsibility for whatever sickness, distress, and injury befall me or mine because of your neglect, whether as touching the property, health, or life of me and mine. As witnesses to this [I call upon] all those who read this letter or hear it read. I commit you to the Lord and to the word of His grace, and likewise all those who are obedient to God in this life and in eternity. Amen.

Written at Eyri on Skutulsfjörður, on 9 January 1657,

        Jón Magnússon the younger[6] (signed with his own hand).
        (This letter was read aloud in the church at Holt
        on the First Sunday after Epiphany, 1657.)

Dean Jón Jónsson's response to the above, addressed to Magnús Magnússon and Gísli Jónsson, dated 19 January 1657

I, Jón Jónson, called and appointed to the spiritual care of this western part of Ísafjarðarsýsla, convey to the honorable magistrates of this *sýsla*, especially

Magnús Magnússon and Gísli Jónsson, deputy to the *sýslumaður* Þorleifur Kortsson, my wishes that they may have grace and peace from God through Jesus Christ.

Herewith I direct your attention to my request and demand (in so far as it pertains to my office) on behalf of *síra* Jón Magnússon, that pious and long-suffering priest at Eyri in Skutulsfjörður—namely, that for the glory of God and the benefit of the Christian Church, and also because of the sore anguish that weighs upon the aforesaid priest, you should with the utmost possible promptness proceed to examine Þuríður Jónsdóttir with regard to the suspicion of sorcery that attaches to her, [treating the matter] with the utmost seriousness according to His Royal Majesty's letter. I also request and exhort you in God's name not to brush aside or neglect this matter in any respect. In this way, with God's help, the truth will be brought to light and the consciences[7] of those involved will be unburdened.

I trust that both your honors will favor me by giving proper consideration to this matter. So that you may see that I am not raising the issue without good cause, I am enclosing *síra* Jón's appeal, so that you may consider his dead earnestness [expressed in] his own handwriting. May God strengthen you and give victory to the truth, to His own glory in the name of Jesus, to whom I heartily and in full faith commend you with my best wishes for your soul and body. In token whereof I herewith subscribe my name at Holt in Önundarfjörður, on 19 January 1657,

Jón Jónsson (signed with his own hand)

(This has been transcribed verbatim from the copy that *síra* Jón Jónsson of Holt sent here by the hand of Sigurður Jónsson of Vatnsfjörður. In witness whereof we who compared [the manuscripts append] our signatures at Skálholt, 31 May 1657:

Þorleifur Árnason (signed with his own hand)
Oddur Eyjólfsson (signed with his own hand)
Sigurður Jónsson (signed with his own hand)

Letter from Magnús Magnússon and Gísli Jónsson to síra Jón Magnússon, dated 30 January 1657

To the esteemed clergyman sr. Jón Magnússon, together with all other honest God-fearing persons who read [this letter] in the parish and judicial district of Eyri. Grace and peace be to you from God, through the merits of Jesus Christ.

This is to let it be known that although we, the undersigned, have had a summons issued and sent written notice to devout men of the nearby districts

Appendix 4 205

that they should without fail attend the assembly that we had scheduled for Friday, nevertheless the assembly is now prevented from taking place because of the following reasons for cancellation. We hope that you, as well as those devout men who have taken the trouble to go there, will assess these reasons fairly and not put an adverse interpretation on them, departing from a just and reasonable view of the matter. You, sr. Jón Magnússon, have [chosen] such an inappropriate time [as this] in which to have your suspicions of Þuríður Jónsdóttir communicated to Gísli Jónsson and myself! Indeed, you have never previously done so at a convenient time, even though both of us, [now] as before, would have been anxious to do our best [to help you] if God had so ordained it—however it may seem [to you]. So you will presumably interpret [our reasons] on this occasion as you have before.

Our reasons for cancellation this time, among others, are the following in particular:

1. First, we cannot manage to get Þuríður any further than here[8] because of the snows and foul weather, and also because [she] is ill.
2. Moreover we did not dare [travel] on Tuesday because of a snowstorm.
3. Thirdly, we both to some extent have legitimate excuses, especially I, Magnús Magnússon, because of injury to my hand.
4. Fourthly, on Thursday we attempted—eight of us in all—to continue our journey. But our guides felt entirely unable to continue the journey any further than Breiðidalur, because of the darkness and foul weather, and so we were forced to turn back. By the time the weather cleared, it was too late to be able to get to the assembly at the [scheduled] time.

For this reason, as things stand, the assembly must wait until another time when better attendance will be possible, at the usual time of the spring assembly. Few of those [who have already come] will want to take the trouble to come again. Besides, it is doubtful whether the weather will permit us to remain longer here [at Holt] if we are to get back home without hindrance, since two holy days are approaching. We are confident—indeed, we know—that Þuríður will not abscond, nor is it likely that she will do you any harm during this period. She will get her just deserts sooner or later from God and men if she is proved guilty, but at this point in the investigation we cannot assert her guilt.

We will not dilate further on the matter. We commit you and all of God's children to the protection and keeping of the word of His grace. You will judge according to your best understanding.

Vale.[9] 30. *januarii anno* 1657, at Holt in Önundarfjörður,

Magnús Magnússon,
Gísli Jónsson.

The Verdict of Five Priests Regarding Reception of the Sacrament by Þuríður Jónsdóttir, Dated 27 May 1657

On the 27th of May, *anno* 1657, at Holt in Önundarfjörður, the respected priest and dean sr. Jón Jónsson presented to us the *casus* (legal case) regarding confession and reception of the sacrament by Þuríður Jónsdóttir, who had come from the parish of Eyri in Skutulsfjörður but did not present a sacramental certificate. The fact is that she has sojourned here for some time and has expressed her wish to receive the sacrament. On the other hand, sr. Jón Jónsson says that he is in no position to grant this, since no such obligation appears in the regulations and ruling of our lord bishop. Therefore, since no provable evidence has been put forward [against Þuríður]—in fact, nothing but insinuation and conjecture—we, the honorable and learned priests assembled here, having reached our opinion with a clear conscience, do declare ourselves agreed, by the moving of God's Spirit, that the aforementioned Þuríður Jónsdóttir should be admitted to private absolution and the reception of the sacrament. (Indeed, we have before us the Ordinance of His Royal Majesty, along with the bishop's ruling[10] regarding this *casus in generali synodo*[11] 1640.) She has been once again examined and exhorted by each one of us individually, according as God has given us the spirit and grace to do so, and we are all agreed that the aforementioned woman seems to display Christian behavior and demeanor. Therefore, having thus examined the matter, we can say in good conscience that, with trust in God, she should be admitted to confession and the reception of the sacrament without doubt and with no impediment, wherever she may be residing.

As confirmation of this we sign our names below, each of us with his own hand, in the same place, year, and day as above:

Jón Jónsson, Hallur Árnason, Gissur Sveinsson, Ólafur Jónsson, Ólafur Þorsteinsson.

Notes

1. The Icelandic texts of these four documents will be found respectively in *Píslarsaga*, 2001 edn., pp. 240–241, 241–242, 138–139, and 231.
2. See p. 146.
3. See Appendix 1 under: Church Attendance ……
4. Sept. 14th.
5. See Appendix 2.
6. Here *síra* Jón is distinguishing himself from his older brother of the same name (see p. 1).
7. "Consciences." Here the 2001 edn. of the Píslarsaga (p. 241, line 5 from below) reads "samviskunnar," but the reading "samviskurnar" makes more sense.

Appendix 4 || 207

8. The word "here" refers to Holt in Önundarfjörður. Þuríður, who was living in Dýrafjörður at the time, was obliged to attend her trial at Eyri, and therefore had to be escorted from Dýrafjörður to Eyri. She and the *sýslumenn* got as far as Holt, but because of winter storms could not cross the Breiðadalsheiði pass from Holt to Eyri.
9. Latin for "farewell."
10. At first sight there seems to be a contradiction between the "bishop's ruling" mentioned here and the absence, mentioned a few lines previously, of any episcopal ruling that would allow Þuríður to receive the sacrament. But perhaps, for some reason, the "bishop's ruling regarding this *casus*" (even though dating from 17 years earlier) had only very recently come to the attention of dean Jón Jónsson and his local synod, while other rulings, of which the dean had been aware earlier, gave no guidance in the matter. (This possibility was suggested by Margaret Cormack.)
11. Latin for "in the general synod."

Appendix 5

Extracts from the Minutes of the Sessions of the Althing in the Years 1656–1659, Regarding the Lawsuits Brought by Síra Jón Magnússon Against the Jón Jónssons, Father and Son, and Þuríður Jónsdóttir[1]

ANNO 1656

The verdicts on the Jón Jónssons

On 1 July 1656, at the *lögrétta*[2] during the meeting of the Althing at Þingvellir, the verdicts that had been reached in trials for sorcery this year in the Ísafjarðarsýsla[3] were officially read out. These verdicts were thought by all God-fearing, honest judges to have been arrived at in a proper, Christian, and praiseworthy manner.

On property left behind by the sorcerers[4]

In the same place and on the same day, the verdict announced by the two *sýslumenn* Þorleifur Kortsson and Magnús Magnússon was publicized regarding [the disposition of] the assets left behind by the sorcerers. [The verdict states] that the priest *síra* Jón Magnússon should receive in compensation ten hundredworths from the Kirkjuból property, and ten hundredworths in personal property derived from the other [younger Jón Jónsson]. In this way the verdict already reached in this affair will not be tampered with. The twelve hundredworths of personal property, or a bit more, that are over and above this amount are to be divided between the king and the heirs. This was approved in the presence of Thomas Nikolajson as representative (Icel. *fógeti*) of [the governor, Icel. *höfuðsmaður*] *herra* Henrik Bjelke.

ANNO 1657

Regarding the charges of síra Jón Magnússon against Þuríður Jónsdóttir

At the same place and time there came before the *lögrétta* that worthy priest *síra* Jón Magnússon, who believes that he has been tormented for a long time by assaults of the devil, for which he holds some persons responsible jointly [with the devil]. He solicits the good advice of the authorities as to how he should proceed, whether he should arraign and bring charges against those whom he considers suspect. As was published in the *lögrétta* last summer, a father and son have already been tried and burned for these acts of sorcery. But if there are still some persons, as yet unpunished, who have an evil reputation for diabolical acts of this sort, or who are found [to be sorcerers] by some evidence or circumstance, then His Royal Majesty's directive[5] obligates all persons in positions of authority, whether ecclesiastical or civil, each according to his rank and position, to report such matters as soon as they become aware of them, and to undertake legal proceedings and impose punishment. [This they must do] if they do not wish to be themselves liable to prosecution as cognizant of and accomplices of such people. And according to the directive contained in His Royal Majesty's letter, the *lögmenn* and *lögréttumenn* do command, charge, and direct the authorities in each *sýsla* to pursue [this matter] earnestly and justly, to the utmost to their ability.

ANNO 1658

Concerning the case of Þuríður Jónsdóttir

The comments and observations of the priests attending the synod regarding the questions that they consider most important to investigate in the case of *síra* Jón Magnússon and Þuríður Jónsdóttir, according to the judgment read aloud at the synod concerning the evidence presented by *síra* Jón:

1) Those persons who lived at Kirkjuból during the upbringing and maturing of Þuríður should be ascertained and questioned as to whether they were aware that she ever studied or practiced magic.

2) It should be ascertained and investigated whether, to anyone's knowledge, a school of magic had been held at Kirkjuból for the children or others who cared to learn it.

Appendix 5 || 211

3) Is it known whether these arts were familiar topics of conversation on this farm, or whether Þuríður was one of those who boasted of the exercise of them?

4) Is it a proved fact that Þuríður displayed clear signs of merriment, with buffoonery and banter, sitting on a chest and dangling her legs, amusing herself by playing with a top and joking, and putting on a velvet cap, when she knew that her father and brother had been burned to death in one and the same bonfire?[6]

5) *Item*, how long a time passed between their burning and her show of buffoonery? It would seem especially worthy of notice and investigation if it can be proved that Jón, Þuríður's father, when he was under arrest at the *sýslumaður's* estate at Eyri, declared that his kinswoman Þuríður would follow him in being consigned to the flames, or whether such words were widely repeated after him.

6) [One should] compare the times of her trip to Hnífsdalur and of the sufferings of the priest; and also of the cow there—their development and final outcome.[7]

7) What evidence did Erlendur Ormsson have when he accused Þuríður so forcibly,[8] as the declaration of Örnólfur Jónsson indicates? Örnólfur is bringing another witness for his statement.

8) Is it true that any honest men saw the escort of devils that followed the priest when he rode home from Kirkjuból, being tormented thereafter by a swarm of gnats and so forth?[9]

9) Erlendur Ormsson should give a full explanation of the accusation that he brought against Þuríður in her absence, and which he wrote and signed at Tunga. He must either disclaim it or be punished for such exaggerated language. The members of the Althing should see to it that this point is followed up.

10) What caused Þuríður to depart so suddenly from Skutulsfjörður, where the priest was suffering? It is incumbent on everyone, so far as he is able, to help in clarifying the points in regard to this question which the *lögmenn* and the *lögrétta* find noteworthy.

11) The suspicion [regarding Þuríður's sorcery] is weakened by the fact that, as the synod notes, to the best of their knowledge it was not aired before Erlendur came on the scene.

Herewith the synod of priests commits this case to the *lögmenn* and the *lögrétta* to settle it as best they can, and commits all of us to [the protection of] the good God.

From the proceedings of the synod at Þingvellir, 30 June 1658.

Signed by: Magister Brynjólfur Sveinsson, *síra* Þorleifur Jónsson, *síra* Þórður Jónsson, *síra* Einar Illugason.

* * *

In regard to Þuríður Jónsdóttir's promise to swear an oath, which she confirmed with a handshake, the *lögrétta* concluded that *síra* Jón should be satisfied if within ten weeks' worth of juridical days[10] she would swear as follows: that she has not by magic or sorcery, by word or deed, either caused or had others cause any of the pains and torments which the aforementioned *síra* Jón Magnússon has been suffering, and that she is not responsible for the practice of any black magic or spells causing illness, injury, or obstacle to *síra* Jón or any other person or livestock. This oath is to be sworn in the presence of *síra* Jón, if he so wishes. Also she is to swear an "oath of twelve" [Icel. *tylftareiður*] along with her compurgators, and this oath is to be sworn at whatever place seems to the *sýslumenn* most appropriate, with the consent of honorable men, and at the conclusion of all investigations.

We pronounce Erlendur Ormsson to be obligated to give a full explanation of his words and his accusation *before* the swearing of the oath. If it so happens that he can give reasoned proof for his statement that she is proved and known to be a practitioner of magic or that she is guilty of the practice of sorcery in connection with the illness of *síra* Jón or others, then let the *sýslumaður* take steps to have her punished according to the law and His Royal Majesty's letter. But if she swears the oath, after a thorough check of the statements and accusation of Erlendur Ormsson, then she is to be acquitted in the lawsuit herein referred to.

Let this decision be communicated to Erlendur in sufficient time for him to come west[11] without inconvenience, to defend and confirm his statements if he is able to do so.

Appeal of síra *Jón Magnússon*

Inasmuch as I, a poor servant of the word of God, perceive that my rights or the assault made upon my life are given no weight—now, so that I may know what amount I should demand [as compensation] from the legacy of Jón the elder who was burned to death, and also whether the portion of the [elder Jón's] farm adjudged to me, according to the settlement as ordered by the *lögmenn* and the *lögrétta*, is appropriate, I appeal my case to the present or future governor [of Iceland], so that I may obtain my rights and not be the cause of any injustice to myself or my heirs or those who seek a settlement.

ANNO 1659

[The conclusion of the trial of Þuríður Jónsdóttir]

The *sýslumaður* Magnús Magnússon appeared before the *lögrétta* and announced the verdicts and the oath involved in the trial of Þuríður Jónsdóttir of the West Fjords. The verdicts were reckoned by the *lögmenn* and the *lögréttumenn* to have been well thought out.

Notes

1. The original Icelandic from which the extracts given in this Appendix are translated is found in *Píslarsaga*, 2001 edn., pp. 299–303.
2. For explanations of the terms *lögrétta, lögmaður, lögréttumaður, fógeti, höfuðsmaður, tylftareiður* occurring in this Appendix, see Introduction, §4.
3. This of course refers to the verdicts (given in Chapter VI of this book) by which the two Jón Jónssons, father and son, were condemned to be burned to death for the practice of sorcery against *síra* Jón Magnússon.
4. This item is mostly an extract from the verdict contained in Chap. VII of this book.
5. See Appendix 2.
6. For what *síra* Jón interprets as the heartless attitude of Þuríður toward the burning of her father and brother, see pp. 160, 161.
7. See p. 137.
8. See p. 138. For more information on Erlendur Ormsson, see Appendix 1 under: Erlendur Ormsson.
9. See p. 139.
10. A "juridical day" (Icel. *sær dagur*) means here a day on which oaths can be sworn officially.
11. It is not clear what place the word "west" refers to.

Appendix 6

The Accusation Brought by Þuríður Jónsdóttir of Kirkjuból Against Síra Jón Magnússon[1]

SPRING 1660

I the undersigned, a pitiful and wretched being in the eyes of God and man, believe that I have for some time, in fact continuously for two years, been the object of assaults and attacks [against me] on the part of sr. Jón Magnússon of Eyri in Skutulsfjörður—violent assaults of various sorts, one after the other, as all the people of this neighborhood know well and also those further away. But the all-knowing God, the Lord, who is seated on high but sees what is low, has now proclaimed and revealed the truth through the agency and assistance of the civil magistrates who are set over me, and also of others whom He has inspired to bear witness to the truth, so that, to the best of my knowledge and information, everything is now settled and concluded. But now my human and fleshly nature and my conscience cannot stand by in silence without making a complaint. I therefore ask the authorities whose duty it is to come to a decision: should I accept as a *fait accompli* the entire unjust accusation and calumny brought against me by sr. Jón in this monstrous case (by whatever name it should properly be called, which time alone will tell)? A person brings complaints at the time when he suffers, and he [sr. Jón] made the first move in this matter.

Accordingly, as it is my understanding that the civil authorities have dealt fully with the accusation brought by sr. Jón, according to the law in a verdict which they will defend, I desire, trusting in the Lord, to determine and have it determined for me, whether or not I am to accept as a thing of the past all that has happened [to me] from beginning to end because of him, since it is better to know rightly than to think wrongly. So I present the document that follows to that honorable priest and dean, sr. Jón Jónsson, and appeal to him humbly and sincerely with the request that (if there is nothing out of order in it) he should look into this case of mine against sr. Jón and give me the satisfaction of knowing—and behaving accordingly—whether or not he could have been blameless in bringing such a charge against an innocent person like me on the ground of his suspicions. Indeed death would certainly have been my lot if his accusations had been judged true, and I was required to present the most weighty oath[2] known to the law.

The first point that I present is to request an opinion on whether it was right or permissible for sr. Jón to bar me from receiving the sacrament for a whole year, on the basis of his suspicions which now turn out to be false. But the decision of the synod of priests in Holt was that I should be allowed to receive [the sacrament], which I subsequently did.[3] Since they reached this decision, that he could not bar me from [the sacrament] in the absence of proof, at a time when they did not know what the verdict would be, it is self-evident that in placing obstacles of whatever sort in my way [sr. Jón] was acting wrongly. I request careful consideration of this point, since whoever bars an innocent person from the holy sacrament is acting in a manner not befitting a priest.

The second point of which I request consideration is whether it was proper for sr. Jón Magnússon, when he visited me [once] on the sabbath day, and on other occasions too, to stir up an unjust lawsuit by his action and behavior which consisted in spitting in my face. He did this in private. Even though witnesses are lacking I shall be glad to prove my claim if need be. Otherwise let him deny it if he can! I confess that for this reason I did not venture to remain at home there any longer, but was obliged to wander westward to Dýrafjörður, homeless and without prospects. For if I had stayed at home he would have kept up his assaults on me. Thus I was forced to part from my mother.

The third item that I present and ask to have looked into is the assertion in *sera* Jón's written accusation that he believes that Þuríður Jónsdóttir is more likely than others to be a sorceress. Since the evidence for this that he adduces is unproved and now shown to be entirely wrong and inapplicable, I want him to give a different proof or present a better justification of his case purporting to show that I am more likely [to be a sorceress] than others. Otherwise I maintain that this assertion of his is extremely questionable, and I request that it be carefully scrutinized to see whether it can be substantiated or whether it should be struck out.

The fourth point is that he attributes to me "adamantine brazenness of spirit." Others wiser than I will understand what this phrase means. But if it means diabolical[4] brazenness, then he is expressing himself in a quite extravagant manner, for he is surely unable to prove it.

In the fifth place I want an investigation of his statement that, in his view, I am under just as much suspicion of sorcery as my father and brother were. He

Appendix 6 | 217

has openly asserted his willingness to be held responsible for this statement before God and his conscience. It is too much to expect that this false suspicion of his should carry no weight. That being so he cannot be without blame in fixing it on me, as if the matter would pass off without blame or reprimand. There is no doubt, and it has often been proved true, that what has been alleged concerning accused persons becomes equally attributed to them [even if they are shown to be] innocent. It is a serious matter that a person who alleges an offense should escape scot-free while the other [the accused] is required to produce a full legal oath in his defense. Suspicion is the first step toward bringing a charge. It is a serious matter if the accuser is to incur no penalty once the suspicion has been rejected by a full proof of innocence according to legal procedure.

There are more and weightier matters to be considered concerning his pernicious charges, all aiming to vilify me. I pray that gracious God will look on them and that good men, who love the truth and are ready and willing to uphold justice, will take the matter in hand, for God Himself has delegated them for this purpose. In addition, I submit to these, and (if necessary) to the Althing, all the hardships that I have been subjected to. Though God and the kind authorities have been so gracious and merciful to me, it is no thanks to sr. Jón. I believe that I am entitled to claim from him all the expenses that I have hitherto incurred, since he has attacked me with a lawsuit which is unjust in all respects. So I now declare in full earnestness that I am bringing a charge against him, and ask to be given satisfaction by those church authorities who I believe will claim jurisdiction over my case against sr. Jón Magnússon. And to that I conjoin whatever charges I may be entitled to bring against him as a result of the charges that he has previously brought against me, whether submitted [by him] in written or spoken form. I bring a charge and ask for a judgment on whatever may be submitted [by me]. I see no reason to spare him since he would not show leniency to me. This is my earnest and wholehearted wish, in affirmation of which I have had two witnesses subscribe their names below, along with my own name.

Notes

1. The suit brought against *síra* Jón Magnússon in this document in the spring of 1660 followed upon the acquittal of Þuríður in 1658 by a local court at Mosvellir in the West Fjords. Þuríður claimed compensation for the pain and suffering inflicted on her by *síra* Jón's unjust and inordinate harassment of her during the preceding years. The original Icelandic of the document here translated is found in the *Píslarsaga*, 2001 edn., pp. 53–55.
2. The *tylftareiður*, i.e., the oath of twelve persons (see the Introduction, §4).
3. See the explanation in Appendix 1 under: Church Attendance, …….
4. The Icelandic word translated here as "adamantine" is *dementískur* (derived from *demantur*, "diamond"). Possibly Þuríður confused *dementískur* with *demónískur*, "demonic."

Illustrations

Illustrations 221

Figure 1. An early photograph of the spit Eyri in Skutulsfjörður, probably taken in 1868. The picture shows debris of ocean ice in Skutulsfjörður. In the center stands the Eyri church, newly erected when the picture was taken. To its left are the churchyard, rectory, and rectory farm. The cluster of buildings to its right is the Danish trading station.

Figure 2. A wooden statue of the Virgin and Child, thought to date from about 1500, which was apparently in the possession of the Eyri church during the incumbency of *síra* Jón Magnússon.

Figure 3. Portrait of Bishop Brynjólfur Sveinsson.

Figure 4. Portrait of *síra* Páll Björnsson.

Figure 5. Portrait of Magnús Magnússon *sýslumaður*.

Figure 6. Aerial view of the modern town of Ísafjörður, looking inland from the Djúp.

Bibliography

Annálar 1400–1800. Annales Islandici posteriorum sæculorum, in 6 vols. Ed. by Hannes Þorsteinsson, Jón Jóhannesson, Þórhallur Vilmundarson, Guðrún Ása Grímsdóttir. Reykjavík: Hið íslenska bókmenntafélag, 1922–1987. (An exhaustive collection of Icelandic historical annals for the years 1400–1800.)

Arnheiður Sigurðardóttir. *Híbýlahættir á miðöldum*. Reykjavík: Bókaútgáfa menningarsjóðs og þjóðvinafélagsins, 1966. (The construction of medieval Icelandic farm-dwellings. In Icelandic.)

Bréfabók Þorláks biskups Skúlasonar, ed. by Þjóðskjalasafn Íslands. Reykjavík: Ísafoldarprentsmiðja, 1979. (Letters of Þorlákur Skúlason, bishop of Hólar from 1628 to 1656. In Icelandic.)

Úr Bréfabókum Brynjólfs biskups Sveinssonar, ed. by Jón Helgason. Reykjavík, 1942. (A selection of letters of Brynjólfur Sveinsson, bishop of Skálholt from 1639 to 1674. In Icelandic.)

Brianchaninov, Bishop Ignatius. *On the Prayer of Jesus*. Trans. from the Russian by Father Lazarus. London: John M. Watkins, 1965.

Burton, Robert. *The Anatomy of Melancholy*, Vol. 3 out of 6 (Third Partition: Love Melancholy, Religious Melancholy), ed. by Thomas C. Faulkner, Nicolas K. Kiessling, Rhonda L. Blair. Oxford: Clarendon Press, 1994.

Caporael, Linda. "Ergotism: The Satan Loosed in Salem?" *Science*, vol. 192 (2 April 1976).

Cormack, Margaret. *The Saints in Iceland, Their Veneration from the Conversion to 1400*. Bruxelles: Société des Bollandistes, 1994.

Eastwell, Harry D. "Voodoo Death and the Mechanism for Dispatch of the Dying in East Arnhem, Australia," *The American Anthropologist*, vol. 84, no. 1, March 1982, pp. 5–18.

Eddu kvæði, ed. by Ólafur Briem. Reykjavík: Skálholt, 1968. (A modern Icelandic edition of the old Eddic poems.)

Eggert Ólafsson. *Ferðabók Eggerts Ólafssonar og Bjarna Pálssonar um ferðir þeirra á Íslandi árin 1752–1757*. Originally publ. in Danish 1772. Trans. into Icelandic by Steindór Steindórsson, in 2 vols, Reykjavík, 1943. (The report, commissioned by the Danish government, of the findings of Eggert Ólafsson and Bjarni Pálsson during their travels around Iceland in 1752–1757.)

Einar Laxness. *Íslands saga*, in 3 vols. Reykjavík: Vaka-Helgafell, 1995. (A history of Iceland, compiled alphabetically by topics. In Icelandic.)

Einar G. Pétursson. *Eddurit Jóns Guðmundssonar lærða*, in 2 vols, with English summary. Vol. 1, Inngangur. Vol. 2, Texti. Reykjavík: Stofnun Árna Magnússonar á Íslandi, 1998. (A detailed study of the life and writings of Jón Guðmundsson the Learned. In Icelandic.)

Ellison, Ruth C. "The Kirkjuból Affair: A Seventeenth-Century Icelandic Witchcraft Case Analyzed." *Seventeenth Century*, 1993 (8th year), no. 2, pp. 217–243.

Ellison, Ruth C. "A Prophet Without Honour: The Brief Career of Erlendur Ormsson." *Saga Book*, XXIV, Part 5, 1997, pp. 293–310.

Flowers, Stephen. *The Galdrabók: An Icelandic Grimoire*. York Beach, Maine: Samuel Weiser, Inc., 1989. (The *Galdrabók* (Book of Sorcery) in English translation and with English introduction and appendices.)

Galdrakver, Ráð til varnar gegn illum öflum þessa og annars heims, in 2 vols., the first being a facsimile of the original manuscript Lbs 143 8vo in Reykjavík, the second containing the Icelandic text and introduction, and with Danish, English, and German translations. Ed. by Emilía Sigmarsdóttir, Rannver H. Hannesson, and Ögmundur Helgason. Reykjavík: Landsbókasafn Íslands—Háskólabókasafn, 2004. (A collection of procedures for the practice of *white* magic.)

Grágás: Lagasafn íslenska þjóðveldisins, ed. by Gunnar Karlsson, Kristján Sveinsson, and Mörður Árnason. Reykjavík: Mál og menning, 1992. (A modern edition of the book of laws of the Icelandic Commonwealth. In Icelandic.)

Guðrún Edda Gunnarsdóttir. *"Herra Jesú, miskunna mér....."*. Reykjavík, 1989. (A study of the Eastern Orthodox practice of the Jesus Prayer. In Icelandic.)

Gunnar Karlsson. *Iceland's 1100 Years: History of a Marginal Society*. Mál og menning, 2000.

Hallgrímur Pétursson. *Passíusálmar*, ed. by Dr. Sigurbjörn Einarsson. Reykjavík: Hallgrímskirkja, 1991. (A modern edition of the *Passion Hymns*. In Icelandic.)

Hallgrímur Pétursson. *Hymns of the Passion*, English translation of the *Passion Hymns*, by Arthur Charles Gook. Reykjavík: Hallgrímskirkja, 1978.

Hannes Þorsteinsson. "Minning sjera Páls prófasts Björnssonar í Selárdal." *Skírnir*, 1922, pp. 53–92. (A biographical sketch of *síra* Páll Björnsson of Selárdalur. In Icelandic.)

Helgi Skúli Kjartansson. *Hallgrímur Pétursson*. Ísafoldarprentsmiðja, 1974. (A biography of the poet-priest Hallgrímur Pétursson. In Icelandic.)

Helgi Þorláksson. *Sautjánda öldin*. Reykjavík: Bóksala stúdenta, 1984 (mimeographed). (A study of the history of Iceland in the 17th century. In Icelandic.)

Helgi Þorláksson. "Aldarfarið á sautjánda öld," *Hallgrímsstefna*, pp. 15–28. Reykjavík: Listvinafélag Hallgrímskirkju, 1997. (An article on Icelandic life in the 17th century. In Icelandic.)

Helgi Þorláksson. *Saga Íslands VI*, ed. Sigurður Líndal. Reykjavík: Hið íslenska bókmenntafélag og sögufélagið, 2003. (The history of the Icelandic Reformation up to about 1640. In Icelandic.)

Hörður Ágústsson. "Íslenski torfbærinn," *Íslensk þjóðmenning I, Uppruni og umhverfi*, ed. by Frosti F. Jóhannsson, pp. 228–344. Reykjavík: Bókaútgáfan Þjóðsaga, 1987. (A detailed description of the construction of Icelandic turf houses. In Icelandic.)

Jóhannes Hraunfjörð Karlsson. *Frá tíund til virðisauka: Saga skatta og kvaða frá upphafi til vorra daga*, Lokaritgerð (meistarapróf) við Háskóla Íslands. Reykjavík, 1996. (A history of tithes and taxes in Iceland up to the present day. In Icelandic.)

Jón J. Aðils. *Einokunarverslun Dana á Íslandi 1602–1787*, 2nd edn. Reykjavík: Heimskringla, 1971. (The Danish Trade Monopoly in Iceland. In Icelandic.)

Jón Árnason. *Íslenzkar þjóðsögur og ævintýri*, 6 vols. Leipzig, 1862 (1st edn.). Reykjavík: Bókaútgáfan Þjóðsaga, 1961. (The most comprehensive collection of Icelandic folktales. In Icelandic.)

Jón Helgason (bishop). *Kristnisaga Íslands frá öndverðu til vorra tíma*, in 2 vols. Reykjavík: Félagsprentsmiðjan, 1925–1927. (A standard history of the Icelandic Church from the Conversion in A.D. 1000 up to the early 20th century. In Icelandic.)

Jón Hnefill Aðalsteinsson. "Þjóðtrú." *Íslensk þjóðmenning, V. Trúarhættir*, ed. by Frosti F. Jóhansson. (On pp. 379–386 there is a short account of the different kinds of magic practiced by Icelandic sorcerers of the 17th century. In Icelandic.)

Jón Magnússon. *Píslarsaga síra Jóns Magnússonar*, ed. by Sigfús Blöndal. Copenhagen: Hið íslenska fræðafélag í Kaupmannahöfn, 1914. (The first printed edition of the *Píslarsaga*. In Icelandic.)

Jón Magnússon. *Píslarsaga síra Jóns Magnússonar*, ed. by Sigurður Nordal. Reykjavík: Almenna bókafélagið, 1967. (The second printed edition of the *Píslarsaga*. In Icelandic.)

Jón Magnússon. *Píslarsaga séra Jóns Magnússonar*, ed. by Matthías Viðar Sæmundsson, with appendices ed. by Þórður Ingi Guðjónsson and Jón Torfason. Reykjavík: Mál og menning, 2001. (The third printed edition of the *Píslarsaga*. In Icelandic.)

Jón Magnússon. *Histoire de mes Souffrances*. A French translation by Einar Már Jónsson of the *Píslarsaga* of *síra* Jón Magnússon. Paris: Les Belles Lettres, 2004.

Jón Steffensen. "Alþýðulækningar," *Íslensk þjóðmenning VII, Alþýðuvísindi*, ed. by Frosti F. Jóhannsson, pp. 103–192. Reykjavík: Bókaútgáfan Þjóðsaga, 1990. (The sicknesses and medical treatments common in Iceland up to the 19th century. In Icelandic.)

Jón Þ. Þór. *Saga Ísafjarðar og Eyrarhrepps hins forna*. Vol. 1, up to 1866. Ísafjörður: Sögufélag Ísfirðinga, 1984. (The history of Ísafjörður and the Eyri parish up to 1866. In Icelandic.)

Jónsbók, with Revisions. Ed. by Ólafur Halldórsson. Odense Universitetsforlag, 1970 (reprinted from the 1904 edition). (The *Jónsbók* was the Icelandic Lawbook, issued by King Magnús Hákonarson of Norway and confirmed by the Althing in 1281. The Revisions were decreed in 1294, 1305, and 1314. In Icelandic, with Introduction in Danish.)

Kristni á Íslandi, in 4 vols. Ed. by Hjalti Hugason, with editorial committee consisting of Sigurjón Einarsson, Helgi Bernódusson, Helgi Skúli Kjartansson, and Jónas Gíslason. Reykjavík: Alþingi, 2000. Vol. 3: *Frá siðaskiptum til upplýsingar*, by Loftur Guttormsson. (The most up-to-date history of Christianity in Iceland, from the Conversion in 1000 up to 2000. The 3rd volume deals with the period from the Reformation up to the Enlightenment. In Icelandic.)

Lawrence of the Resurrection, Brother. *The Practice of the Presence of God*. Trans. into English from the French by John J. Delaney. Image Books, 1977.

Lindqvist, Natan (editor). *En isländsk Svartkonstbok från 1500-talet*. Uppsala, 1921. (The *Galdrabók*, with text in Icelandic and with Swedish translation and commentary.)

Loftur Guttormsson. "Læsi," *Íslensk þjóðmenning 6, Munnmenntir og bókmenning*, ed. Frosti F. Jóhannsson, pp. 118–144. Reykjavík: Bókaútgáfan Þjóðsaga, 1989. (An article on the extent of literacy in Iceland, especially during the 16th to 18th centuries. In Icelandic.)

Luther, Martin. *Luther's Works*, 55 vols. Edited by Jaroslav Pelikan (vols. 1–30) and Helmut T. Lehmann (vols. 31–55). Concordia Publishing House and Fortress Press, 1957–1986. (An English translation, from the German and Latin, of Luther's important writings.)

Magnús Már Lárusson. "Íslenskar mælieiningar." *Skírnir*, 1958, pp. 208–245. (Traditional Icelandic units of measurement. In Icelandic.)

Manntal á Íslandi 1703, tekið að tilhlutun Árna Magnússonar og Páls Vídalín, ásamt manntali 1729 í þrem sýslum. Reykjavík: Ríkisprentsmiðjan Gutenberg, 1924–1947. (The epoch-making census carried out in Iceland in 1703 by Árni Magnússon and Páll Vídalín. In Icelandic. See also under Þorsteinn Þorsteinsson.)

Matthías Viðar Sæmundsson. *Galdrar á Íslandi: Íslensk galdrabók*. Almenna bókafélagið, 1992. (A complete edition, with Inroduction and Commentary, of the *Galdrabók*, the only surviving manual of magic, both "white" and "black," as practiced in 17th-century Iceland. In Icelandic.)

Matthías Viðar Sæmundsson. *Galdur á brennuöld*. Reykjavík: Iceland Review, 1996. (A concise history of sorcery as practiced in Iceland in the 17th century. In Icelandic.)

Njörður P. Njarðvík. *Dauðamenn*. Iðunn, 1982. (A short novel, based on the *Píslarsaga* of Jón Magnússon. Its main character is Jón Jónsson the younger, whose story it tells from the standpoint of Jón Jónsson himself rather than from that of *síra* Jón Magnússon. This novel is reviewed by Helgi Skúli Kjartansson in *Tímarit Máls og menningar* 1983 (vol. 44), pp. 446–450. The review is favorable on the whole, though critical in detail. In Icelandic.)

Ólafur Davíðsson. *Galdur og galdramál á Íslandi*, in 4 parts. Reykjavík: Sögufélag, 1940. (A classic account of the sorcery practiced in Iceland and the trials for sorcery that took place there in the 17th century. In Icelandic.)

Ólína Þorvarðardóttir. "Merkingarheimur og skynjun: Sekt og sakleysi í *Píslarsögu síra* Jóns Magnússonar," *Tímarit Máls og menningar*, 1992, no. 4, pp. 37–42. (An analysis of the *Píslarsaga*, in which the author proposes an influenza epidemic as the source of the sufferings of *síra* Jón and his household. In Icelandic.)

Ólína Þorvarðardóttir. *Brennuöldin, Galdur og galdratrú í málskjölum og munnmælum*. Háskólaútgáfan, 2000. (A thorough survey of all aspects of the 17th-century practice of witchcraft in Iceland, with special emphasis on the treatment of witchcraft in Icelandic folklore. In Icelandic.)

Óskar Halldórsson. *Bókmenntir á lærdómsöld 1550–1770*. Reykjavík: Hið íslenska bókmenntafélag, 1996. (A survey of Icelandic literature in the "Age of Learning," 1550–1770. In Icelandic.)

Óttar Guðmundsson. "Schizophrenian og *Píslarsaga* sr. Jóns Magnússonar," *Pressan*, fimmtudagur, 17. maí, 1990, p. 25. (An Icelandic psychiatrist discusses the question of whether Jón Magnússon suffered from schizophrenia. In Icelandic.)

Óttar Guðmundsson. *Tíminn og tárið. Íslandingar og áfengið í 1100 ár*. Reykjavík: Forlagið, 1992. (1100 years of alcoholic drinks in Iceland. In Icelandic.)

Páll Björnsson. *Character Bestiae (Kennimark kölska)*, ed. by Lýður Björnsson. Reykjavík: Ísafoldarprentsmiðja, 1976. Reviewed by Einar G. Pétursson, *Saga*, 1977, vol. 15, pp. 229–232. (*The Mark of the Beast*, by Páll Björnsson, the outstanding work on magic produced in 17th-century Iceland. In Icelandic.)

Páll Eggert Ólason. *Saga íslendinga. 5. bindi, Seytjánda öld, Höfuðþættir*. Reykjavík: Menntamálaráð og þjóðvinafélag, 1942. (A classic history of 17th-century Iceland. In Icelandic.)

Reisubók Jóns Ólafssonar Indíafara, Samin af honum sjálfum (1661), ed. Völundur Óskarsson. Reykjavík: Mál og menning, 1992. (The Travel Book of Jón Ólafsson, voyager to India, written by himself. In Icelandic.)

Rémy, Nicolas. *Daemonolatreia*, 1595. Trans. into English by Montague Summers. London: John Rodker, 1930. (One of the classical texts of the demonology that dominated the western Church during the period of the witchcraft craze.)

Russell, Jeffrey Burton. *Witchcraft in the Middle Ages*. Cornell Univesity, 1972.

Sigfús H. Andrésson. "Þorleifur lögmaður Kortsson," *Skírnir*, 1957, pp. 152–171. (A biographical sketch of Þorleifur Kortsson, the principal 17th-century Icelandic magistrate involved in the burning of sorcerers. In Icelandic.)

Siglaugur Brynleifsson. *Galdrar og brennudómar*. Reykjavík: Mál og menning, 1976. (A good and relatively brief history of the outbursts of witchcraft in Iceland in the 17th century. In Icelandic.)

Sigurður Nordal. "Galdrarit," *Samhengi og samtíð*, vol. 2, pp. 122–132. Reykjavík: Hið íslenska bókmenntafélag, 1996. (In this article the distinguished Icelandic literary scholar Sigurður Nordal points out that *síra* Jón Magnússon was not typical of his age, and that Icelanders of his century occupied their minds with other things than witchcraft. In Icelandic.)

Sigurjón Jónsson. *Sóttarfar og sjúkdómar á Íslandi 1400–1800*. Reykjavík: Hið íslenska bókmenntafélag, 1944. (A doctor's description of the principal illnesses that plagued Icelanders during the period 1400–1800. In Icelandic.)

Snorri Sturluson. *Heimskringla*, Íslensk fornrit, vols. 26, 27, 28. (A history of the kings of Norway, one of the major works of medieval Norse literature. In Icelandic.)

Sprenger, Jacob, and Heinrich Kramer. *Malleus Maleficarum*, 1486. Trans. from the Latin into English by Montague Summers. London: John Rodker, 1928. (*The Hammer of Witches*, the treatise which laid the foundation of the European witchcraft craze.)

Tambiah, Stanley Jeyaraja. *Magic, Science, Religion, and the Scope of Rationality*. (From the Lewis Henry Morgan Lectures presented at the University of Rochester 1984.) Cambridge University Press, 1990.

Þorsteinn Þorsteinsson. "Manntalið 1703," *Andvari*, vol. 72 (1947), pp. 26–50. Reykjavík: Ríkisprentsmiðjan Gutenberg. (An analysis of the 1703 census of the population of Iceland. In Icelandic.)

Þorvaldur Thoroddsen. *Landfræðisaga Íslands. Hugmyndir manna um Ísland, náttúruskoðun þess og rannsóknir, fyrr og síðar*, in 2 vols. Reykjavík: Hið íslenska bókmenntafélag, 1892–1896, 1898. (The best-known work of the geologist and geographer Þorvaldur Thoroddsen, who was the first in modern times to draw attention to the *Píslarsaga* of Jón Magnússon. In Icelandic.)

Trevor-Roper, Hugh R. *The European Witch-Craze of the Sixteenth and Seventeenth Centuries and Other Essays*. New York and Evanston: Harper Torchbooks, 1969.

Trevor-Roper, Hugh R. *Galdrafárið í Evrópu*. Trans. into Icelandic from the original *The European Witch-Craze of the Sixteenth and Seventeenth Centuries*, with an Introduction, by Helgi Skúli Kjartansson. Reykjavík: Hið íslenska bókmenntafélag, 1977.

Ware, Kallistos. *The Power of the Name. The Jesus Prayer in Orthodox Spirituality*. London: Marshall Pickering, 1989.

The Way of a Pilgrim and The Pilgrim Continues His Way, anonymous. Trans. from the Russian by R. M. French. London: S.P.C.K., 1963. (The original Russian, under the title *Otkrovennye Rasskazy Strannika Dukhovnomu Svoemu Ottsu*, was published in Paris by YMCA Press in 1948.)

Witchcraft and Magic in Europe: The Eighteenth and Nineteenth Centuries, ed. by Bengt Ankarloo and Stuart Clark. Philadelphia: University of Pennsylvania Press, 1999.

Witchcraft in Europe 1100–1700. A Documentary History, ed. by Alan C. Kors and Edward Peters. Philadelphia: University of Pennsylvania Press, 1972.

Writings from the Philokalia on Prayer of the Heart. Trans. from the Russian by E. Kadloubovsky and G. E. H. Palmer. London: Faber & Faber, Ltd., 1957.

Index

a priori probability   36, 56 n125, 166
æðigaldur (madness magic)   72, 73, 171
Ægishjálmur (helmet of awe or terror, magical stave)   22, 181, 182
Aeneid of Virgil   68
Æsir (pre-Christian Norse gods)   111
Agrippa, Cornelius (German philosopher, 1486–1535)   5, 9, 16
Álftafjörður   71, 81 n2, 141, 145, 146, 178
Algiers   103 n2
Althing at Þingvellir, Öxará Assembly, Öxarárþing   2, 6, 7, 10, 11, 12, 14, 20, 30, 32, 78, 120, 127, 147, 148, 162, 163, 167, 179, 196, 197, 198, 202, 211, 217
   Minutes of the Althing   198, 209–213
Anatomy of Melancholy — see Burton, Robert
Andrés Hallsson   105
angels of God, nearness and protection of   101
Antikvarisk-Topografiska Arkivet, Stockholm   21
apologetic tracts — *see* supplementary tracts
Aquinas, St. Thomas (Italian theologian and philosopher, 1225–1274)   45 n8
Aristotelian classification of kinds of causality   90, 91, 96 n4

Arnardalur   25, 71, 72, 73, 74, 75, 80, 81 n2, 84
Arngrímur Jónsson (Icelandic priest and scholar, 1568–1648)   23
Árni Jónsson   83
Árni Magnússon (manuscript collector, 1663–1730)   51 n75, 194 n2
Árni Oddsson (*lögmaður*, 1592–1665)   46 n20, 167, 170 n41
Ásgrímur Björnsson   117
Ásmundur Guðmundsson   79, 108, 195, 197
Ásta Narfadóttir   63, 106, 196
Augnaþuss (magical stave)   110, 114 n17
Augustine of Hippo, St. (N. African Christian theologian and phiosopher, A.D. 354–430)   17
aurar — *see eyrir*

baðstofa (communal room)   13, 79, 86, 89, 101, 125, 140, 142, 149, 150, 171, 175, 176
Bakki (farm)   25
Barðastrandarsýsla   72, 79
Benidikt Þorleifsson   197, 198 n4
Bessastaðir   11
Bible   9, 89
Bjarni Jónsson   199 n7
Bjarni Snorrason (stepson of Jón Magnússon)   26, 76, 86, 166
Bjarni Þorgeirsson   105
Bjarni Þorleifsson   195

Bjelke, Henrik (governor of Iceland, 1615–1683) 11, 210
Björn Bjarnason (of Arnardalur) 72, 73
Björn Jónsson (of Engidalur) 75, 76, 78, 82 n17, 108, 109, 181, 196, 197
Björn Jónsson (*lögréttumaður*, annalist, of Skarðsá, 1574–1655) 198 n4
Björn Pálsson (son of *síra* Páll Björnsson) 185
Blönduós (modern town) 26
Bodin, Jean (French philosopher, 1529–1596) 6, 45 n9, 186
Bolungarvík (town) 89, 100, 150
Breiðadalsheiði (mountain pass) 24, 102, 103 n8, 176
Breiðidalur 205
Brynjólfur Bjarnason 77, 105, 117, 120, 142, 195
Brynjólfur Sveinsson (bishop of Skálholt, 1605–1675) 9, 10, 14, 16, 19, 21, 168 n4, 174, 176, 183, 186, 197, 211
Burton, Robert (author of *Anatomy of Melancholy*, 1577–1640) 33

calendar, Julian, Gregorian, old Icelandic 171, 172
Canon Episcopi 45 n8
Cardano, Girolamo (Italian mathematician, 1501–1576) 5, 16
Census and Farm Register (of 1703) 25, 51 n75, 51 n76
Christian III (king of Denmark 1534–1559) 8
Christian IV (king of Denmark 1588–1648) 14, 16, 30, 31, 112
Decree of 1617 14, 16, 30, 31, 112, 113 n6, 193–194, 201, 202, 203, 210, 212
Christianity in Iceland, adoption of 7
Christmas Register 109, 114 n12
church attendance (in 17th-century Iceland) 172
Church Ordinance, Lutheran 8, 46 n17, 128

clairvoyance, *see* second-sighted
Commonwealth Period (in Iceland) 8, 175
compurgator 12, 28, 78, 212
confession 172
Copenhagen, University of Copenhagen 9, 10, 183, 194
Cormack, Margaret 207
Council of State 193

Dagverðardalur 24
Danish Houses, *see* Trading Stations
Danish Trade Monopoly in Iceland, *see* Trading Stations
De Occulta Philosophia (by Cornelius Agrippa) 9
De Praestigiis Daemonum (by Johann Weyer) 45 n12
deacon (Icel. *djákni*), choir deacon (Icel. *kórdjákni*) 65, 173, 174
dean (Icel. *prófastur*), deanery (Icel. *prófastsdæmi*) 174
Decree of Absolutism 11
Denmark 5, 8, 178
Deuteronomy, Book of 111
diocesan schools 10
dramatize his feelings, Jón Magnússon's urge to 35
Dýrafjörður, West Fjords 216

Eastern Orthodox Christianity 38, 39, 187
economic causes of sorcery lawsuits 49 n50
Eddic poetry 50 n66
Egede, Hans ("apostle of Greenland", 1686–1758) 56 n135
Eggert Björnsson (*sýslumaður*) 185
Eggert Ólafsson (pioneer of Icelandic Enlightenment, 1726–1768) 55 n116
Egill Pálsson 108, 196, 197
Einar Arnórsson 108, 195, 197
Einar Illugason (priest) 211
Einar Már Jónsson 44 n2, 51 n68, 151 n4, 170 n44
ell (unit of value) 190

Engidalur (farm)   24, 25, 75, 143
England   5, 178
ergot-poisoning   34, 55 n115
Erlendur Eyjólfsson (burned for sorcery)   185
Erlendur Ormsson (vagrant and "prophet")   29, 30, 52 n89, 133, 134, 138, 139, 144, 160, 163, 174, 175, 211, 212
Exodus, Book of   111, 186
extrasensory perception, clairvoyance *see* second-sighted
explanatory document (*transskriftarbréf*)   109, 111, 114 n11
Eyrarkirkja (church at Eyri)   24, 31, 133, 145
Eyri (in Seyðisfjörður)   126, 134 n2, 211
Eyri (farm and spit, in Skutulsfjörður)   24, 79, 103 n8, 105, 117, 125, 142, 143, 145, 146, 147, 149, 151, 158, 176, 177, 188, 195, 202, 203, 204, 206, 215
eyrir (unit of value, plural *aurar*)   191

Fáfnir (mythical serpent)   181
Fáfnismál (Eddic poem)   181
farm dwellings, construction of Icelandic   12, 47 n25
Farm Register, *see* Census of 1703
farting runes   182
Fjölnir (magical stave)   182
Flowers, Stephen   21, 181–182
fógeti (bailiff, representative)   11
Fossar (farm)   25
Frederick III (king of Denmark 1648–1670)   180
Fremri-Arnardalur (farm)   25
Fremri-Hnífsdalur (farm)   25

ghost (*draugur, sending*),   69 n15
Gísli Einarsson (priest in Vatnsfjörður)   26
Gísli Jónsson (*lögsagnari* and *sýslumaður*)   28, 72, 76, 77, 105, 106, 117, 129, 145, 146, 175, 177, 195, 197, 198, 201, 202, 203, 204, 205
Gísli Oddsson (bishop of Skálholt 1632–1638)   16, 26
Gissur Ísleifsson (bishop of Skálholt 1082–1118)   7, 188
Gissur Sveinsson (priest)   206
God, the Lord, the Most High, the holy Trinity   15, 35-end passim
Golnisþey (magical stave)   110, 114 n17
governor of Iceland (Icel. *höfuðsmaður, hirðstjóri*)   11, 119, 210, 212
Graduale (liturgical book)   9
Grágás (Lawbook of the Commonwealth Period)   7, 8, 13, 48 n35, 112, 115 n27, 175
Kristinréttur (Church law)   112, 115 n27, 118, 175, 178
Greenland   23
Guðbrandur Þorláksson (bishop of Hólar 1571–1627)   9, 14, 18, 172, 176, 179
Guðlaug Gunnlaugsdóttir   151
Guðmundur Ásmundsson   117, 195
Guðmundur Einarsson (priest of Staðarstaður)   14, 194 n1
Guðmundur Ísleiksson   73, 74, 145, 151, 196
Guðmundur Þorleifsson   108, 117
Guðmundur Þorsteinsson   105, 195
Guðríður Símonardóttir (wife of Hallgrímur Pétursson)   103 n2
Guðrún Bjarnadóttir (wife of the elder Jón Jónsson and mother of the younger Jón Jónsson, Þuríður, and Þorgerður)   118, 138, 140, 148, 160, 163, 178, 216
Guðrún Guðmundsdóttir   151, 196
Gunnlaugur Skeggjason   108, 144, 195
Gyða   111

Hafrafell (farm)   25, 139
Hagallinn blá (magical stave)   110, 114 n17

Halla Arnórsdóttir   144, 151
Hallbjörg Ólafsdóttir   151
Halldór Finnbogason (burned for persistent blasphemy)   20
Halldór Ólafsson (brother of Jón Ólafsson *Indíafari*)   141
Halldór Pálsson (son of *síra* Páll Björnsson)   185
Halldóra Jónsdóttir (wife of the dean *síra* Jón Jónsson)   29, 52 n92, 142, 146, 177, 201
Hallgrímur Pétursson (poet and priest, 1614–1674)   19, 56 n123, 103 n2, 103 n3, 176, 177
   Passion Hymns   19, 176
Hallný (of Kirkjuból)   160
Hallur Árnason (priest)   206
Hallur Tindsson (of Engidalur)   164
Hamburg, Germany   189
Hannes Þorsteinsson   184, 185, 186
Hattardalur   146
Hávamál (Eddic poem)   50 n64
Helga Halldórsdóttir (wife of *síra* Páll Björnsson)   184–186
Hemmingsen, Niels   49 n48
héraðsdómur (local district court)   12
Hercules   168
Herdís Arnórsdóttir   144
Hildur Halldórsdóttir (wife of Sigmundur Guðmundsson, daughter of Randíður Ólafsdóttir)   141
Hjaltadalur   176
Hjarðardalur   142
Hnífsdalsvík   73
Hnífsdalur   25, 74, 89, 130, 137, 164, 211
höfuðsmaður, see governor
Hólar (in Hjaltadalur, school and diocesan seat)   7, 8, 10, 20, 176, 179
Hóll   100
Holt (in Önundarfjörður, parish of the dean *síra* Jón Jónsson)   30, 143, 146, 165, 166, 173, 176, 201, 202, 203, 204, 205, 206, 216

homespun (Icel. *vaðmál*, a measure of value)   190
House Reading (Icel. *húslestur*), evening wake   175, 176, 179
hreppur   105, 117, 146, 177
Hrútafjörður   72, 86
Hugrás   14
huldufólk ("hidden people," elves)   14, 16, 18
humiliation and degradation of Jón Magnússon   94
humility of Jón Magnússon   41
hundredworth (unit of value)   117–120, 190, 209
Hvalfjörður   39, 99, 103 n4

illusions (Latin *fascinum*)   158, 165
India   178
influenza epidemic   34, 69 n16, 81 n4
Ingibjörg Ívarsdóttir   130
Ingibjörg Pálsdóttir   144
Innocent VIII (pope 1484–1492)   4
insanity, mental illness   17, 35, 48 n35
inventory of church property (*máldagi*)   24
Ísafjarðardjúp (Djúp for short)   23, 24
Ísafjarðarsýsla   12, 28, 175, 203, 209
Ísafjörður (town)   1, 24
Isaiah, Book of   112
Íslandslýsing (Description of Iceland, by Bishop Oddur Einarsson)   9
Íslendingasögur (Sagas of the Icelanders)   13
Íslensk galdrabók (Icelandic Book of Magic)   21, 181–182, 194 n3
Íslenskar þjóðsögur og ævintýri (Icelandic Folktales and Legends, by Jón Árnason)   182

James, Epistle of   132
Jesus Christ   18, 39, 99, 100, 113, 129, 131, 164, 187, 202, 204
   the Passion of Jesus   100
John the Baptist   102, 132, 133, 143, 144, 157, 164

Index

Jón Arason (last Roman Catholic bishop of Hólar 1524–1550) 8, 9, 179
Jón Árnason (collector of Icelandic folktales, 1819–1888) 190
Jón Espólín (*sýslumaður*, annalist, 1769–1836) 198 n4
Jón Guðmundsson (the Learned, 1574–1658) 10, 14
Jón Guðmundsson (member of a court) 105
Jón Helgason (burned for sorcery) 185
Jón Jónsson (of Eyri) 145, 149, 151, 196
Jón Jónsson (of Fossar) 79
Jón Jónsson (of Hnífsdalur) 130
Jón Jónsson (member of a court) 105, 108
Jón Jónsson (priest and dean at Holt in Önundarfjörður, West Fjords, died 1680) 29, 84, 117, 126, 146, 147, 173, 174, 176, 177, 201, 202, 203, 206, 216
Jón Jónsson the elder (of Kirkjuból) 1, 3, 26, 62-end passim
Jón Jónsson the younger (of Kirkjuból) 1, 3, 26, 62-end passim
Jón Leifsson (burned for sorcery) 185
Jón Magnússon (*sýslumaður*, of Dalasýsla) 197
Jón Magnússon the elder (priest and poet, brother of Jón Magnússon the younger, 1601–1675) 1, 26
Jón Magnússon the younger (priest, nicknamed *þumlungur*, the subject of this book, ca. 1610–1696) passim
  letters written by 53 n99
  castigates magistrates for their negligence in investigating sorcery cases 95, 96, 129, 161, 163, 183
  spits in Þuríður's face 216
Jón Ólafsson (of Arnardalur) 72, 73, 78, 177, 178, 197

Jón Ólafsson *Indíafari* (1593–1679) 75, 82 n13, 83, 178
  Travel Journal of Jón Ólafsson *Indíafari* 178
Jón Pétursson 64, 109
Jón Sigurðsson (priest at Eyri after Jón Magnússon the younger) 2
Jón Steingrímsson ("fire-priest", 1728–1791) 50 n67
Jón Steinþórsson 99
Jón Sveinsson (executioner) 79, 80
Jón Sveinsson (priest and dean at Holt in Önundarfjörður, half brother of Bishop Brynjólfur Sveinsson) 177
Jón Þórðarson 105
Jón Þorsteinsson (of Tunga) 108, 143, 144, 164, 195, 197
Jón Þorvaldsson 195
Jón Vídalín (bishop of Skálholt 1698–1720) 44 n3, 56 n123, 184
  Vídalín's Postil 184
Jonah, Book of 94
Jónsbók (Lawbook) 8, 13, 47 n22, 106, 112, 175, 178
  Mannhelgi (Personal Rights) 106, 112, 114 n7, 118, 119, 121 n9, 169 n12, 178
Judas (the disciple who betrayed Jesus) 63
judges, High Court 159
juridical days 212, 213 n10

Kaldaðareyri 149
Kalmar Union 8
Katrín Ísleiksdóttir 142
Kennimark kölska, see Páll Björnsson
Kirkjuból (in Korpudalur) 145
Kirkjuból (in Langidalur) 113, 120
Kirkjuból (in Skutulsfjörður) 25, 27, 29, 31, 61, 62, 72, 75, 76, 80, 106, 111, 120, 126, 133, 139, 140, 144, 148, 158, 160, 164, 165, 166, 173, 178, 201, 209, 210
Kirkjubólskirkja 26, 81, 155
Klemens Bjarnason (sentenced to exile for sorcery) 20

Kramer, Heinrich (Dominican monk, coauthor of *Malleus Maleficarum*) 4
Kristín Ólafsdóttir 142, 151
Kristín Sigmundardóttir (wife of Sturli Bjarnason) 140
Kristinréttur, see Grágás
kúgildi 118, 121 n7

Landfræðisaga Íslands, see Þorvaldur Thoroddsen
Langadalsströnd 146
Langebek, Jakob (manuscript collector) 2
Lassi Diðriksson (burned for sorcery) 185
Latin 10, 34
Lawrence, Brother (French monk contemporary with *síra* Jón Magnússon, 1614–1691) 57 n141
leiðarþing (informative assembly) 149, 179
Lesser Catechism (of Martin Luther) 180
Leviticus, Book of 111
Lindqvist, Natan 21
literacy (Icel. *læsi*) 179–180
lögmaður (plur. *lögmenn*) (law-man) 11, 86, 120, 147, 197, 198 n4, 210, 211, 212, 213
lögrétta (law council of the Althing) 7, 11, 12, 167, 197, 199 n7, 209, 210, 211, 212
lögréttumaður (plur. *lögréttumenn*) 11, 71, 147, 198 n4, 210, 213
lögsagnari (deputy) 12, 28, 76, 175
Luther, Martin (founder of the German Reformation, 1483–1546) 5, 45 n13, 180
Lutheran Church in Iceland 8, 9

Macarius, St. 45 n13
magic pragmatically efficacious 35
magical spells (Icel. *særingar*), staves (Icel. *galdrastafir*) 22, 110, 111, 114 n17, 180–182, 193

Magnús Björnsson (*lögmaður*) 46 n20, 199 n7
Magnús Björnsson (burned for sorcery) 185
Magnús Einarsson (priest) 145
Magnús Guðmundsson 195
Magnús Jónsson (of Engidalur) 143, 163, 164
Magnús Jónsson "*prúði*" (poet, *sýslumaður*, ca. 1525–1591) 183
Magnús Magnússon (*sýslumaður*, 1630–1704) 12, 27, 28, 71, 72, 73, 75, 76, 80, 81, 86, 105, 106, 108, 113, 117, 120, 125, 126, 128, 129, 137, 142, 146, 149, 150, 165, 166, 175, 177, 183, 195, 196, 197, 198, 201, 202, 203, 204, 205, 209, 211, 212
Magnús Sigurðsson 197, 198 n4
Malachi, Book of 112
Malleus Maleficarum 4, 5, 6, 18, 53 n98
Mannhelgi, see *Jónsbók*
manuals of sorcery 15, 21, 50 n59
Margrét Arnórsdóttir 130, 137, 162, 164
Margrét Þorvaldsdóttir 140, 144, 145, 163
Markús Brandsson (of Seljabrekka) 110, 114 n15, 140, 143
Matthías Viðar Sæmundsson 2, 21, 33, 44 n4, 45 n13
meðhjálparar 173
"mental epidemic" 32, 33
mind (Icel. *hugur*) of the sorcerer 23
monasteries and convents 8
monastic proprietor 8
mörk (plur. *merkur*, a unit of value) 191, 199 n7
Moses 17
Mosvellir (West Fjords, site of acquittal of Þuríður Jónsdóttir) 30, 202

National Library of Iceland 19
National Museum of Iceland (Þjóðminjasafn Íslands) 25

Neðri-Arnardalur (farm)   25
Neðri-Hnífsdalur (farm)   25, 89
Neoplatonism, Platonism   5, 9
neurasthenia, neurosis   32, 35, 40, 54 n106
Nikolaison, Thomas   199 n7, 210
Nineveh   94
Njáll (hero of *Njáll's Saga*)   143, 152 n16
Nordal, Sigurður (professor and author, 1886–1974)   2, 32, 33, 34, 38, 40, 43, 49 n50, 54 n108, 56 n135
Norway   7, 8, 175, 178

Oddur Einarsson (bishop of Skálholt 1589–1630)   9, 14, 20, 26, 35, 172
Óðinn (Norse god)   50 n64, 111
Ögur (in the West Fjords)   26
Ólafur (cook)   110, 111
Ólafur Jónsson (priest)   206
Ólafur Sigmundsson   196
Ólafur Þorsteinsson (priest)   206
Ólína Þorvarðardóttir   44 n3, 55 n114
Ólöf Bjarnardóttir   100
Ólöf Guðmundardóttir   144
Önundarfjörður (West Fjords)   24, 103 n8, 145, 164, 166
Örnólfur Jónsson   138, 163, 211
Óttar Guðmundsson (psychiatrist)   56 n124
Öxarárþing, *see* Althing

Páll Björnsson (priest of Selárdalur, 1621–1706)   10, 16, 17, 18, 20, 28, 29, 132, 183–187
    Kennimark kölska (The Mark of the Beast)   16, 49 n39, 186
Páll Egilsson (of Hafrafell)   142
Páll Jónsson (bishop of Skálholt 1195–1211)   24
Páll Vídalín   51 n75
pallur (platform)   13, 67, 73, 75, 86, 101
Passion Hymns, see Hallgrímur Pétursson

Paul, St. (apostle)   38, 57 n149
permission for Þuríður to receive the sacrament   202, 206
Personal Rights (*Mannhelgi*), *see Jónsbók*
Pétur Einarsson (of Eyri, Skutulsfjörður)   140, 145, 151
Pétur Einarsson (annalist, 1597–1666)   44 n3
physical signs of "demonic attacks," as described by *síra* Jón
    satanic spirit on his feet, like a mouse or rat   62
    unnatural sleep   64, 106, 148, 181
    repulsive sensation as of a cat rustling at his feet   64
    a dog digging its claws like red-hot needles into his neck   64
    burning in his hand after handshake with Jón Jónsson the younger   65, 108, 110
    spasms of pain in the arm and wrist   65
    pounded and trampled while praying in the church   66
    hissings in his ear   66
    swarms of fiends in his house   66
    insects fluttering in the rooms   66
    devil walking in the shape of the Jón Jónssons   66, 108
    his people harassed with itching, lethargy, heat and cold, lumps in the throat   68
    terrifying creatures, loud frightening crashes   68
    biting wind struck his right ear, as if from a gaping dog, making a disgusting sound   72
    æðigaldur (madness magic), to rob him of his wits   72, 73
    one girl struck down and speechless   73
    men out fishing felt a demon on board; one stricken almost fatally   73, 74
    devils crawling over Jón Ólafsson *Indíafari*, who was nauseated   75

physical signs of "demonic attacks," as
    described by *síra* Jón (*contd*)
  Gísli Jónsson suffers pain in the foot
    and optical illusions   76
  concourse of fiends churning up the
    sea as if by an earthquake   78
  executioner visited by fiends in the
    form of the Jón Jónssons, and
    stabbed   79
  haunted by a riotous multitude of
    demons   80
  Magnús Magnússon struck with a
    frightful pain in one foot   81
  Jón Magnússon's wife afflicted by
    demons   84
  tortures worse than any physical
    sickness: crushed under huge weight,
    jabbed with red-hot needles, impaled
    with a spike, lying in blazing fire,
    piercing cold, flesh crawling with
    ghastly seething worms   85, 86
  blowing as of whales under his pillow
    89
  fiery embers burning his head   89
  his neck and chest swollen, with
    intense headache   90
  strange insect flew in the face of a
    priest who was praying for Jón
    Magnússon   90
  whelp crawling in *síra* Jón's belly and
    internal parts   91
  mouth screwed up and squeezed
    over to one cheek   92
  snake writhing around him   92
  shot up into the air, then cast down
    into a bottomless abyss   93
  indescribable tortures, the torments
    of hell   93, 94
  jabbed in the side by the younger
    Jón Jónsson   127
  thrown out of bed   130
  demonic assault after admonishing a
    man involved in runes   133
  disorder in the hand after the same
    man took *síra* Jón's hand   133
  numbness and convulsions of a girl
    who nursed a bewitched cow
    137, 162
  ring of darkness around Þuríður
    138, 163
  agonizing torments, face attacked by
    biting gnats   139, 211
  drawn out limb from limb   139
  devil in Þuríður's likeness, with black
    cassock and broad-brimmed hat
    142, 165
  devil in Þuríður's likeness riding a
    brown mare   142, 165
  devil in the likenesses of various
    suspected sorcerers   142, 143
  Magnús Jónsson struck by the devil
    after refusing Þuríður an escort
    143, 164
  Jón Þorsteinsson pained in his side
    after riding with Þuríður on his
    horse   144, 164
  shocks and buffets felt by various
    women near Þuríður   144
  flying sparks coming out of a door
    when Þuríður was alone indoors
    144, 163
  fireball over Kirkjuból where Þuríður
    was alone. A dog followed *síra* Jón
    144, 145, 163
  evil female spirit precedes Þuríður
    and Snæbjörn on their way to
    Önundarfjörður   145
  síra Jón felt a fireball over his head
    when Snæbjörn was in church   145
  one who also saw these visions was
    struck down and made speechless
    145
  devilry so escalated that one man of
    síra Jón's household lay at death's
    door   146
  attack lasting from Christmas into
    þorri, when apparitions dwindled
    147
  mice creeping and jumping over him
    148

Index

painful sleep, from which he awoke by the lashing of an angel 148
his wife, under a tent, heard rain falling, though in fact there was no rain 149
Þuríður forced to move from Kirkjuból; demonic attacks on *síra* Jón subside 149, 150
farting spells 159, 160
síra Jón attacked with sorcery on berating Þuríður, as on berating the Jón Jónssons 163
those who refused to escort Þuríður suffered strange nocturnal phobias 164
likewise those who had refused to swear to the innocence of the Jón Jónssons 164
death of a goat due to sorcery of one of the Jón Jónssons 164
injury to Sigmundur because he refused to escort Þuríður over the mountains 166
magic practiced on one who read *síra* Jón's letter to the dean in Þuríður's presence 166
demonic rampages escalated on Þuríður's arrivals and died down on her departures 166
pirates 24, 99, 103 n2
Prayer of Jesus 38, 92, 187
Protestant, *see* Reformation
Proverbs, Book of 57 n146
public opinion regarding the two Jón Jónsons and Þuríður Jónsdóttir 53 n94

quarter (unit of value) 191

Randíður Ólafsdóttir 41, 141, 152 n12
Rannveig Snorradóttir (stepdaughter of Jón Magnússon) 26, 27, 108
Reformation, Protestant Reformers 5, 8
refusal of Jón Magnússon to allow the younger Jón Jónsson to marry his stepdaughter 108
Remy, Nicolas (French judge) 6, 45 n9, 186
Renaissance 9
"repentance" of sorcerers 126, 127, 128
revealed interpretation of the word of God 101
Revelation, Book of 57 n140, 87 n4
Reykjavík (present capital of Iceland) 7, 176, 188
ríkisdalur (Danish unit of money) 194
Rome, Roman Catholic Church 5, 8
Romans, Epistle to the 57 n138, 57 n149
Royal Library of Copenhagen 2, 31
Royal Society of London 20, 184
runes, runic alphabet 20, 22, 23

sacrament of the Lord's Supper, mass 61, 63, 106, 128, 172, 173, 180, 206, 216
sacramental certificate 143, 172, 173, 174, 202, 206
Sagas of the Icelanders (Icel. *Íslendingasögur*) 13
Samuel (prophet) 165
Satan, the devil 4, 5, 6, 28, 119, 120, 164, 165
saving sorcerers from damnation 129
schizophrenia 56 n124
school of sorcery 161
Scot, Reginald (English doctor) 5, 6
second-sighted, clairvoyant 23, 36, 62, 66, 78, 142, 147, 158
Selárdalur (West Fjords) 29, 183, 184
self-abasement of Jón Magnússon 35, 141
Seljabrekkunaust 142, 149
Seljaland (farm) 25, 73, 140, 152 n12
sending (evil spirit sent to hurt one's enemies) 187–188
Settlement Age 6, 188

sex ratio of sorcery defendants 48 n36
shooting at a demon 67, 69 n15
side-alcove (of a church) (Icel. *stúka*) 66, 188
Sigfús Blöndal 2, 32, 33
Sigmundur Björnsson (stepson of Sturli Bjarnason of Kirkjuból) 150, 166
Sigmundur Guðmundsson (of Seljaland) 79, 108, 133, 140, 141, 195
Sigmundur Jónsson 108
Signý Ólafsdóttir (wife of Björn Jónsson of Engidalur) 143
Sigurbjörn Einarsson (bishop) 134 n11, 169 n19
Sigurdrífumál (Eddic poem) 115 n21
Sigurður (mythical Norse hero) 181
Sigurður Jónsson (of Eyri) 102, 103 n6, 144, 163
Sigurður Jónsson (priest of Vatnsfjörður) 204
Sigurður Nordal, *see* Nordal
Sigurjón Jónsson (doctor) 44 n3, 56 n124
Simmingh, Petrus (Swedish priest) 44 n3
Skagafjörður 176
Skálholt (diocesan seat and school) 7, 8, 10, 20, 21, 26, 35, 100, 103 n4, 176, 188
 Skálholt School 188
 Skálholt manual of magic 21
skáli (guest bedroom) 13, 74, 79, 140, 148, 188–189
Skötufjörður 90
Skutulsfjörður 1, 24, 25, 81 n2, 133, 156, 165, 211
Snæbjörn Pálsson (head of a household at Kirkjuból) 26, 61, 62, 64, 76, 143, 145, 146, 178
Snæbjörn Torfason 105, 113, 117, 120
Snæfellssýsla 174
Snorri Hákonarson (priest) 26
Snorri Jónsson (son of Jón Magnússon and Þorkatla Bjarnadóttir) 26, 31, 74

Solomon's Seal (magical stave) 110, 182
sorcery, magic, witchcraft passim
 "school of sorcery" at Kirkjuból 161
spells and talismans, *see* magical spells and staves
Spirit of God 101
spiritual experiences of Jón Magnússon 39–42, 95, 99–102, 131
 Jesus Prayer is not "work-righteousness" 40
 sweetness came out of his wretchedness and self-deprecation 95
 first temptation, in 1627 99–100
 practice of prayer, revelation of meanings of scriptural texts 100–101
 angelic protection 101
 words spoken to him by God's Spirit 101
 visions, dreams, and revelations of devout people 102
 "I shall be victorious tomorrow" 131
 is told to approach Randíður Ólafsdóttir with humility 141
spiritual life a bulwark against insanity 38
spiritual signs of "demonic attacks" according to *síra* Jón
 weird, impure, and evil thoughts 64
 coldness and dryness of heart, no devotion 72
 physical torments as nothing compared to those that harrow the soul 91, 93
 he lay like dead turf or a clod of earth, battered and kicked 91
 if he loses control of his speech, let his people sew his mouth shut 92
 though drained of all pious feeling, at least let his tongue be active in prayer 92
 he would be the only one among the damned to be calling on God 92

Index

he felt his mouth and face distorted, so that he might not be able to pray 92
he prays not silently but crying aloud 93
hellish filth and spiritual foulness were stamped upon his heart 93
his mind perverted God's word into blasphemy 93
he has known the agonies of souls in hell 93–94
his heart was harder than steel or stone 130
also Randíður Ólafsdóttir withstood prolonged assaults of the devil 141
Sprenger, Jacob (Dominican monk, coauthor of *Malleus maleficarum*) 4
Stefán Brandsson 108, 118
Strandir, Strandasýsla 146, 158, 165
Sturli Bjarnason (of Kirkjuból) 26, 108, 133, 138, 140, 164, 165, 178, 197
Sturlunga Saga 13
Súðavík 71, 73, 78, 80, 81 n2, 141, 203
supplementary (apologetic) tracts 3, 32, 44 n6, 168 n11, 169 n14, 169 n15
Svalbarð family 175
Sveinn Árnason 20
Sveinn Símonarson (priest and dean, father of Bishop Brynjólfur, ca. 1559–1644) 176
synod (of priests) 10, 31, 173, 202, 206, 210, 211, 216
sýsla (district), *sýslumaður* (sheriff, plur. *sýslumenn*) 11, 12, 28, 74, 75, 80, 105, 108, 118, 120, 146, 147, 148, 160, 161, 177, 199 n7, 210, 212

tax-farmers (Icel. *skattbændur*) 180
telepathy 32, 34
þing (assembly) 7

Þingvellir, *see* Althing
Þóra Einarsdóttir 138, 143
Þórarinn (of Borg, Skötufjörður) 90
Þorbjörg Guðmundsdóttir (mother of dean Jón Jónsson of Holt) 177
Þordís Símonsdóttir 199 n7
Þorður Jónsson (priest) 211
Þorgerður (younger sister of Jón Jónsson the younger and of Þuríður Jónsdóttir) 62, 178
Þorkatla Bjarnadóttir (wife of *síra* Jón Magnússon) 26, 73, 74, 84, 94, 119, 120, 131, 132, 148, 150
Þorkell Árnason 105
Þorlákur Arason (*lögréttumaður*) 71, 105, 195
Þorlákur Skúlason (bishop of Hólar 1628–1656) 20
Þorleifur Árnason 204
Þorleifur Jónsson (priest) 211
Þorleifur Kortsson (*sýslumaður* and *lögmaður*, ca. 1620–1698) 1, 12, 16, 28, 72, 76, 86, 105, 117, 120, 129, 142, 146, 150, 175, 185, 186, 189–190, 203, 204, 209
personal qualities of 189
burning of sorcerers 189–190
Þorleifur Þórðarson 75, 159, 162, 190
þorri (month of the old Icelandic calendar) 85, 147, 172
Þorskafjörður assembly 105
Þorvaldur Thoroddssen (geographer and naturalist, 1855–1921) 2, 32, 33, 44 n1
Landfræðisaga Íslands 32, 54 n105
Thumás Jörundarson 109
Thumás Þorvaldsson 108
Þuríður Jónsdóttir (of Kirkjuból) 1, 3, 29, 30, 31, 32, 33, 35, 41, 47 n22, 53 n96, 69 n11, 93, 103 n6, 128, 130, 133, 134, 137, 138, 139, 140, 142, 143, 144, 145, 146, 148, 149, 150, 155, 156, 158, 159, 160, 161, 162, 163, 164, 165, 166, 167, 168 n11,

Þuríður Jónsdóttir (of Kirkjuból) (*contd*) 173, 174, 178, 179, 180, 201, 202, 203, 204, 205, 206, 209, 210, 211, 212, 215–217
"hardhearted" behavior of Þuríður 29, 56 n122, 160, 161, 168 n11
Þuríður Ólafsdóttir (burned for sorcery) 185
Þverdalsheiði 145
Þyrill (mountain) 99
tithe (Icel. *tíund*) 117, 118
Tithe Law 7, 121 n2
Tómas of Snæfjöll (priest) 90
Torfi Jónsson 118
Torfnes 139
torpedo fish 68 n9
torture 4, 5, 15, 37, 94, 129
trading stations, Danish houses, Danish Trade Monopoly 12, 24, 47 n24, 51 n71, 86, 87 n9
Trékyllisvík (West Fjords) 28, 168 n7, 189
Tunga (farm) 25, 102, 108, 143, 144, 164, 211
Tungudalur 24
turf roofs, construction of Icelandic 13
two levels, compartments, of Jón Magnússon's mental life 42, 43, 57 n149
Tycho Brahe (Danish astronomer, 1546–1601) 9, 20
tylftareiður (oath of twelve) 12, 28, 30, 47 n22, 77, 105, 113 n5, 199 n7, 202, 212, 216

units of value 190–191
University of Copenhagen, *see* Copenhagen
Unnur (of Kirkjuból) 160
Urnir (magical stave) 110, 114 n17

Vatnsfjörður (West Fjords) 26
Vestmannaeyjar 99, 103 n2
Vídalín's Postil, *see* Jón Vídalín
Vilchin (bishop of Skálholt 1391–1405) 24, 51 n72
Virgin and Child in the Eyri church, image of 51 n73
Voodoo death 35, 55 n118

West Fjords 23, 24, 28, 48 n36, 145, 165, 167, 175, 178, 189, 213
Weyer, Johann (doctor, from Brabant, ca. 1515–1588) 5, 6, 16, 17, 18, 19, 45 n12
white and black magic 4, 14, 15, 22, 23, 47 n29
windows 13
Witch of Endor (*I Samuel*, chap. 28) 165
witchcraft trials in Iceland, general characteristics of 15, 48 n36
witchcraft and the western Church 4–6
witches' sabbaths 4, 5
wrath of God against magistrates who do not enforce the laws against sorcery 95, 96
"wrestling magic" 110